THOSE WHO SAW HER

SAW HER

REVISED EDITION

Also by Catherine M. Odell

The First Human Right: A Pro-Life Primer
(with William Odell)

Father Solanus: The Story of Solanus Casey, O.F.M. Cap.

THOSE WHO SAW HER

REVISED EDITION

Apparitions of Mary

Catherine M. Odell

Our Sunday Visitor Publishing Division
Our Sunday Visitor, Inc.
Huntington, Indiana 46750

Library of Congress Catalog Card Number: 85-63143
International Standard Book Number: 0-87973-664-X

Cover design by Monica Watts
PRINTED IN THE UNITED STATES OF AMERICA
664

Contents

Introduction

*D*ying upon the cross, Jesus bequeathed to us His own Mother. As He gazed upon Mary and the beloved disciple who represents all followers of Christ, He proclaimed for all generations to hear: "Behold your Mother" (cf. John 19:26-27).

Throughout the ages, Mary has exercised this maternal role. The Second Vatican Council accentuated this loving care of Mary: "This motherhood of Mary in the order of grace continues uninterruptedly from the consent which she loyally gave at the Annunciation and which she sustained without wavering beneath the cross, until the eternal fulfillment of all the elect. Taken up to heaven, she did not lay aside this saving office but by her manifold intercession continues to bring us the gifts of eternal salvation. By her maternal charity, she cares for the brethren of her Son, who still journey on earth surrounded by dangers and difficulties, until they are led into their blessed home" (*Constitution on the Church*, No. 62).

One of the many ways by which Mary fulfills her role as Mother of all is by lovingly manifesting herself to chosen witnesses, usually innocent, simple children who typify those who enter the kingdom of her Son (cf. Matthew 18:3). Her message is always an insistence upon the Gospel proclamation as lived, taught, and prayed by the Church. Her purpose is always to center us on her Son, the "one Mediator between God and man, the man Christ Jesus" (1 Timothy 2:5).

With scrupulous care, Holy Mother the Church carefully examines these prophetic phenomena before presenting them to the faithful as worthy of credence. Of the numerous claims of appearances of Our Lady, relatively few have been so approved by the Church. Some of the sites of these manifestations of Mary have become shrines and pilgrimage centers, attracting thousands upon thousands every year.

As the appearances themselves, so, too, these shrines are truly *Marian:* they are centered upon Christ and His Body, the Church. Where is the Eucharistic Lord more venerated than at the magnificent Eucharistic shrine of Lourdes? Where are people in such numbers turning to the Lord in a truly evangelical conversion than at the great center of prayer and penance, Fátima? All authentic apparitions of Our Lady, and pilgrimage centers that grow up around them are, like the Mother of God herself, centered on Jesus the Lord. Through these appearances of our loving Mother, we are led to imitate her, the first disciple, and "hear the word of God and keep it" (Luke 11:28).

The Church has been blessed through these appearances of Our Lady. Her universal love for all the brethren of her Son is manifest in these apparitions, which are not limited to one nation or one age. They have taken place throughout the history of the Church and in diverse areas of the Church. Mary is truly the Mother of us all, calling every generation to prayer and penance so that we may turn more fully to her Divine Son.

These apparitions of Mary are, therefore, too important to be ignored by the faithful. They should be studied, for their evangelical message helps us constantly to renew our life in Christ and strengthens our Catholic faith.

We are indebted, therefore, to Catherine Odell for having compiled this careful narrative of some of the more important appearances of Mary, the Mother of the Lord. Her concise overview of the person of Our Lady and the manner by which the Church examines the reported apparitions is also of great benefit. May this book be widely read, for it helps us to understand the reality of Mary's maternal love for us. The more that people open their hearts to her care, the more intensely will the

Holy Spirit form Christ within them and thereby renew the Church, for the glory of God the Father.

JOHN JOSEPH CARDINAL CARBERRY
St. Louis, Missouri
February 11, 1986
(Feast of Our Lady of Lourdes)

Preface

*I*n our times, Christians and Catholics have been part of an unprecedented Marian revival. Pope Pius XII, who was consecrated as a bishop on May 13, 1917 — as Our Lady began her visits to Fátima — was understandably a man who kept his eyes on Mary. Recalling the apparitions of the Virgin at Rue de Bac in 1830, La Salette in 1846, Lourdes in 1858, Pontmain in 1870, and at Knock in 1879, he called the nineteenth century the "century of Marian predilection." But then, Pope Pius did not live to see very much of the last half of the twentieth century.

In many ways, our own century could have a greater claim as a "Marian Age." Mary is with us in many ways, making herself at home with every age-group and in every part of the world. One of the ways that Mary is most vividly and intimately with us, of course, is through apparitions.

In the last three decades, the claims of supernatural apparitions have overwhelmed the Church and the faithful. "One of the signs of our times," admitted the Vatican's Cardinal Joseph Ratzinger, Prefect of the Congregation for the Doctrine of the Faith, "is that the announcements of 'Marian apparitions' are multiplying all over the world." Many of them are probably false and can sooner or later be identified as the products of wishful thinking or delusions. Often, the pastoral challenge of the Church is to study and assess such claims.

On the other hand, as this book maintains, Mary has returned to see her children on this planet in the past. Why would we presume that she wouldn't appear again to encourage us, to warn us, and to turn us once again toward Jesus? Looking at the injustices and miseries of our era, no one could say that heaven's help is no longer needed, no longer relevant.

In the heart of the book, the reader will find accounts of the best-known Marian apparitions of the last several centuries. These include the stories of Guadalupe, Rue de Bac, La Salette, Lourdes, Pontmain, Knock, Fátima, Beauraing, and Banneux.

Also presented are five modern apparition accounts: Akita, Japan; Kibeho, Rwanda; Medjugorje, Croatia; San Nicolás, Argentina, and Betania, Venezuela. Of these, Akita and Betania have received the fullest approval of the local Church. They are the third and fourth apparitions approved as supernatural in origin and "worthy of belief" in our century.

On the other hand, the apparitions of Kibeho and San Nicolás are shared here because they have profoundly touched the countries where they occurred but are largely unknown throughout the rest of the world. Kibeho and San Nicolás carry a limited level of approval from the bishops of the dioceses where they were reported. A further and fuller approval could come for these reported apparitions in future years.

The same could be said for the reported apparitions at Medjugorje (Chapter 14). In 1991, nineteen bishops of Yugoslavia reported that they could not yet "affirm that supernatural apparitions or revelation are involved" at Medjugorje. Study of the events there continues.

The first three chapters of the book attempt to give the reader an understanding of the mindset and method of the local Church when it examines apparitions, such as those at Kibeho, San Nicolás, or Medjugorje. Catholics might more easily see the love and wisdom included in the caution that characterizes the judgment of the Church.

The best efforts of this book, however, can only dimly describe the glory known by "those who saw her." A small girl once asked Sister Marie Bernarde (Bernadette of Lourdes) if

the Blessed Virgin was truly beautiful. "Oh," replied Bernadette with a remembered reflection of paradise in her eyes, "so
beautiful that when one sees her once, he longs to die to see
her again!"

1

Who is Mary?

*W*ho, indeed, is Mary?

That question has taken centuries to answer in the Church that Jesus founded. As recently as 1950, the Church issued dogmatic statements about her and her unique relationship to heaven and earth. In that year, Pope Pius XII proclaimed that Mary was taken into heaven body and soul at the end of her earthly life. Many Christians had believed, at least as early as the seventh century, that such was her happy and appropriate fate. A final assurance of her Assumption, however, was gratifying, joyful news.

To believe that God had preserved this person from the taint of sin to allow for her divine Motherhood and her Assumption was consoling. She was humanly good in a way that would never be repeated. Surely, the faithful reasoned, Mary would not leave the world behind her and forget it. And since her life began, she has not forgotten. Believers knew something of her origins as a simple, faith-filled girl in Galilee.

This was the Mary of history.

There was a time, twenty centuries ago, when this slim young Jewish maiden, living in Palestine, meant almost nothing to the known world. She was called "Miriam" by her parents, who are traditionally known as Joachim and Ann. Hers was a very common name in Palestine, wrote French historian Henri Daniel-Rops in *The Book of Mary*. This seems to be verified in Scripture, which referred to other "Miriams," or "Marias," the Latin form of "Miriam." The Gospels speak of Mary the wife of Clopas, Mary Salome, Mary Magdalene, Mary the mother of Mark, in addition to Mary the Mother of Jesus.

To Joachim and Ann, who lived in the tiny village of Nazareth in Galilee, their own Mary was very special. But, to be practical, few people besides themselves, and their few relatives and friends, would have given the child a second thought.

Almost nothing is known of her life before the Angel Gabriel arrived with an astounding message (see Luke 1:26-38). She was probably in her fifteenth or sixteenth year. Until then, as far as anyone could tell, her life had traced the predictable patterns established by Jewish society for young women.

One thing undoubtedly true of Mary was that she knew the Scriptures intimately, but she was no exception here. It was not uncommon for Hebrew children of this era to study the Scriptures. The "Magnificat" (Luke 1:46-55), the beautiful prayer-poem that Mary spontaneously created when greeted by Elizabeth, is a primary example. Scripture scholars say there is not one line in the prayer that does not allude to other passages of Scripture, or even incorporate whole phrases.

Mary's life as a woman was already unique in the history of humankind. She had been conceived without the inherited stain of original sin. Yet, as far as could be seen by others of her time, she was normal.

At the age of fourteen or fifteen at the latest, she was betrothed to Joseph, although they were not yet living together. If Joseph was typical of men about to marry then, he was considerably older than Mary. St. Luke's Gospel states clearly that they were bound in a marriage agreement at the time of the Annunciation. "It was at this age that the daughters of Israel married," author Daniel-Rops wrote. Jewish society placed primary importance on procreation. Marriages were arranged with this obligation in mind. To remain unmarried was unthinkable in the world in which Mary lived.

Yet Mary seems to have been committed to virginity at the same time she was engaged to be married to Joseph, as her response to the Angel Gabriel suggests. This was most unusual, given the societal stress on the value of children.

"But how can this come about, since I am a virgin?" she answered when informed she would be the Mother of the Son of the Most High. Her answer indicated that her virginity was not merely temporary — until her marriage to Joseph. Mary was clearly puzzled about how such a conception could ever take place. The commitment, not unknown in Jewish society among men, was a sacred one, one that Joseph must have known about and accepted. In fact, he must have made the same decision, proposing marriage only to provide for her in a culture in which women did not remain single.

Then, in the light of the angel's coming, Mary learned that the conception to take place within her womb would be miraculous. It would be accomplished by the power of the Holy Spirit. She would be a Virgin Mother. The Savior would be her Son. Her aged cousin Elizabeth was also with child, she was told. This, too, was a sign for her. She agreed to it all, but undoubtedly with a trembling heart: "Let what you have said be done to me" (Luke 1:38).

In the days that followed, Mary rushed to visit her cousin Elizabeth, whose barren condition had been so miraculously redeemed. Mary knew all the prophets' promises that the Savior would be born of a virgin, a descendant of the House of David. *She* was a virgin, a descendant of the Davidic line. Like other children of Israel, she had learned all the scriptural prophecies about the Messiah. Now they were taking flesh in her own body. "Of all women you are the most blessed, and blessed is the fruit of your womb," Elizabeth said when she greeted Mary (Luke 1:42).

If Mary was a living flame of faith in her God, her betrothed was also an admirable model of the same virtue. Only Matthew wrote of this part of Joseph's story (see Matthew 1:18-25). Joseph's understandable doubts about Mary were resolved, and the family that would welcome the Christ was established. Apocryphal "Gospels" and accounts of the hidden years of this Holy Family are numerous. But, with the exception of several references in Luke, nothing is really known about them.

Some idea of what Palestine was like during the first century is available, however. The Jewish historian Flavius Josephus left detailed accounts of daily life.

The family's home in Nazareth was no doubt partly comprised of a cave or grotto. Palestine was filled with such caves in its hills. People commonly built a small house or room off the front of the caves. Ordinarily, the kitchen was to be found in this portion of the house, with a fireplace for cooking and for heat.

In the kitchen, Mary prepared the food for meals. According to scholars, Palestinian families of this era typically ate barley bread or biscuits, lentils prepared with oil or honey, onions, asparagus, tomatoes, and a wider range of fruits, including peaches, pears, figs, melons, dates, and pomegranates. Meat was a rarity, and fish was a food found only at celebrations.

Mary also had to mend the family's clothing, which usually consisted of linen garments in the summer and wool in the winter. Her own clothing was probably made up of two basic floor-length garments, one worn like a tunic over the other. A man's clothing was similar. A veil usually covered the woman's head. Sandals, when they were worn, were fashioned of wood or leather.

Possibly in a nearby cave, Joseph would have pursued his trade of carpentry. It is probable that he made some household furniture like tables and benches, but more likely such things as yokes for oxen. In the second century, it was said that the plows made by Joseph, the foster-father of Jesus, were still in existence.

Jewish law insisted that fathers instruct sons in a trade. Jesus undoubtedly spent time with Joseph learning carpentry. Carpenters of that time identified themselves by slipping a chip of wood behind their ears. To humor the boy struggling to learn the arts of cutting and sizing, Joseph must have sometimes playfully slipped such a token behind the ear of Mary's Son.

Three times each day, Mary, Joseph, and Jesus stopped for prayers. On the Sabbath, all work stopped and the day was given over entirely to Yahweh. The family then walked to the synagogue in Nazareth. Like all synagogues of this era, it overlooked the community from high ground. It was from this synagogue that Jesus was expelled much later, after He told Nazareth that the prophecies about a Savior were being fulfilled in their own day.

For Mary and everyone else of her times, the routines of life in Palestine were more or less unchanging. According to commentators, only Jewish feasts and festivals joyfully broke the endless grind of daily domestic monotony. It was during one of these Passover feasts that Mary and Joseph became separated from Jesus and had to return to Jerusalem to find Him (see Luke 2:41-50).

For the Mother of Jesus, the beginning of her Son's public ministry marked a new time in her life. She was apparently a widow by this time, wearing the solemn black prescribed by tradition. She knew, however, that her reasons for grief would greatly multiply as the teaching of Jesus challenged Israel.

All of this was as it had to be, however. Even the suffering of Mary — called a sword that would pierce her soul (Luke 2:35) — came through the suffering of her Son. But Mary's life was lived in close connection with that of Jesus. It was only after she had died and been assumed into heaven that the followers of Jesus began to gradually understand how powerful that connection was.

Although the Gospels of Matthew and Mark briefly mention Mary as the Mother of Jesus, the other two evangelists provide the texts on which the Church of Jesus finally based its teaching about her.

This was the Mary of the Scriptures.

Luke is the primary source of the briefly chronicled events in the life of Mary that are of crucial Christian significance. These are the events that related to the fact that Jesus was miraculously conceived and born of this Virgin through the power of the Holy Spirit (Luke 1-2:20). Luke later told of the presentation of the Child in the Temple in Jerusalem and the prophecies given there to Mary by Simeon and Anna (Luke 2:22-38). This Gospel also told the well-known story of the anxious search by Mary and Joseph for Jesus when the boy was twelve (Luke 2:41-50).

John's "Marian texts" told of her role at both the beginning and at the end of her Son's work. At the beginning, she encouraged His intervention at the wedding feast at Cana (John 2:1-12). "Do whatever He tells you," she told the servants. The result, the changing of water into wine, was the first miracle of Jesus. The Church has always thought of Mary's advice as the first rule of discipleship. And Mary, it came to be seen, was her Son's first disciple.

John also reported Mary's presence at the cross during the death of Jesus (see John 19:25-27). This last reference was to take on great significance for the Church. From His cross, Jesus said to His Mother: "Woman, this is your Son." To John, He said: "This is your Mother." As the centuries moved by, the Church began to see that Jesus had wanted His whole Church, all of His successors, to see that "This is your Mother."

In addition to these texts, two critical scriptural references to Mary are found outside of the Gospels. One in Genesis, the Bible's first book, is a prophetic portrait of Mary's future motherhood of the Redeemer. "I will make you enemies of each other: you and the woman, your offspring and her offspring," Yahweh God warned the serpent. "It will crush your head and you will strike its heel" (Genesis 3:15).

The other text occurs at the opposite end of Scripture, in the last book of the Bible, the Book of Revelation. In chapter twelve, a heavily symbolized portrait is presented of a struggle in heaven between a woman and a dragon. She is "adorned with the sun, standing on the moon, and with the twelve stars on her head for a crown." The woman, obviously a queen of the heavens, gives birth to a son (Jesus) whom the dragon tries to eat (see Revelation 12:1-6).

Dogma concerning Mary came to hinge on two realities: that Mary really was the Mother of Jesus Christ, who is God, and that Mary was a Virgin-Mother. These two truths needed doctrinal confirmation by the Church. Out of these came the doctrines concerning Mary's Immaculate Conception and her Assumption into heaven.

This was the Mary of theology.

These were theologically difficult realities to sort out, however. In the centuries following the foundation of His Church, many believers struggled with these teachings. Nestorius, patriarch of Constantinople, heretically taught that in Jesus Christ were two persons merged together — God the Son and Jesus the Son of Mary. Nestorius refused to agree that Mary was therefore "*Theotokos*," the "God Bearer," or "the Mother of God." The Council of Ephesus refuted Nestorius, teaching that in Christ there was one person with two natures, human and divine. Though Mary herself was in no way divine, she really was the "Mother of God," the council restated in 431.

The conviction that Mary was perpetually a virgin also grew after the Council of Ephesus. In the same century, the great Doctors of the Church, Augustine, Ambrose, and Jerome, developed and refined this belief. If Mary had originally consecrated her life and virginity to God, she would not have retracted that vow because of the birth of Jesus, the Church Fathers affirmed. Mary's whole life was a model of faithfulness and selfless giving.

The doctrine touching on Mary's holiness was much longer in development. St. Augustine approached this vital issue and theorized that God would naturally preserve the Mother of His Son from sin. Her body, after all, was like the Ark of the Covenant of the Old Testament. It held and carried God. Gabriel's words of greeting to the Virgin in Nazareth also seemed to point to this exceptional freedom from the stain of original sin. "Rejoice, O highly favored daughter. The Lord is with you" (Luke 1:28).

The Church in the East echoed this belief in Mary's preservation from sin, her "Immaculate Conception," in the seventh century. The Franciscan Duns Scotus significantly added to the thinking about the subject in the fourteenth century. Five hundred years later, in the nineteenth century, the doctrine of the "Immaculate Conception" was formally pronounced by Pope Pius IX in 1854. Just four years later, the Virgin Mother of God is said to have confirmed the dogma to a fourteen-year-old at Lourdes, France. "I am the Immaculate Conception," she told Bernadette Soubirous.

The Assumption of the Blessed Virgin Mary had been marked and celebrated by the Christian Church as early as the seventh century. This belief by Christians down the centuries eventually blended with confidence about Mary's freedom from the stain of sin (although belief in the Assumption preceded belief in the Immaculate Conception and was accepted even by people who rejected the latter). If God had so preserved her soul from sin, the theory maintained, He would also have preserved her body from corruption, one of the fruits of original sin. In 1950, during the pontificate of Pius XII, the assumption of Mary, body and soul, into heaven was dogmatically proclaimed to have occurred after her death.

Closer to our own times, discussions of Mary's role and reality with respect to the Church have grown without additional dogmatic statements, but they have grown.

"Compare Vatican II to all previous councils of the Church," suggested Cardinal John Carberry, a Marian authority and a participant at the Vatican Council. "It becomes evident that no other ecumenical council has spoken at such length and with such beauty about Mary as did Vatican Council II." Elaborating on the council's attention, Pope Paul VI released the apostolic exhortation *Marialis Cultus* ("Devotion to the Blessed Virgin Mary") in 1974.

What did the recent council and the popes of our own era have to say about Mary?

The first council document, the constitution *Sacrosanctum Concilium*, dealt with the liturgy. In this document, it was pointed out that Mary is undeniably linked with the life, death, and Resurrection of Jesus. Because of this life linkage, the liturgy, too, must reflect Mary's position, the document insisted.

In the last chapter of *Lumen Gentium*, the "Dogmatic Constitution on the Church," the council examined the issue of "The Blessed Virgin Mary, Mother of God, in the Mystery of Christ and the Church," more fully. For the modern world, it stated, it wished a fuller look at "her who occupies a place in the heavens which is the highest after Christ and also closest to us" (*LG* 54).

There is just one mediator between God and men, the council fathers continued. That is Christ. Nonetheless, "Mary's function as Mother of men in no way obscures or diminishes this unique mediation of Christ but rather shows its power." Mary's positive influence in the world flows not from her own merits, they added, but "from the superabundance of the merits of Christ" the Redeemer. Because of this role as "Mother of the Church," which flows from the salvation given from Christ, the Blessed Virgin can be properly invoked as "Advocate, Helper, Benefactress and Mediatrix" (*LG* 62).

In this light the council and *Marialis Cultus* reaffirmed devotions to Mary such as the Rosary, a purely scriptural prayer. The Rosary, a prayer based upon Mary's role as "Advocate" and "Mediatrix," would never be outmoded, the council said.

And in Mary, the council said, there was to be found a model of the Church. "Seeking after the glory of Christ, the Church becomes more like her lofty type," the document pointed out. The Church, therefore, was right to look to her "who gave birth to Christ, who was thus conceived of the Holy Spirit and born of a virgin, in order that through the Church he could be born and increase in the hearts of the faithful" (*LG* 65).

In bringing the relationship of Mary to the Church into twentieth-century light, the council was continuing the unbroken tradition of respect for her that began with the apostles. Mary's unique and privileged role in salvation had always been in the mind of God. She was immaculately preserved from the consequences of sin and became a unique and loving ambassador between her Son, Jesus, and all humanity.

In 1987, Pope John Paul II announced that a "Marian Year" would begin at Pentecost in 1987 and conclude with the Feast of the Assumption in 1988. Extraordinary blessings were available that year to those who made pilgrimages to Marian shrines. It was only the second Marian Year in the two-thousand-year history of the Church. To prepare the way for the year, th pope issued his encyclical *Redemptoris Mater*, "The Mothe of the Redeemer."

2

Why does Mary come?

*F*or almost the lifespan of the Church, the Blessed Virgin Mary has been returning to the world that she left almost twenty centuries ago.

But why? Why would she come back at all? What's more, why would she return again and again? What could be the reason for an apparition just off a busy Paris street, or near pagan Aztec temple ruins, or on a banana farm near a Venezuelan village called Betania? What in the world calls her from her realm — paradise — that she earned so fully, so faultlessly?

The answers are not written down catechism-style in any reference volume in any archives. Rather, they lie in the heart of Mary, which is the heart we should come to understand. And the answers lie in the needs of the world, which we understand all too well. Apparitions have always had something to do with her heart and the world's needs.

Theological authorities have a very precise way of looking at apparitions in our day. An apparition, one authority said, is the "manifestation, perceived by a subject of a being, the vision of whom in this place and in this moment is unexplainable according to the normal course of things."

That is the working definition by Father René Laurentin, the French theologian and authority on Mary's remarkable returns. Fellow theologian and Mariologist Father Eamon Carroll, O. Carm., who focuses on function, refers to them as "simple echoes of the Gospel, Church teaching or practice, with some application to the circumstances of the time."

When not purely imaginary, apparitions always involve the sense of sight, but the other senses are often touched as well. Many apparitions involve hearing messages from the Mother of God. And the senses of touch, taste, and smell are often channels for her message, too.

Catherine Labouré never forgot a certain sensation that occurred when Our Lady appeared to her in 1830 in Paris. Catherine had lost her own mother at the age of nine. When the radiant and exquisite Virgin sat down in a chair in the sanctuary of the convent chapel, the young nun dropped to her knees in front of her. But then the needs of a daughter's heart took over. She placed her hands on the silk-robed knees, the understandable response of a devoted daughter. "I am sure that this was the happiest moment of my life," she wrote twenty-six years later.

Apparitions, on the first level of influence, touch the "subjects" in this very human way, but at a very supernatural depth.

Mary's appearances were once called examples of "private revelation," even if the messages seemed intended for an audience far beyond the visionary or visionaries. Father Laurentin and others today prefer to call them "particular revelations." They are messages given to help live out the teaching of fundamental Revelation in that "particular" time and place. Revelation refers to the revealed truth, the total truth about God and salvation. Scripture and Tradition (doctrine transmitted by the apostles but not in Scripture) comprise Revelation. The Church is essentially *apostolic*: it can proclaim only the message received from the apostles. Nothing *new* can be incorporated into this, even though it may be true.

Since the Church maintains that this Revelation completely supplied the necessary body of truth regarding God and salvation two thousand years ago, "particular revelations," including apparitions, can really add nothing fundamental. This is the reason why belief in apparitions, even those like Lourdes and Fátima, is optional. *The Teaching of Christ*, a catechism by Bishop Donald W. Wuerl et al., states: "The Church does not give any definite teaching on the authenticity or nature of such apparitions." So Catholics are not obliged to believe that Mary has appeared anywhere at any time on earth since the Assumption.

But if Mary comes to repeat, to remind, to restate, she also comes to prophesy, Church authorities believe. The Mother of God, some maintain, is the true prophet of the New Testament. Even from a historical perspective, this prophetic function of her apparitions isn't difficult to defend. Mary's visits here on earth were reported very early in the history of the Church.

Some of the first apparitions were reported in the East in the earliest centuries. Gregory the Thaumaturge saw her before his death in 270. She also came to St. Athanasius in the fourth century and to St. John Damascene in the eighth century. Both were Doctors of the Church. The Basilica of St. Mary Major in Rome was said to be located by Mary's appearance with a summer snow. Many founders of religious orders also apparently knew the favor of her personal appearance. Apparitions by Mary and other saints, it is said, were well received and perhaps even anticipated in the infancy of the Church.

Father Laurentin contends that Mary was, and remains, uniquely qualified for this continuing role as New Testament prophet.

Authentic apparitions, first of all, are manifestations of God, he explains. "Mary, as the one closest to God and to Christ, is logically the first one called to communicate in the name of God and as a sign of God. This corresponds to the role of the Virgin Mary as the servant of the Lord for the Salvation in which she cooperated. It is also in conformity with her mission as Mother, which was given to her by Christ at Calvary."

But the Assumption of Mary body and soul into heaven prepared her for this role even more. The unique preservation and glorification of Mary's body along with her soul particularly equips her to be an intermediary between heaven and earth, Father Laurentin maintains. "She is more endowed to communicate on a sensible level [to the senses] than those who exist as separated souls."

In a certain sense, therefore, though she had already lived out her life here on earth, she can resume it, at a gloried level, at any given time or place. She reenters the world much as one would enter or exit a house through a door. One of the seers of Fátima, ten-year-old Lucia, described the disappearance of Our

Lady in just about that way. It followed the second apparition on June 13, 1917.

"Pronto!" Lucia said, watching the Lady recede into the sky in the east above the Cova da Iria. "Now she can't be seen any more. Now she is entering heaven. Now the doors are being shut."

Mary has continually reentered the doors to our sphere for reasons that only heaven could ever verify. It is clearly a presumption to try to mind-read the Mother of God, whose goals must perfectly match the will of God. And yet, it seems clear enough that apparitions intended for many on this side of the door repeatedly show the same purposes. Many historians of Marian apparitions believe that her goals flow from purposes like those on this list from Father Laurentin. Apparitions are intended:

1) to manifest the hidden presence of God;
2) to renew community life;
3) to convert hearts;
4) to reawaken and stimulate faith; and
5) to renew hope and dynamism in the Church.

If this indeed captures the general secret behind her appearances, it seems she indeed wishes to make bold strokes. It is not just individual hearts and spirits that are the goal of her conversion efforts. The Virgin is after the revitalization of communities and of the Church at the same time. She never wishes to do any less. Yet it would seem that some apparitions are poorly received, and that some might carry a heavier societal and spiritual challenge than others.

In the apparitions at Guadalupe, Mexico, in 1531, for instance, the Mother of God crossed into men's time and space at a delicate moment for the Indians. The cultural and religious future of Mexico and the Americas was waiting to be shaped.

Less than a generation before the Guadalupe appearance, Spanish conquistadors had invaded Mexico, completely conquering it. Spanish abuse followed, but the conquest was genuinely a blessing for the hundreds of native tribes. They had lived under the domination of the Aztec chief Montezuma. Pagan cults fed on brutal forced labor and human sacrifice on a massive scale. When the bloodied temples of sacrifice were pulled down, Christian churches went up. Christianity had a toehold in the nation. The Indians were good ground, waiting for the seed of faith.

The Virgin knew the right moment to cross over the threshold. She appeared to Juan Diego, a Christian, leaving behind a miraculous portrait of herself on Juan's *tilma*, or cloak. Like a mother fully aware of the particular needs of her children, she knew that Juan's people needed to find a new faith in a more literal way.

In the phenomenal image of Our Lady of Guadalupe, she graphically reaffirmed the Christian faith before their eyes. Symbols of the pagan cults had dominated their lives with cruelty and fear. But on the cloak, these symbols, especially the sun and moon, were absent. (They were painted in later and shown under her domination.) Instead, the Lady displayed a more potent symbol — the cross. On cloth of rough cactus fiber, the apparition of Guadalupe seemed to be frozen in time. Juan's people were touched. Eight million were converted within the decade.

Yet no statistics could begin to suggest the societal and spiritual impact that the Guadalupe visit created. In significance, Father René Laurentin contrasted the event to the Reformation taking place simultaneously in Europe. The apparitions reconciled and blended the budding Christianity of the Indians with that of the conquering Spaniards. The Reformation, on the other hand, had the opposite effect. All across Europe, Christians were divided and separated from one another in hatred and fear.

The multicultural scope of Guadalupe's purpose and power isn't found in every apparition by the Blessed Virgin.

The single evening apparition by Our Lady at Knock, Ireland, Father Eamon Carroll believes, was primarily "a message of consolation to support a suffering people," the Irish of that era. This apparition, which took place in August of 1879, was strictly visual. But the apparition of the Blessed Virgin, St. Joseph, and St. John the Evangelist was visible to everyone in the Knock village who came to see it.

The Irish faith had been sorely tested in the nineteenth century, historians affirm. Before the Virgin and the accompanying saints appeared at Knock in County Mayo, millions in Ireland had suffered horribly from the potato famine and from religious persecution. The vision seemed to be fashioned simply to sustain Irish hope.

The remarkable apparition at Pontmain also had its first and deepest meaning for the French at war in 1871. Prussia was rolling over France in a war that had begun in the autumn of 1870. Panic and a heaviness dragged on the French spirit. The nation had endured revolution and political upheaval during the nineteenth century. Prussia's easy mastery over France diminished any remaining sense of national pride and seemed to predict doom.

But then the Virgin descended upon France, very close to the actual battle lines. She came to Pontmain, a village where a true religious spirit and the French faith were still alive and healthy. There, in the sky, early on a winter evening, she appeared to four children. As at Knock, the Virgin Mary did not speak. But there was a "written" message given to Pontmain, for the whole country.

A banner unfurled just below the woman's feet in the apparition near Pontmain. Letter by letter, the children read the message mysteriously created to strengthen the hope of believers. "God will hear you in a little while," one message consoled them. Then it concluded with a lesson about prayer and its power — "My Son allows himself to be touched." The Son of God, in other words, could be moved to intercede whether the need was peace between nations or a family's "daily bread."

Other apparitions seem to be primarily intended for the future and a worldwide communication.

The apparitions at Fátima in 1917 are the best and most powerful example of a Marian message apparently given in this way. Our Lady of the Rosary did make prophecies about Portugal, the native land of the three children. She also gave each of the three young visionaries secrets that they were not to share with anyone. But the fundamental character of Fátima, as the Church continued to study it, seemed to be profoundly prophetic and even apocalyptic.

At the Cova da Iria, the Lady spoke not only of the war in which Portugal was then engaged. She also warned of the danger of a future, more terrible world war. She specifically prophesied that "when you see a night illuminated by an unknown light," war would be imminent. In 1938, Lucia believed that the sign arrived with the strange manifestation of the aurora borealis seen all over Europe and in North America. World War II began within months.

In 1917 at Fátima, the Virgin also told the children — and the world — that Russia, if it was not converted, would "scatter her errors through the world, provoking wars and persecutions of the Church." This statement was made in July. Nikolai Lenin took full control in Russia to establish Communism in autumn. Until the peaceful dissolution of the Soviet Union in 1991, Russia's "errors" had truly been a concern for the whole world. But in the end, as the Fátima Virgin predicted, "my Immaculate Heart will triumph.... Russia will be converted."

Each time the Mother of God passes through the portals separating eternity from the present, something precious is gained by mankind: healing springs of water (Lourdes, La Salette, Banneux and Betania); a sign of comfort for a hungry nation (Knock); a medal fashioned with heaven's design (the Rue du Bac), or a miracle of the sun to alert an endangered century (Fátima).

It seems clear that what she gives is part of the larger plan of her Son, who gave and continues to give salvation. Some responsible Christians maintain that her Son's gift should be sufficient to sustain His people today. And in a way, at first glance, the functions of faith and the incidence of apparitions seem to present the believer with contradictory principles.

"Blessed are those who have not seen and yet have believed" (John 20:29), Jesus told the Apostle Thomas. The Letter to the Hebrews added to the praise of faith that requires no visible manifestations of the God who gives it. "Only faith can guarantee the blessing that we hope for, or prove the existence of the realities that at present remain unseen" (Hebrews 11:1).

Nonetheless, in the room where the apostles were gathered, Thomas, the doubting disciple, received his chance to touch the wounds of the Risen Christ. And on the road to Damascus, Saul of Tarsus was laid low by a flashing light from heaven and the resounding voice of Jesus of Nazareth.

The apparitions of Mary seem to continue this generosity of a God who often bolstered belief by touching people where and when they needed it. They seem to be perceivable examples of a generous love in Mary and in her Son. The goodness that visionaries see on her face is her motivation to come.

"The Lady looked at everyone and with so much love and affection," Bernadette said, following one of the later apparitions. "Sometimes she seemed to be looking one by one at the people there, and now and again her look would rest on someone for a moment as though she had recognized a friend."

3

The Church and apparitions

*W*hat is the best way to see when what must be looked at is invisible? How is it possible to humanly judge something said to come from heaven? When is it necessary to state a position publicly when the experience is claimed as a "private" one?

Fundamentally, these are the questions, the dilemmas, that the Church must face when supernatural apparition claims are made. They are the hard questions, which long centuries of pastoral experience of the universal Church have scarcely made much easier. Nonetheless, the Church has always, and continues to, address these concerns. It does so, after all, with faith. The same Lord who creates apparitions has also fashioned the institution that must sometimes measure them.

In the minds of some Christians, even approved apparitions are to be feared as flash points of fanaticism where a foolish faith can go astray. After all, they maintain, apparitions do not contribute anything to the essentials of faith. Although this is true, the response seems to surface from a fear of the spontaneous, the unpredictable, the supernatural, which apparitions and all genuine charismatic phenomena represent.

That is not the thinking of Rome or its long line of pontiffs. From the beginning, the role of apparitions, miracles, and other supernatural manifestations has been recognized and welcomed. However, that acceptance has always been accompanied by a built-in prudence, a caution that the Church believes is its responsibility. Ironically, its approach echoes that of the Pharisee Gamaliel. His sensible spirit of prudence was profiled in the Acts of the Apostles. Gamaliel suggested a procedure for evaluating the new Christian teachings, which were upsetting Jewish leaders.

Gamaliel was a respected member of the Sanhedrin, the Jewish Supreme Court, which had ordered the arrest of Peter and other apostles in Jerusalem. The Sanhedrin, angered at the new religious message, wanted to crush the new movement. Its members wanted to kill the apostles. Gamaliel suggested patience and strength, which could wait long enough to see the fruits of Christianity:

"If this enterprise, this movement of theirs, is of human origin, it will break up of its own accord; but if it does in fact come from God you will not only be unable to destroy them, but you might find yourselves fighting against God" (Acts 5:38-40).

The guideline is as good in the hands of the Church as it was in the hands of the Sanhedrin. And it has been of value since the first apparitions of Mary were reported in the apostolic age. When an apparition of Mary is reported, therefore, the first role of the Church is to keep in mind what Gamaliel suggested. God must and will sustain the validity of the experience if it is from Him. If it is "of human origin, it will break up of its own accord."

According to an authority on Marian apparitions, however, the Church will often find itself pulled in opposite directions during the time of waiting and study. On the local or diocesan level, a commission is typically organized to gather information about a reported apparition. The opposing pulls or tensions the Church feels begin to be felt at the early stage of study.

Father René Laurentin has said that these are the tensions between authority and prophecy. Since genuine apparitions have a prophetic function and a tone of urgency, it is often difficult for the Church to maintain the cautious pace that careful judgment or discernment requires.

"The word of ecclesiastical authority will appear very pale to those who have *seen*" the Blessed Virgin or others from heaven, commented the French theologian. There is an immediate danger, he believes, that "seers risk setting themselves up as a parallel and competitive magisterium" because they have seen. Perhaps the Virgin's apparent preference for children and the unpretentious as visionaries has blunted that tendency. In the apparitions acknowledged by the Church, tensions between prophecy and authority have always been reconciled, although not always with sensitivity.

On March 25, 1858, Bernadette Soubirous was making her way to the rectory to deliver a message to her pastor, Abbé Peyramale. The message, in fact, was the prophetic confirmation of the Marian dogma the Church had proclaimed in 1854.

For weeks, the gruff pastor had been insisting that Bernadette learn the name of the Lady who had been appearing since February 11. "She is having a lot of fun with you!" the pastor had scoffed when Bernadette told him earlier that the Lady had answered her repeated questions with a smile. Authority needed and demanded confirmation.

Finally Bernadette came to knock on the pastor's door with an answer.

"I am the Immaculate Conception," the fourteen-year-old blurted out in the rectory study. The forty-seven-year-old pastor paled. His mind reeled with the reality. The Mother of God! But then he was in mental agony over the confusing way the Virgin had described herself — "I am the Immaculate Conception."

"You are mistaken!" he told Bernadette after he'd thought about it a little more. "Do you know what that means?" he demanded to know.

The seer shook her head no.

"Then how can you say the words if you did not understand them?"

"I kept repeating them along the way," Bernadette admitted.

"Go back home. I will see you another day," the priest told her. What he did not tell her she learned later in the day. The "Immaculate Conception" was the Blessed Virgin Mary, she was told. At about the same hour that Bernadette was welcoming this news with joy, Abbé Peyramale was once again considering the way in which Our Lady had identified herself. As he turned it over and over in his mind, he saw the meaning.

The Mother of God was the very essence of purity from her first moment. "I am the Immaculate Conception." It was a figure of speech, heaven's figure of speech. It was a great truth.

Eventually at Lourdes, the prophetic witness of the apparition and the authority of the Church to validate and support it were perfectly balanced. But Bernadette's ability to bend to authority and to carry her message to authority were necessary for the balance. And, though she could not have known it, this ability was another sign that the apparition was truly from God.

"One of the criteria that a vision comes from God is that it does not divide the Church, but remains in charity, order, and obedience," explains Father Laurentin. Those qualities were visible in events at Akita, Japan, in the late 1970s when bitter accusations of fraud were hurled at Sister Agnes Sasagawa and her convent. The visionary and her sisters suffered silently and continued to respect and obey their superiors.

The other criteria and methods for assessment of apparitions have been progressively shaped by the Church since the sixteenth century.

In 1516, at the Fifth Lateran Council, the Church of Rome first formally addressed the matter of apparitions and private revelations. But the focus at that time was the problem of publicizing the messages that apparitions invariably produced. That was properly the concern of the total Church, the council believed, because erroneous teaching could mislead the faithful. The council, therefore, forbade the publication of predictions or other apparition messages unless there was approval of it from Rome.

At the Council of Trent in 1563, the basic guidelines for investigation of "miracles" (which included apparitions) were established and given for use to the local churchmen. It required the establishment of a diocesan commission to study apparition claims, a procedure still used.

"No new miracles may be admitted ... without the recognition and approbation of the bishop," the council declared. "The bishop, from the moment he is informed, will take the counsel of theologians and other pious men, and will do what he estimates to be conformed to the truth and to piety."

In the eighteenth century, the Church refined the understanding the faithful needed to have about approved apparitions. The explanation was written by Prospero Lambertini, who later became Pope Benedict XIV. This statement supplied the Church with the working attitude it would maintain concerning supernatural visits:

"It is necessary to know that the approbation given by the Church to a private revelation is *nothing other than a permission accorded*, after an attentive examination, *to communicate this revelation* for the instruction and good of the faithful. *To such revelations, even those approved by the Church, one must not accord an assent of Catholic faith*. It is necessary only, according to the law of prudence, to give to them an assent of human belief to the degree that such revelations appear probably and piously credible."

On behalf of approved apparitions, the future pope advised that believers could certainly and legitimately refuse to believe in apparitions "provided this is done with suitable modesty, for good reasons and without contempt." Into the twentieth century, many have welcomed at least part of the Lambertini guidelines. They do not particularly believe in Guadalupe, Lourdes, Fátima, or any of the others. Or if they don't believe, it's with "suitable modesty."

Approved apparitions should also exhibit certain characteristics, it was found. If they truly sprang from a divine source, they would: manifest a hidden presence of God, renew community life, convert hearts, reawaken and stimulate faith, and renew hope and dynamism in the Church.

Generally, experience proved, there were categories into which studied apparitions eventually fell. The lowest category of evaluation labels a reported apparition as "not worthy of belief." It does not, according to the judgment, exhibit the anticipated characteristics or hallmarks of an apparition of supernatural origin.

The second category assigns a somewhat neutral judgment to the event — "nothing contrary to the Faith." The local church, in its own best light, suggests that the reported event might or might not be the result of a supernatural intervention.

The third category includes the apparitions that are today called "approved" or "recognized" by the Church. These, it is said, are "worthy of belief" by the faithful and show the distinguishing traits of an occurrence arranged by God.

With a knowledge of all of this, bishops in modern times have been better equipped to respond when the most remarkable visits of all are reported. It has been easier to deal with apparitions that they have had to assess for the sake of the faithful. Dealing with apparitions that are still uncategorized or those already judged "unworthy of belief," however, has been a difficult pastoral problem. And in a sense, it is a fairly modern problem for the Church.

The "approved" Marian apparitions of the nineteenth and the early twentieth centuries whet the popular appetite for such events.

But after each claim that the Church later confirmed as valid, an "echo-phenomenon" was noticed. During the weeks of Bernadette's apparitions at Lourdes, similar claims rained down so frequently upon Abbé Peyramale, the local pastor, that he was barely civil when he spoke with the real seer.

Following the apparition of Our Lady of Beauraing to five Belgian children in 1932-33, twenty "visions" were reported in Belgium within weeks. Only one, the acknowledged apparition to Mariette Beco at Banneux, was eventually confirmed at the same time as Beauraing. The proclivity to see visions has continued well into the twentieth century.

From 1923 until 1975, according to theologian Bernard Billet's international study, two hundred thirty-two separate occasions of Marian visits were reported in thirty-two countries. Other authorities suggest that hundreds of apparitions have been reported just in the last decade or two.

These "apparitions," explained Father Billet, will probably remain "unapproved" or "unrecognized" as far as the Church is concerned. Judgments were made on the local level as in the case of two reports from the United States. They were seen not only as "unrecognized" but also "unworthy of belief."

In 1970, Veronica Lueken claimed to be a visionary of Marian apparitions in Bayside, New York. After careful study, the Diocese of Brooklyn, New York, said it did not believe that this was the case. In fact, it reported that the events there seemed to be "inauthentic."

Diocesan spokesmen explained that the judgment emerged from holding Bayside events up to the criteria set out by the Church. The Bayside message, one representative maintained, "has condemned all the changes in the Church." A negative attitude recurring through the so-called messages of Mary seemed to attack the legitimate authority of the Church to institute the liturgical changes mandated at the Second Vatican Council.

A similar local assessment was made regarding the claims of Mrs. Mary Ann Van Hoof, who believed she saw visions of Mary dating from 1950 until her death in early 1984 at Necedah, Wisconsin. There, too, the Church did not find the necessary attributes that indicated an "authentic" experience of Mary.

Apparitions reported between 1961 and 1965 at Garabandal, Spain, were referred back to the local bishop for judgment. At the end of an investigation in 1965, the bishop ruled that no supernatural events had occurred. Later, however, a new commission was organized to study Garabandal.

Before the recent approval of apparitions at Akita (1981) and Betania (1987), no approvals had been granted from the Church since 1947, when recognition confirmed the authenticity of the Belgian apparitions at Beauraing and Banneux. Certain sanctuaries and pilgrimages, however, have received authorization. But the major expression of Church endorsement for Marian apparition sites has focused on places like Lourdes and Fátima. Though the Church must use prudence, even in the statements it makes regarding those apparitions, pilgrimage visits to Fátima and Lourdes by popes in recent years solidify their prestige among the faithful.

Does the cessation of Church approval indicate that the Mother of God herself has ceased to visit our world? Not necessarily, theorizes Father René Laurentin. There is a tension between authority and prophecy (the Church and apparitions) that must work itself out again and again.

The tension will continue, but there is little need to be concerned that it will damage the Church. Because Mary has assured us that she is indeed Mother of the Church, it is safe — and even necessary — to believe that she will always be near. And when the time is right and the needs of the Church warrant it, she will be close enough for eyes to see.*

*If you would like more information on this subject, simply call toll-free 1-800-348-2440 (customer service) and ask for a free copy of Our Sunday Visitor's booklet, "Marian Apparitions and the Church" by J. Michael Miller, C.S.B.

Guadalupe, Mexico

1531

For fifty-seven years, Juan Diego had lived near the shore of Lake Texcoco in a village hugging Tlatelolco, the Aztec capital. As he walked toward that city on a chilly morning in 1531, his thoughts returned to the years of Aztec pagan rites and despicable human sacrifice. Later, the Spanish conquistadors had overwhelmed the Aztec chieftains who had ruthlessly ruled the Indian tribes. For Juan and fifteen million Indians, a new time and spirit then began in his homeland.

In Juan's own mind, only the last six of his years had been truly joyful. In 1525, he and his wife, Maria Lucia, had been baptized as Christians. On most days, well before dawn, Juan was somewhere on this road, headed to or from Mass. His village was called Tolpetlac, near Cuauhtitlan. This day, December 9, 1531, was a Saturday, a day on which a special Mass was said in honor of the Virgin Mary.

For some time, his early morning walks had been solitary as he crossed the hill of Tepeyac and the Tepeyac causeway to Tlatelolco, the future Mexico City. Juan's wife had died. There was only his uncle, Juan Bernardino. Juan Diego thought of his dead Maria Lucia many times as he made his way. There had been no children, and she had been precious to him.

As Juan approached the crest of Tepeyac Hill, he saw a cloud encircled with a rainbow of colors. Then he heard strange music coming from the hill as well. Could it be from some sort of rare bird? he wondered. He stared up at the hill with the sun now rising behind it. A woman's voice was calling above the music. He was fascinated but confused.

"Juanito, Juan Dieguito ..." the voice came, urging him. Since it seemed to be coming from behind the top of the hill, he ascended to the crest to look. A young woman, strikingly beautiful, stood there beckoning him. She radiated such light and joy that Juan Diego could think of nothing more to do than drop to his knees and smile at her.

Everything around her seemed to catch the sweet fire she

glowed with. The leaves of the plants surrounding her on the hill were aglow; the branches of the trees and bushes shone like polished gold. Around the whole hill a rainbow of multicolored light seemed to have descended.

"Juanito [Little John], my sweet child, where are you going?" the woman asked him in Nahuatl, his own tongue.

"My Lady and my child," he replied in an Indian idiom of endearment, "I am on my way to the church at Tlatelolco to hear Mass."

Then, with no further introduction, the shining young woman spoke very seriously and yet lovingly to Juan Diego. He listened with an intensity born of instant devotion. The woman was so beautiful, so gracious, that he could not do otherwise.

"You must know and be very certain in your heart, my son," she began, "that I am truly the perpetual and perfect Virgin Mary, holy Mother of the True God through whom everything lives, the Creator and Master of Heaven and Earth.

"I wish and intensely desire that in this place my sanctuary be erected so that in it I may show and make known and give all my love, my compassion, my help and my protection to the people. I am your merciful Mother, the Mother of all of you who live united in this land, and of all mankind, of all those who love me, of those who cry to me, of those who seek me, of those who have confidence in me. Here I will hear their weeping, their sorrow, and will remedy and alleviate their suffering, necessities, and misfortunes.

"And so that my intentions may be made known, you must go to the house of the bishop of Mexico and tell him that I sent you and that it is my desire to have a sanctuary built here."

Overwhelmed at knowing the identity of the woman, Juan then bowed in obedience to her request. Immediately, without turning back, he took leave of her and hurried toward the causeway into the city. He knew where to find the house of his excellency Don Juan de Zumarraga, the recently named bishop of Mexico (New Spain).

Juan rapped on the door of the bishop's house and waited. It was still early morning, shortly after dawn. The bishop's servants opened the door to him with looks of scorn in their eyes: *This Indian! Who was he to think of imposing on the lordly bishop, and at this hour!* But Juan was eventually admitted into the bishop's study.

With patience, the Spanish-born bishop listened as Juan told of his encounter with the Mother of God at the top of Tepeyac Hill, translated from the Indian's Nahuatl dialect by an aide. Bishop Zumarraga was understanding, but he did not really believe Juan's words. Tepeyac, the bishop had learned, was the site of the temple of the Aztec corn goddess, Tonantzin. Perhaps this story was a jumble of that tradition and newfound Christian beliefs the Indian claimed.

The bishop told Juan Diego that he would think over what he had said. "Come back to see me in a few days," he suggested.

Juan Diego was indeed trusting. He had not anticipated that Bishop Zumarraga would doubt him. The image of the Virgin was so sharply and beautifully impressed upon his own spirit. It was hard to believe that anyone else would deny her wishes. Heavyhearted, he headed back to Tepeyac, thinking himself a failure.

As Juan climbed the rise to Tepeyac once again, the Lady was suddenly standing toward the top. He ran closer, dropped to his knees, and dropped his head as well. He was ashamed, but hoped that she would understand that he had tried. With deep regret, he told her of his attempt to convince Bishop Zumarraga and of the bishop's doubting eyes and puzzling smile. This man of God thought that Juan Diego was a liar or a fool.

Burdened by his own littleness, the quiet, good-hearted Indian broke down. Perhaps, he suggested, the Lady could find a more eloquent, more persuasive messenger.

If anything, as Juan Diego later told it, his recitation of failures warmed her smile and her apparent affection for him. Her words were consoling. There were many others she could send, she admitted, but she had chosen him. Her request would be answered through his efforts, she promised.

Courage and self-esteem once again flickered inside of him. Taking leave of "my Dear One, my Lady," Juan made his way now to his home. On the following day, Sunday, December 10, he planned to visit the bishop's house once again.

The next day was chilly, and Juan Diego made his way to Mass somewhat later than usual in the morning. His coarse cloak was needed, and he thanked the good God for it as he made his way to Mass. His spirit was at peace concerning the challenge after Mass. The Virgin told him that he would be the one to get her message across to the only man who could have a church built.

At the home of the bishop, Juan's heart was once again thumping wildly with anxiety and fear. This time, Bishop Zumarraga listened more closely. His eyes did not wander all over the Indian's face, looking for a sign of instability or a penchant for lying. He looked straight into Juan's dark eyes as he spoke, with an aide interpreting. Still, when Juan Diego was finished with his story — the same story as the day before — the bishop again refused to commit himself. He needed proof, he said.

"Perhaps you can bring me some sign of the Lady as a tangible proof that she is the Mother of God and that she definitely wants a temple built at Tepeyac Hill," he said. Then Bishop Zumarraga smiled at Juan and left it at that.

Simply and humbly, Juan agreed. But the bishop was thoroughly surprised by the Indian's consent to provide a miracle. As Juan left, Bishop Zumarraga sent two servants after him to track his movements. Outside of the city, the men from the bishop's house lost sight of Juan Diego. He seemed to disappear into thin air, or into the sunset then settling over the land.

In fact, Juan Diego had again entered that special realm

where his time and space were meshed with the Virgin's on Tepeyac Hill. He greeted her and told her of the bishop's request for proof. Gently, and with a smile, she assured Juan that there would be a sign on the following day. The bishop would have no more doubts.

If Juan was as happy as a man could be when descending the hill, the joy soon vanished. When he reached home, he found his uncle, his only relative, deathly ill. Juan Bernardino had a soaring fever.

On the following day, Juan Diego could not leave his uncle's side. He was frightened that the old man would die. There seemed to be no break in the fever's grip. Juan Diego's spirit was heavy, and heavier still when he thought about his forsaken appointment with the bishop. When he thought of the beautiful Virgin Mother waiting for him to fulfill his promise, he was sick at heart. He almost wished that he too were on his deathbed.

Night brought no relief for Juan Bernardino. The sick man asked his nephew to leave early on the following morning for the monastery of Santiago Tlatelolco. He wished to receive the Anointing of the Sick and the Holy Eucharist.

Once he was on the road again, Juan began to fear meeting the Virgin. It was just before dawn on Tuesday, December 12. The day before, he was to have taken the verifying sign to the bishop for "his Dear One, his Lady." How could he tell her that he had failed once again? The most direct route to the monastery would take him near Tepeyac and the shining Mother of God. He decided to take the long way around.

As he was skirting the hilltop where he had seen her, Juan Diego was suddenly face to face again with the heavenly Lady. He shrank with embarrassment, but her greeting dispelled it.

"What troubles you, my dear son? Where are you going?" she asked.

Juan raised his eyes to her then and told her of the illness of his beloved uncle, Juan Bernardino. He had to care for him, he explained; there was no one else to do so. He begged her forgiveness for delaying in the mission she had given him. The Blessed Virgin Mary's response was reassuring:

"Listen and be sure, my dear son, that I will protect you; do not be frightened or grieved or let your heart be dismayed, however great the illness may be that you speak of. Am I not here, I who am your Mother, and is not my help a refuge? Am I not of your kind? Do not be concerned about your uncle's illness, for he is not going to die. Be assured, he is already well. Is there anything else that you need?"

With these words, the world of Juan Diego was once again washed with the clear, bright light of hope. Whatever the Virgin had said would surely come to pass. He listened as she gave him instructions about carrying the providential sign to Bishop Zumarraga. He would carry a bouquet of roses, Castilian roses, miraculously flowering on Tepeyac, on a barren hill in winter. These he was to take to the bishop.

The Virgin directed him to climb to the top of Tepeyac Hill. He was to pick the roses now growing there where only cactus, thistles, and thornbush had previously been seen. Juan's eyes grew wide at the lush abundance of roses of every color. He began to pluck them in great bunches and carry them back down to the Virgin. She arranged them in his *tilma*.

When it was heavy with the fragrant and radiant roses — heaven's own hybrids — Juan carefully put the folded cloak over his head once again. He tied one corner to the top of the *tilma* at his shoulder to keep the flowers from tumbling out. Then, with a loving smile and farewell to the Lady, he was off again to the bishop's residence. Talk to no one but the bishop, the Virgin had warned Juan. It was the last of four apparitions of the Blessed Virgin to Juan Diego at Guadalupe. He did not realize it as he left her, but Juan would only see the Virgin again in the image she would leave behind.

At the home of Bishop Zumarraga, Juan Diego was admitted for the third time in four days. There was no scorn on the faces of the bishop's servants this time. With open curiosity, they tried to see what he was carrying in the fold of his *tilma*. But Juan only held the ends of the garment closer to his chest, pushing the curious back. The roses were not to be crushed!

When he was in the presence of Bishop Zumarraga this time, Juan bubbled with his message. The bishop stared at the *tilma* he was clutching. He listened as his interpreter struggled to keep up with the unbroken litany of Nahuatl enthusiasm. Juan Diego shared the whole story about his uncle's sickness and his inability to come the day before, about the day's encounter with the Virgin once again, about her insistence that a church be built on Tepeyac Hill.

Finally, Juan told of gathering the roses and of the way the Holy Mother arranged them with care in his cloak. With a smile of the purest joy, Juan then dramatically let loose the bottom of his *tilma*. The roses would fall to the floor in a rainbow cascade of glory at the bishop's feet ... or so Juan thought.

The bishop did watch as several roses fell to his carpet, but then his eyes moved back up to the *tilma* and filled with tears. He fell speechless to his knees before Juan, who was still wearing the cloak, and began to beg pardon of the Virgin. There on the rough cactus-fiber *tilma* was an exquisite full-length portrait of the Virgin Mother of God, just as Juan had described her.

Now Juan Diego himself looked down at the front of his much-used cloak. Below him was a rendering of the heavenly woman he had so recently seen bending and arranging the roses in his cloak. She had been attired in a dark turquoise mantle, just like the figure in this portrait emblazoned on his old *tilma*.

A pink robe also adorned the image, just as the Lady had looked on Tepeyac. Her dark black hair could be seen beneath the mantle. Her posture was an attitude of humility and prayer, with her small, delicate hands joined, her head bowed to the left, her dark eyes half-shaded by the eyelids. Her eyes seemed patient, submissive. The facial features of the Virgin were delicate, beautiful, Indian in character but universal in appeal.

By now, Juan's heart was in his throat, choking him with joy and tears. He started to lift the cloak up over his head, and the bishop quickly rose from his knees to help him with the treasure. After some hesitation, Bishop Zumarraga carried it respectfully to his chapel and laid it before the Blessed Sacrament. By now, his entire household and a number of priests were also gathered around the miraculous portrait. Prayers rose in the chapel as groups of twos and threes spontaneously approached the *tilma* to kiss the bottom of it.

On December 13, the following day, Juan, who had stayed with the bishop overnight, began the trek back to Tepeyac Hill. This time his journey trailed a retinue of believers and the curious. Bishop Zumarraga asked the visionary to take him to see the place where Our Lady had touched New Spain.

Following this, Juan Diego hurried to his home. He had told the bishop about the illness of his uncle, but believed, as the Lady had promised, that he would find him well. Juan Bernardino *was* well. In fact, he was fully recovered and told his nephew that the Virgin had visited him, too:

"I too have seen her. She came to me in this very house and spoke to me. She told me, too, that she wanted a temple to be built at Tepeyac Hill. She said that her image should be called 'Holy Mary of Guadalupe,' though she did not explain why."

Juan de Zumarraga, a man who had left a Franciscan priory to come to this new land, was stirred to his depths. Our Lady of Guadalupe was known to the Spanish as an ancient statue depicting the divine motherhood of the Blessed Virgin.

Some questions were to continue throughout history concerning this name. Some authorities suggested that Zumarraga and the others heard a Nahuatl word, *Coatalocpia* (pronounced "Cuatlashupe"), which meant, "Who crushed the Stone Serpent." The serpent beneath the feet of the Virgin on Juan Diego's cloak was a symbol for the Indians. It brought to mind the pagan symbol of their Aztec religion, demanding human sacrifice.

In compliance with the wishes of the Virgin, Bishop Zumarraga planned to have an *hermita*, a little chapel or church, built there by Christmas. In the next two weeks, Indians flocked to Tepeyac Hill to erect the shelter for their Lady. On December 26, 1531, the day after Christmas and precisely two weeks after the miraculous image appeared, a procession was held. With great pomp, the cloak of Juan Diego was carried from the bishop's church to the chapel.

Accounts of the procession say that the Indians of the region had strewn the four-mile route with herbs and flowers. Dressed in bright costumes and adorned with feathers, hundreds danced as the image was borne past. But a near-tragedy along the way spread the devotion to Our Lady of Guadalupe.

As part of the celebration, the Indians reenacted a mock battle by the lake near Tepeyac Hill. In the excitement, one of the Indians was accidently pierced with an arrow in the neck. He died near the feet of the bishop and others who were escorting the precious *tilma*.

With grief, but with faith too, he was picked up and placed in front of the mounted image of Our Lady of Guadalupe. Within moments, the "dead" man sat up. The arrow was carefully withdrawn, with no apparent damage except for a scar where the arrow had entered. Tepeyac Hill went wild with joy. Spaniards and the Aztecs, recently released from the horror of a pagan cult, had discovered a living Mother who cared for her children.

To say that the life of Juan Diego was never the same is to state the obvious. He gave the cornfields and the small house that he owned to Juan Bernardino. A small hut was then built for the visionary on Tepeyac Hill. He acted as sacristan at the *hermita*, telling and retelling the story of the apparitions, the blessed *tilma*, and the wonders.

Bishop Zumarraga granted Juan the permission to receive

the Eucharist at Mass three times a week, an unusual concession in that century. Juan made use of it but never with any sense of superiority or prestige. A major interrogation of natives of the area in 1666 revealed that, in those years following the apparitions, Juan was called "The Pilgrim." Villagers living near Tepeyac recalled that their grandparents or great-grandparents often saw Juan making his way to Mass. He was always alone, always aglow with a special peace and joy.

In 1548, Juan Diego and Bishop Zumarraga died within a few days of each other. Juan was seventy-four; Bishop Zumarraga died at seventy-two. In the decade following the apparitions and the creation of the Guadalupe image, eight million Indians were baptized, and the growth of Christian conversion and devotion continued throughout the century.

The image of "Holy Mary of Guadalupe" has its mysteries for each century and culture to solve. In the century of its origin, the sixteenth, the picture of the Virgin functioned as a sort of graphic catechism for the Indian culture. In writing, the Aztecs used a form of picture writing, which was similar to Egyptian hieroglyphics used thousands of years earlier.

Here was a beautiful maiden of their own kind. She stood with an attitude of peace and prayer. When they viewed the portrait as a whole, the Indians could see and "read" that this new maiden was more powerful than any and all of their pagan gods, and she did not demand their blood. Her kindness, her care for them, offered them her Son's body and blood instead. Jesus Christ would sustain them; His Mother would be their Mother and Protector.

Added to all this, the Indians could see that the Lady wore a brooch or pin at her throat with a black cross on it. This was the symbol used by the Franciscan friars who had come with the conquistadors early in the century. She was of heaven, and represented heaven's power.

In 1709, a massive basilica was erected at the base of the hill to house the revered image on Juan Diego's cloak. For over two centuries it drew pilgrims from Mexico and all over the world. In 1921, a bomb hidden in a bouquet of flowers was placed on the altar just beneath the Guadalupe image. Since 1917, the national constitution had fostered an intensely anti-Catholic rule in Mexico. The bomb went off during Mass and shattered parts of the altar. However, no one attending Mass in the Guadalupe basilica was touched and the *tilma*, too, was unharmed.

In 1976, a new Basilica of Our Lady of Guadalupe was dedicated in Mexico City, while the older one was left standing on ground said to be sinking. An estimated fifteen million people visit Guadalupe each year. Processions still bring thousands on their knees to the feet of the Virgin.

In a different way, scientists of the twentieth century have also had to bow to the image.

Dr. Philip S. Callahan, an infrared specialist, biophysicist, and entomologist for the U.S. Department of Agriculture in Gainesville, Florida, studied the Guadalupe image in the spring of 1979. His work was done on behalf of the "Image of Guadalupe Research Project."

After four hundred forty-eight years, the rough fabric on which the image was imprinted was still in fine condition. Essentially, the fabric could be compared to gunnysacking, Callahan said. The pigments that created the image, the researchers discovered, were similar to earth pigments that would have been in use during Juan Diego's lifetime. Their color and quality was still rich, while the painted embellishments added in later decades had begun to fade and crack.

There had been no sizing or preparatory paint laid upon the surface of the fabric. There was no hint of preliminary sketching lines underneath — a shock to those who claimed that the painting was made by human hands. But on close inspection, the golden sunrays, stars, gold trim on the mantle, the moon, and the angel were found to be human "embellishments." They were added to the original portrait of the Virgin over the centuries. All these additions to the image — sunburst, crescent moon, etc. — were found to be deteriorating, while the original portrait showed no sign of wear, tear, or fading.

Another remarkable discovery related to the *tilma* was found in the eyes of the Virgin. Greatly enlarged photos of the eyes revealed a human figure resembling Juan Diego. Though this finding might be dismissed as an illusion, the *tilma* itself cannot be.

The Guadalupe *tilma* is an object that the most rigorous examinations of modern science can't explain. There is a great mystery in the rough cactus-fiber cloak that an Indian wore across his back on a December day many centuries ago. The *tilma* and its history have also been a great source of pride for the Mexican people. Seeing the fervor of pilgrims, Pope John Paul II remarked, "Ninety-five percent of the Mexican people are Catholics, but ninety-eight percent are Guadalupeans."

The apparitions of Our Lady of Guadalupe were never officially confirmed as "worthy of belief" in the same way that other apparitions were in later centuries. Perhaps the life-sized image miraculously produced on the *tilma* of Juan Diego made that unnecessary. In 1754, however, Pope Benedict XIV authorized a Mass and Office under the title of Our Lady of Guadalupe for celebration on December 12, her feast day. Mary was also named patroness of New Spain (Mexico), and in 1910, Our Lady of Guadalupe was named patroness of Latin America. Pope Pius XII proclaimed the patronage of the Guadalupe Madonna over both continents (North and South America) in 1945.

In 1990, Pope John Paul beatified Juan Diego, the visionary of Guadalupe. The celebration of Juan's wonderful life and holiness was to be remembered as an optional feast on December 9.

Rue du Bac, Paris

1830

*I*t is only understandable that a young nun, a newcomer to convent life, would spend some sleepless nights considering the awesome turn her life had taken. Yet Catherine Labouré, a simple and largely unschooled country girl, had suffered none of that midnight misery in the hot Paris summer of 1830. In fact, the six months since her acceptance as a novice by the Daughters of Charity had been her happiest. There was no nostalgic looking back. And during this first spring and summer spent at the motherhouse at 140 Rue du Bac (Street of the Ferryboat), the young postulant had happily reversed the educational deprivation of her girlhood. Though her spelling always had a certain mysterious quality to it, she had learned to read and write for the first time in her life.

Born May 2, 1806, in the tiny village of Fain-les-Moutiers in the French province of Burgundy, twenty-four-year-old Catherine had longed for religious life since she was thirteen. Because she was born on the feast of St. Zoé, the second-century Christian martyr, this eighth child of the Labourés was always called "Zoé," though she was baptized "Catherine." In the convent she reclaimed her baptismal name, "Catherine," and was ever after known as *Soeur Catherine* (Sister Catherine) or *Soeur Labouré*.

She was always a pious, hardworking girl, but especially so after the death of her mother when little Zoé was nine. She and her younger sister, Antoinette, or Tonine, tried to shoulder the burden of Madeleine Labouré's death for their father's sake. Privately, however, Catherine was devastated by the loss.

As it often does, the grief had its own saving grace. A few months after her mother had died, a servant found Zoé in the bedroom her parents had shared. She was perched on top of a massive bureau, where a large statue of the Blessed Virgin stood. She threw her arms around the figure and wept. "It is you, then, who are going to be my Mother," she sobbed. Apparently there was a feeling of security that Zoé received from her heavenly Mother.

Her piety and virtues had grown in the adolescent years. To Tonine's never-ending surprise and chagrin, Catherine rose before dawn several times a week so that she could walk to a nearby village to hear Mass. Also, her family discovered that from the age of fourteen she had fasted on Fridays and Saturdays.

Catherine loved summer best, though she and Tonine had extra work then. They tended to the poultry yard as well as to the stables and the garden. The housework had been their exclusive and year-round responsibility since the year that Catherine was fourteen and Tonine was twelve.

Tonine always recalled that the Labourés' seven hundred or eight hundred pigeons were Catherine's special joy and she delighted in feeding them. "They would fly to her, circling about her head, getting caught in her hair and sitting on her shoulders. She would pause happily in the midst of them, and it made a charming picture to see her there."

Like her older sister Marie-Louise, Catherine was determined to enter religious life. Marie-Louise had joined the convent of the Daughters of Charity in Paris, and Catherine prayed for the same fate. But her father, Pierre, opposed Catherine's choice of a religious vocation. Perhaps he felt that giving one daughter to God was enough. Catherine never knew the reason for his position. However, in January of 1830, she went to the Daughters of Charity with her father's grudging approval, though he refused to provide her trousseau or dowry. Those came through a friend.

The hopes of many of her years had brought her to the hot, humid Paris summer of 1830. And it would also have to be said that a very remarkable faith was alive in her as well. Though no one except her confessor knew of it, she had already experienced visions just days after she moved into the convent of the Daughters of Charity.

She told the priest that she had seen the heart of the order's founder, St. Vincent de Paul, on April 30. She also relayed the prophetic messages she had then received concerning the future of France and two religious orders, the Daughters of Charity and the Priests of the Mission, or Lazarists. St. Vincent, the apostle to the poor, had founded them both. Not long after these occurrences, in April and May, she began to see Christ, who appeared to her during the Mass at communion time and during exposition of the Blessed Sacrament.

By midsummer of 1830, probably none of the one hundred fifty nuns of her convent would have guessed that the thin, quiet postulant with the pretty blue eyes had received any spiritual favors. She was the very picture of a shy, retiring country girl. In fact, as most saw her, there was absolutely nothing remarkable about her. And yet it was this postulant who was awakened late at night on July 18, 1830, for a rendezvous with the Mother of God.

Catherine awoke with a start. A child's voice was calling, "Sister, Sister, Sister Catherine!" Catherine sat up, rubbed her eyes, and pushed aside the net curtain that hung around her bed. Standing there by her bed was a small boy of about five or six, dressed all in white.

The child was literally glowing with some sort of interior light, Catherine explained in her memoir of the events twenty-six years later. "The Blessed Virgin awaits you!" the child told her. A mixture of joy and wild anticipation began to flood into the postulant. But there was also a sudden nagging fear, a very human fear. Many other postulants slept in this common room, where the beds projected from alcoves adjoining the main dormitory room. Had her sleeping sisters been awakened?

"Do not be troubled," said the child, seeming to read her thoughts as she joined him in the hallway. "It is half past eleven and everyone is asleep. Come, I am waiting."

This was the prelude to a midnight meeting with the Mother of God that is perhaps the most charming, most tender, of all such accounts. The warm, simple joy of the experience is so easy to find in the reminiscences of the middle-aged Sister

Catherine, who wrote down her memories of the apparition more than a quarter of a century later.

The glowing child led her through the long convent corridors to the chapel, Catherine wrote. To her surprise, the place was brightly lit all along the way, even though the schedule at the motherhouse called for the sisters to be in their beds by eight o'clock at night.

As they reached the chapel, the child lifted his finger to touch the heavy wooden door. It swung open as though it were on springs. Catherine was amazed. Inside, every candle and torch was lit. It looked, she thought to herself, as though midnight Mass, maybe a Christmas Mass, were about to begin.

Nonetheless, as the eyes of the young nun scanned the room, she couldn't find the promised Blessed Virgin. She was not there. Just then, however, the child beckoned her to follow him toward the sanctuary. There he told her to kneel beside the chaplain's chair.

Catherine later wrote of the event: "I heard the rustling of a silken robe coming from the side of the sanctuary. The 'Lady' bowed before the tabernacle, and then she seated herself in M. Richenet's chair." After some interior confusion about how she should react, Catherine recalled, "I rushed forward and knelt before the Blessed Virgin with my hands on her knees. I cannot express what I felt, but I am sure that this was the happiest moment of my life."

Her first thought on seeing her heavenly Mother was a silly one, Catherine admitted. The chaplain's chair resembled the one in a painting of St. Anne that hung in the choir. When the young sister beheld the Virgin seated in this chair, her first thought was that she did not resemble St. Anne, her mother.

Then, however, the love that she had always felt for her two mothers melted the reserve. Seated before her was the Mother she had claimed when her own mother died. For two hours or more, Catherine was poised at the Virgin's knees, listening to instructions that would be needed throughout her life. The Blessed Mother advised her to rely on prayer when her heart was troubled. And there were other matters that she would have to understand. Our Lady paused, as if listening, and then spoke again to Catherine.

"My child, God wishes to entrust a mission to you," Our Lady told the young woman. "It will be the cause of great suffering to you, but you will surmount it with the thought that it will work to God's glory.

"You will know later what this mission is to be," the Virgin also informed her. "You will be contradicted; but do not fear, grace will be given to help you. In your prayers, inspiration will be given to you."

And then, the Mother of God spoke of the world's future in sad tones.

"The times are very evil. Great misfortune will come to France: her throne will be overthrown. The whole world will be upset by evils of every kind.... There will also be victims among the clergy of Paris. The archbishop himself will die. The cross will be insulted; blood will flow in the streets."

As she shared these words of prophecy with Catherine, the Blessed Mother wept. Finally, she could no longer speak of the great tragedies in store for France and for religious orders in France in the coming years.

Catherine, overwhelmed with empathy for her weeping Mother, was frightened, too, for her nation. She dared not ask it aloud, but she wondered when some of these horrors would befall her native land. As though she had asked it aloud, an answer came to her: "In forty years."

Finally, however, the messages the Virgin had come to give her ceased. When the Queen left her, Catherine wrote, "she disappeared like a shadow, as she had come." The child, whom she thought of as her guardian angel, escorted her back to the dormitory room and to her bed.

"When I returned," Catherine said, "it was two o'clock in

the morning, for I heard the hour strike. I went back to bed; but I did not sleep again that night."

Who can imagine what was behind the simple smile of the country novice that next morning? What was in her mind at breakfast, at recreation time, at adoration time, and during her hours of work in the kitchen? The world would have to imagine, and the convent could not have guessed. Catherine shared none of it except with Father Aladel, her confessor. The Blessed Mother had told her it should be that way. Catherine never yielded to the temptation to discuss her good fortune, her great gift, with another human being.

Much of what she learned and heard remained Catherine's private revelation, yet much of it was clearly given to her so that she could give it to the world. In the short run, however, none of it made any sense to the chaplain of this house of nuns. At thirty, perhaps he had already dealt with sisters who were inclined to see and hear heaven a bit too easily. Catherine was very much aware that he did not believe her. She also knew that he hadn't believed her when she had earlier told him of the apparitions of St. Vincent's heart and of Christ in the Eucharist.

Although the twenty-four-year-old's life continued uneventfully through the hot Paris summer and fall, surely she must have been anxious. The one person to whom she was permitted to tell her story did not believe her. Not only that, but the Blessed Mother had clearly said that she would be entrusted with a mission. What was it?

Late in November she had her answer. November 27, 1830, was the eve of the first Sunday of Advent, the season of the Lord's coming. In the chapel at the convent on the Rue du Bac, the novices were gathered at 5:30 P.M. for quiet prayer. White-veiled heads were bowed; the church was silent.

All at once Catherine, who had been kneeling at her place like all the others, heard once again the rustle of heavenly silk. She raised her head and eyes. There on the right side of the main altar, right in front of her, the Blessed Virgin stood as though suspended in solemn and stately glory. "So beautiful I could not describe it," Catherine said later, and yet hers were the only pair of eyes in the church who could see it.

The Virgin was clothed in a white silken robe that fit close to her neck and draped down over her shoulders and arms. A long veil covered her head, which left just enough of her hair in view for Catherine to see that it was braided and held by a piece of lace.

As before, the vision was not static. The Virgin raised her eyes to heaven, and Catherine then noticed also that she stood upon a green snake coiled over a white sphere. At the level of her breast she held a golden ball surmounted by a cross. Catherine felt that the Lady was offering the ball — the world — to God.

As the other novices breathed quiet prayers into their hands, Catherine stared hard at the scene, which altered once again in front of the altar.

Suddenly the golden orb was gone and Our Lady lifted her hands toward heaven. Each finger of her hand exhibited beautiful precious jewels of differing sizes and colors. From some of these stones light rays began to fall upon the white sphere beneath her feet. From some of the stones there was no light.

Catherine again heard, inside herself, an answer to an unspoken question. She was wondering what the stones meant when she "heard" a voice explaining that the stones represented graces. The Queen of Heaven had these graces in hand, so to speak, and could direct them to those who asked for them. Many went unclaimed.

Once again, the apparition evolved.

Before Catherine's unblinking blue eyes, an oval frame appeared around Our Lady's form. Words materialized inside this frame that said: "O Mary conceived without sin, pray for us who have recourse to thee."

"Have a medal made after this pattern," the inner voice again said to the young nun. "Those who wear it blessed about their necks, and who confidently say this prayer, will receive great graces and will enjoy the special protection of the Mother of God." Then the frame reversed and the other side of the medal appeared.

"A large M," Catherine wrote, was "surmounted by a cross, having a double bar under it. Beneath this M, the holy hearts of Jesus and Mary were placed, side by side, the first crowned with thorns, the other pierced by a sword. Around the whole were twelve stars."

And so Advent began that year with Catherine Labouré finally understanding what her mission was. Dutifully, she went again to her confessor and told of her commission to "have a medal made after this pattern." Again, Father Aladel was polite but dubious, and he did nothing.

Catherine, the powerless novice, on the other hand, did something. As the Virgin had advised her, she prayed often for a solution to the impasse, wondering some days how Our Lady would fit things together.

Following the medal apparition, there were three more apparitions of the Blessed Virgin to Catherine Labouré in less than a year. In December of 1830, March of 1831, and in September, the Virgin visited the quiet sister from the country. In September, 1831, the Blessed Mother told Catherine that she was displeased that no progress was being made on behalf of the medal. She told her also that Catherine would not see her again in that life. Instead, Catherine was to hear her Mother's voice in an interior way during prayer.

In fact, the medal was out of Catherine's hands. She did not make judgments about what to tell or not to tell Father Aladel. She merely told him what she was told, describing what she had seen. In the massive motherhouse on the Rue du Bac, Catherine went about her work.

When Catherine told the young cleric about the Holy Mother's disappointment, he became uneasy for the first time.

Suddenly, he was not completely sure that the sister was sadly, yet piously, hallucinating.

Sometime in the fall, on a visit to the Archbishop of Paris, Father Aladel shared the story of the nun and her medal in a way that did not betray the confidentiality of the confessional. The archbishop could find no fault with the revelations being given through the young sister. At the end of the conversation, he encouraged production of the medal and said that he himself wished to have the first one struck.

Fall leaves scattered down the Rue du Bac, only to be followed by fluttering snowfalls, which were followed by spring rains. Only then was something about to be done concerning the medal. In the meantime, in February 1831, Catherine was assigned to the Hospice of Enghien, a facility for the care of poor elderly.

Enghien was about two miles from the motherhouse where the apparitions had taken place, and it was just across a garden from another larger facility. This, too, was run by the Daughters of Charity. The sisters at Enghien would walk through the garden to share prayer and recreation with the nuns there.

And so the world of Catherine Labouré became this treasured triangle of houses — Enghien, the house across the garden, and the motherhouse on the Rue du Bac. Under her own roof, *Ma Soeur Labouré* (My Sister Labouré) was soon loved for her gift of making fine, nutritious meals from meager stocks. Sister Labouré was the cook and the seamstress for the hospice where fifty men and women made their home.

In June of 1831, the medals became a reality. Going first to a Parisian engraver named Vachette, Father Aladel had arranged for the production of 1,500 medals. When given one, along with the other sisters of her house, the inscrutable sister who had experienced the apparitions was as pleased and gracious as the rest. "I will wear it with veneration," she said, "but the important thing now is to make it widely known."

The two orders founded by St. Vincent de Paul — the

Lazarists and the Daughters of Charity — now worked to spread the use of the medal. The medals were given and taken so quickly all over Paris and France that Vachette, the engraver, reluctantly had to share his booming business with others. In Paris alone, more than two million medals had been distributed by 1836.

In the rest of France, the numbers kept moving at the same pace. Millions were cast, cooled, and sold almost as soon as they were laid upon the counters. The "Medal of the Immaculate Conception," the "Mary's Medal," or the "Medal of the Daughters of Charity," was more popular than Father Aladel could have been persuaded it would be.

Part of the popularity of the medal, as France was learning, had to do with reports by those who wore it. Within two years of its issuing, the medal almost everywhere was called "the Medal that cures," or the "Miraculous Medal."

In one of the houses of the Daughters of Charity, cholera broke out among the girls. A child with a very serious case was given a medal and was completely cured within minutes. A distraught mother pinned a medal on a five-year-old who had never been able to walk. On the first day of his mother's novena to the Blessed Virgin, the boy began to walk. The marvels of the medal designed by heaven's direction continued nonstop into the twentieth century. Millions of the medals are in use today.

Sister Labouré, it is certain, heard of these wonders, as did her sisters throughout Paris. Often they were the talk among the sisters during recreation time. Sister Cook, it was sometimes thought, was conspicuously quiet when the subject moved to the apparitions, the medal, or its wonders.

After 1836, she was given overall responsibility for the old men at Enghien Hospice and also for the poultry yard. Now thirty, she loved both added tasks. Care of the poultry yard, after all, had been given to her and to Tonine as children. They had loved feeding and caring for the chickens and pigeons.

And Soeur Labouré treated her old men with the same tenderness as her mother hens had used in rounding up chicks. She spoiled the penniless fellows when their spirits were low, but she kept them under control and in good health.

One day, a young nun being visited by her parents pointed to Catherine and described her as the visionary of the Rue du Bac apparitions of 1831. The girl's father rushed over to meet Soeur Labouré, telling her how honored he was. Catherine merely shrugged off his comments and gave him a very confused look. The man bowed apologetically and backed away. "It is not always wise to believe all that one hears," she told the embarrassed young nun, who later came to see her. She had not denied that she was the visionary, but cautioned that she might not be.

This was Catherine's unwavering response to the suggestion that she was the sister who saw the Mother of God in the chapel. It was important, she believed, to place the emphasis on the Blessed Virgin, not on the insignificant nun she chose to pass along her message. She told one living person of her experiences, but not her family, not her superiors or closest friends in religious life. Only Father Aladel, the confessor.

Forty years of the seer's life passed by, with the years largely following the same pattern. Gradually, her sisters at Enghien came to see the rare facility the quiet Soeur Labouré had in performing almost any task. Yet the superior, Soeur Dufès, was not so sure.

Soeur Dufès found Catherine somewhat simple — in more ways than one. Catherine's self-effacing behavior could be confusing. When an opportunity arose to name an official assistant at the little community at Enghien, her fellow nuns hoped it would be Sister Labouré, to honor her for her many years of humble service. Instead, a much younger sister was named by the superior, and Catherine bowed in smiling acceptance.

As the years bent her over with arthritis, Catherine began to worry that another request of the Virgin would go unfulfilled.

Our Lady had wanted an altar to mark the apparition site in the chapel. There was also to be a statue fashioned after Mary's appearance at the apparition of the Miraculous Medal. None of that was being done.

Father Aladel, himself aging, appeared to believe that there was no hurry once the medals had been distributed. In 1865, the confessor died and was succeeded by Father Chinchon. Sister Labouré dutifully went to him and shared the wonders that only Father Aladel had ever heard. And yet, to Catherine's great sorrow, Father Chinchon also did nothing to fulfill the Virgin's request for a chapel and a statue — simple requests.

In 1876, Sister Catherine learned that Father Chinchon was to be relieved of his duties as confessor to the Daughters of Charity. She was profoundly disturbed. To try to convince a new priest of the necessity of giving the Virgin what she wanted seemed insurmountable. The cool, calm Catherine almost broke down. She knew that her time was limited; she was seventy years old, and in failing health.

In desperation, Catherine went to her superior, Soeur Dufès. Weeping over the problems that now seemed hopelessly complicated, she told the other nun that she was indeed the sister who had received the apparitions. Soeur Dufès was shocked. She was also ashamed of the way she had treated the woman she had seen as foolishly simple.

The superior agreed to help complete the work assigned so many years before by the Mother of Christ. In short order, the efficient nun had commissioned a Parisian sculptor to cast a statue that followed the descriptions of the apparition's only eyewitness. Nonetheless, it was still twenty years before the statue of Our Lady of the Globe stood upon the requested altar in the chapel.

Catherine did not live to see the final fulfillment of Our Lady's wishes. She lost strength throughout 1876. A worsening heart condition and asthma took their toll. Sister Catherine Labouré died December 31, 1876. She had predicted that she would not see the new year, and that her burial would not require her sisters to arrange for a hearse to take her to the cemetery.

As news of her death circulated throughout Paris, many came to honor her. For a few years, it had been suspected that she was the nun who had spoken to the Blessed Virgin. Catherine would not admit it during her lifetime, but in death the truth was almost impossible to hide. Her face, they noticed, was beautiful. The wrinkles had smoothed away and she was young again. Crowds passed by her bier, touching rosaries and Miraculous Medals to her habit.

Almost at the last moment, the Daughters of Charity recalled that there was an unused vault in the chapel at Reuilly, near the Enghien Hospice where Catherine had spent her life cooking, mending, and caring for old men and chickens. In the presence of hundreds of her sisters and priests from the Lazarists, she was carried to her resting place in early January, 1877.

It was not until 1895, however, that her cause for sainthood was seriously undertaken by her order. Perhaps Sister Catherine's self-effacing style had its effect even after death. She was beatified May 28, 1933, and canonized July 27, 1947.

A few months before her beatification was announced by Pope Pius XI, it was found that her body was remarkably preserved. It was moved back to the chapel at the motherhouse on the Rue du Bac. After all, this was the same chapel to which an angel had led a young nun for a miraculous meeting more than a century before. Catherine must have been happy to return and to know that a new altar had been built there. On the altar was placed an image of Our Lady of the Globe, offering the world to God.

La Salette, France

1846

*T*he air was still very clean and fresh near Corps and Ablandins, mountain villages nestled in the southeastern quarter of France. A bulge from the midsection of the nation there seems to push France right into Italy to the east and toward Switzerland to the north. Grenoble, the most notable city of this region, lies about fifty miles from little Corps.

The Alps rise pretty steeply there, but the climb scarcely bothered the two young cowherds on a bright, brisk September day in 1846. They had risen early to walk the eight cows and one goat they tended up into the foothills. They were headed for high pasture on this Saturday, September 19.

As it happened, both eleven-year-old Maximin Giraud and Melanie Mathieu, almost fifteen years old, were from Corps, but they had just recently met. Both were hired out to farmers in adjoining towns. All the way up to the plateau from Ablandins that morning, Maximin had played with his dog Loulou while following the cows. He had her do tricks, threw sticks for her to fetch, and laughed uproariously at such silliness all the way up to the meadow. Melanie would have preferred to herd alone, but that was risky.

Both children were small for their ages. Many people looked at the wild boy with thatchy black hair and pitied his parents. In fact, it was wasted pity. Maximin's father frequented taverns, and his son seldom spent much time with him. The boy tried to stay away from his stepmother, who spent most of her energies and affection on the younger children, her own.

Melanie, slight and thin, had straight, pretty facial features, but her eyes seldom met those of anyone who spoke to her. For years she had been hired out by her impoverished family to tend the cattle or sheep of other families — people who had more to feed her than the Mathieus had.

The children could tell when it was noon because the bells of the parish church at La Salette rang out the "Angelus." They didn't stop to pray, as the bells traditionally asked. Neither one knew more than a haphazard version of the "Hail Mary" or the "Our Father." The Giraud and Mathieu families were no worse than other nonpracticing Catholic families of the region, but they were no better.

Melanie unwrapped the bread and cheese that constituted the herder's lunch, and the children ate with gusto. Maximin, to Melanie's delight, was silent, at least while he ate. Their contrasting personalities made them strange companions. He was a carefree and careless boy. She, on the other hand, was somber and solitary. They showed very different responses to the grinding rural poverty that put them on this mountain to herd cows for so little pay.

The day, which had started out cool before dawn, was now warm, lulling. After they had eaten, both children were surprised to find themselves drowsy. They soon surrendered to the warmth of sun and slept, curled up against the slope. It was two hours before Melanie raised her head and shook it. She could see by the sun that their nap had not been brief, and she could also see that the cows were gone.

"Memin," the girl called to the slumbering boy. "Memin, get up at once. We must look for the cows. I don't know where they are."

The boy grabbed his heavy staff and ran after her. At the top of the ravine, above the spot where they had been sleeping, they would have a panoramic view. Melanie shouted with relief as she reached the crest. Down the other side were the eight cows and the goat. Chastened by the close call in losing sight of the animals, the girl turned back down to the spot where they had dropped their knapsack. The cattle would need water again soon, then they would drive them back toward the village.

Suddenly, as she approached the spot near the edge where they had rested, she let out a shriek. There, down in the ravine, almost within touching distance, was a large glowing circle of light. It was similar to a sun glowing and reflecting color like a diamond. "Memin!" she called again, but the boy was already there, as transfixed as she was.

Terrorized, the girl dropped her heavy herder's staff. Maximin, however, was preparing for the threat and grabbed his staff all the tighter. "Hold on to that staff of yours," he advised. "If that attempts to hurt us, I will give it a hard whack!"

But what was there to whack?

As the children continued to watch, the globe became even more dazzling. Then, incredibly, it began to open, as if it were a wondrous shell or a magic egg. As it opened further, the two could see a woman inside. She was seated, bent forward, with her face buried in her hands and her elbows resting on her knees. It was the very picture of a woman weeping as though she had suffered the greatest loss of her life. The glowing globe of light faded away into the afternoon sun.

"Oh my God," exclaimed Melanie in a sort of prayer. At this moment, she stared at the shimmering figure, fearing that something evil rather than good would soon befall her. She was thinking of something Grandma Pra had warned her about. The elderly mother of the man who employed her had been shocked that Melanie did not say her prayers. The devil would carry her off if she did not change her ways, the old woman had predicted.

This glorious weeping woman now stood up. Her hands fell away from her face and crossed upon her breast. Melanie and Maximin were struck by her beauty. She was exquisite, the girl thought to herself. Her face was so beautiful, even though both children could see that the tears hadn't stopped.

The woman wore a long white dress, which seemed to glitter with small pearls of light. A lucent white headdress covered her head, where a tall crown rested. Across her shoulders she also wore a shawl, which was trimmed with roses, and there was a large yellow apron tied about her waist. White slippers fixed with pearls and gold buckles were on her feet. The children also saw that a cross was hung on a chain around her neck.

"Come to me, my children," she said to them. The words were spoken tenderly; she addressed them in French. "Do not be afraid. I am here to tell you something of the greatest importance."

Until this moment, fear had gripped their hearts. Now it melted quickly, as the Alpine snow that disappeared quickly on a warm, sunny day. Melanie and Maximin felt free. They descended the ravine in short order and crossed the dry streambed, where she stood. The woman, with a queenly bearing, moved slightly toward them. The globe of shimmering light that had enclosed her now enveloped all of them.

"If my people will not obey, I shall be compelled to loose my Son's arm," she told the children. "It is so heavy, so pressing, that I can no longer restrain it. How long have I suffered for you!" But the woman, though still crying, noticed the confused look Melanie gave to Memin.

"Ah, you do not understand French, my children," she said, smiling. Then she began again in the local patois. The beautiful woman in white began to explain the reasons for her Son's anger and her own struggles to protect them:

"I have appointed you six days for working. The seventh I have reserved for myself. And no one will give it to me. This it is that causes the weight of my Son's arm to be crushing."

And she continued:

"The cart drivers cannot swear without bringing in my Son's name. These are the two things that make my Son's arm so burdensome."

God was being dishonored, the woman insisted, and the price of such abuse would be costly. "If the harvest is spoiled, it is your own fault," she said. The potato crop, which had been destroyed the year before, would yield no better during this year, she predicted. Even walnuts and grapes grown in the region would rot before they were ripe. And the grain, too, would never be productively gathered. It would never find its way into the bread that sustained them, she said, shaking her head in sorrow.

"A great famine is coming," she told the children then. But before that food shortage would occur, many of the young children of the area would die of a serious disease. Their parents would be helpless; there would be no help for the young ones.

Then something even more mysterious happened. The woman faced the children in turn and spoke to each one individually. As she spoke to one, the other could hear nothing. Melanic could see that Maximin nodded his head yes and seemed to know what she was saying. Then the Lady turned toward her, and Melanie understood. She heard words of encouragement and advice from this visitor. Her heart was won over, she knew. There was nothing the girl would not have promised or done to make this still-weeping but precious woman happy.

"Do you say your prayers well, my children?" the glowing woman suddenly asked so that both could hear. Maximin kicked at a stone. "No, Madame," they both answered. "Hardly at all," Melanie confessed.

"Ah, my children, it is very important to do so, at night and in the morning," she responded, with firmness but kindness, too. "When you don't have time, at least say an 'Our Father' or a 'Hail Mary,' " and when you can, say more.

"Only a few rather old women go to Mass in the summer," added the woman, returning to the complaints she had to make. "Everyone else works every Sunday all summer long. During Lent, they go to the butcher shops like dogs."

This woman then reminded Maximin of an occasion when, with his father, he had seen spoiled wheat. She related the exact circumstances of the incident and reminded him of what he had said and what his father had told him. The boy was overwhelmed. He and his father had been alone that afternoon.

"Well, my children, you will make this known to all my people," she said. These were her last words, and she turned from the children and moved slowly down the ravine and up the slope. Maximin and Melanie accompanied her, noticing that her feet never touched the earth but seemed to glide above it.

As she reached the top of the slope, she rose slowly into the air. As the children watched, a peaceful, joyful expression spread across her features. The tears, the look of anguish and heartbreak, were gone. The globe of light surrounded her again, and with a last look toward them and one more toward the southeast, she disappeared.

Maximin had tried to slow her departure. He grabbed after one of the flowers on her feet, but his hand came away with nothing. The woman was gone, with no trace left behind except in the hearts of two children, which were changed forever. They stared at empty space, the unseen door that she had entered, for a very long time.

"Perhaps," ventured Melanie finally, "she was a great saint."

"If we had known she was a great saint, we should have asked her to take us with her," answered the boy. They were both lost in the dream of it, the fresh yet painful memory of the grace that had visited them. Who was she? Why had she visited them? Was it really real? This — the first, last, and only apparition at La Salette — was over in just about a half hour.

The children now moved to round up the cows, the one goat, and their knapsacks. It was time to return to the village, to the things that had previously constituted the "real world." Maximin was surprised to find Loulou snoozing near the ravine. She had not been disturbed by the wondrous woman who had come with so much splendor and beauty.

Maximin and Melanie seemed to think that their shining visitor would have been seen by others near the village of Ablandins, but there was no talk of anything unusual as they slapped and pushed the cows to hurry them into the barnyard that evening. They were late. At least Memin's boss, Pierre Selme, thought *Memin* was. And why hadn't Maximin come back to the field after watering the cattle at noon? he wanted to know. That was the agreed practice.

With very little if any self-consciousness, the eleven-year-old explained that he and Melanie had been stopped from doing so. A beautiful woman had met them and talked with them. Selme laughed heartily. If the boy was going to have an excuse, it might as well be a fantastic one.

With no more prodding, Maximin proceeded to tell the man the entire story. From his fear about retrieving his knapsack when he first saw her, to his agony of heart when he saw her leaving, he told it all. The farmer snorted once again at the preposterous tale — but the boy's manner while he talked had been disturbing. To end it all and put the fear of God into the little fibber, Selme promised Maximin that he would ask Melanie about it after supper. He knew her to be a serious girl — no trickster.

Later at the home of Baptiste Pra, the boy told his story once again to the head of the house. The Pras let their soup grow cold. Melanie was still in the barn with the cows, and she had said nothing yet. Grandma Pra, who had befriended the child, went to fetch her.

At first, Melanie, the shy one, maintained that there was no use in her telling the story they had just heard of Maximin. But she began her own account all the same. In every way, it matched the boy's.

"You hear, then?" Grandma Pra said suddenly, turning to her son, Baptiste. "You hear what the Blessed Virgin said to this child? I suppose you're still going to work tomorrow — Sunday, remember — after that!" The woman was the first to believe in the children, but her son scoffed. Would the Blessed Virgin appear to children like these? Melanie, he pointed out, didn't even say her prayers.

And with this domestic disagreement, the controversy over the apparition of La Salette began. However, it did not remain the household affair of Baptiste Pra and family.

Grandma Pra called the woman "the Blessed Virgin." Maximin and Melanie had not thought of her that way. The two of them were scarcely well enough informed on religious matters to have guessed it could be she. Baptiste Pra, in the practical way of looking at things, had a point.

Outside the house where the Pras, Selme, and the two children talked the matter out, a gathering of neighbors took place. In a hamlet like Ablandins, there were few secrets older than a day. As the villagers crowded into the home of the Pras, asking again and again for a report from Memin or Melanie, the night grew cooler.

Finally, Selme took matters in hand. He would take the children to see the pastor, Father Jacques Perrin, in the morning. Father Perrin, although soon to be transferred, was still assigned to the parish of La Salette, serving a dozen or so hamlets, including Ablandins and Corps.

Father Perrin listened to the children tell of the shining woman and believed them completely. Within an hour, he was tearfully repeating the tale from the pulpit at Sunday Mass. His premature approval of the apparition at La Salette disturbed the bishop. It set the story racing down the mountain valleys like a spring runoff. The account seemed to have an ecclesial verification of authenticity, but that would not be given officially for some time.

Life changed dramatically for the two children that week. They were constantly under scrutiny. Sometimes the scrutiny was friendly and flattering. Just as often, however, Melanie and Maximin were being studied to build the case against them and the apparition. A number of people could not believe that the Blessed Virgin would visit two scamps in a cow pasture.

One of the local mayors tried to bribe Melanie with thirty francs not to repeat the story. That was three months' wages for a girl who herded cows. She was smart enough to see how much this could mean to her impoverished family. Yet the vision of the shining, exquisite face came back to her. She threw the francs back on the table and refused. Then the mayor went to threaten Maximin with imprisonment for fraud, but with no better result. The boy shrugged and stuck to his story.

Within months, it seemed that the Virgin's warnings had taken root in this French terrain. The new pastor, Father Melin, noticed the change immediately. There were conversions, long lines for confession and for the Eucharist, and a full church on Sundays. Even Maximin's father had been deeply touched.

Mr. Giraud had listened and grumbled when he first heard his son telling about the Virgin's message. Then one day Maximin said to him, "The Lady spoke of you, too."

"Of me? What did she say?" responded the astonished wheelwright.

The boy then told his father about the Lady's detailed knowledge of the time that the two of them had looked at the spoiled wheat. The lad told how the Virgin had repeated the words of father and son precisely. Giraud said nothing but was impressed. When his wife told him soon after that she wanted to take the trip to the site of the Virgin's visit, he did not protest. And a little later, he himself went. The asthma that he had suffered from for many years was gone after his visit. He returned to the Church and to the sacraments, abandoning his wasteful ways.

On September 19, 1847, the first anniversary of the apparition, a massive procession made its way up to the mountain where the apparition had taken place. Fifty thousand to sixty thousand people crowded in around a covered altar where commemorative Masses were celebrated on this joyful day. Nearby, water gurgled from the spring, which had dried up just the year before. It had erupted anew soon after the apparition.

Twenty-three cures had already been reported by those who maintained that Our Lady of La Salette had answered their prayers in a miraculous way. Bishop de Bruillard, the head of the Diocese of Grenoble, established a commission for inquiry into the La Salette claims and into the apparition itself.

As events were under study, so were the children. Following the apparition, they became boarding students with the sisters in the convent of Corps. Since their religious training had been so deficient, the nuns worked hard to prepare them for First Communion.

Melanie had great difficulty in memorizing her prayers, while Maximin was forever restless in the exclusive company of women. And hardly a day went by without visitors arriving at the convent asking to talk to the young boy and girl who had seen the Holy Virgin. Melanie and Memin grew tired of it all.

After four years of schooling, the children longed to move on. In September of 1850, Maximin was taken to see the revered Curé of Ars, the future St. John Vianney. The nation already believed the Curé to be a saint and waited to hear what he thought of the boy who had seen the Virgin at La Salette.

But the meeting was disastrous! Maximin could scarcely understand the almost toothless John Vianney. And the day before the meeting, the lad had endured an interview with the arrogant and abrasive assistant pastor at Ars, Father Raymond. Sadly, the Curé concluded that the La Salette story was false. Eight years passed before the saintly Father Vianney asked the Virgin for a sign about La Salette's authenticity. The answer he asked for was given to him, and his faith in the apparition and in Maximin was restored.

In the meantime, Maximin entered the minor seminary at Grenoble, while Melanie entered the convent of the Sisters of Providence at Corenc. Both struggled with the studies and disciplines that the life required. Maximin's father died, and the young man then had no home where he felt welcome.

In 1851, both Melanie and Maximin were told that Pope Pius IX had asked for them to tell him, in writing, the secrets that Our Lady of La Salette had given to them. In fact, the request and pressure came from other sources, but the letters were taken to Rome anyway. The Pope, it is said, rose from his desk and took the sealed envelopes over to his window to read in silence. He smiled while reading the words that Maximin had received from the heavenly Mother. Melanie's letter, however, apparently contained grave warnings about the world. The pontiff's expression changed and became worried.

Toward the end of that year, Bishop de Bruillard released a pastoral letter that told the people of his diocese that the claim of an apparition at La Salette "bears in itself all the marks of truth, and the faithful have grounds to believe it indubitable and certain." The letter concluded with an authorization of what the bishop called "the cult of Our Lady of La Salette."

Official sanction of their stories did not make life untroubled for Maximin Giraud and Melanie Mathieu. And ironically, religious life was not the fulfillment that either of them would find.

Though he struggled with his decision, Maximin finally determined that the priesthood was not the life for him. He dabbled in the study of medicine, later at becoming a pharmacist, then a mechanic. Unscrupulous investors solicited his name in promotion of a liquor. Always short of funds, he agreed. It was embarrassing to all those concerned about one who had seen the Virgin Mother of God. He even journeyed to Rome to join the papal Zouaves, the Vatican guard. Their uniforms and glorious role had always attracted him. In six months, that dream, too, was done.

On March 1, 1875, Maximin Giraud died at the age of forty. He had begun to suffer from asthma, just as his father had, but the many years of drifting and poor care of his health had also conspired to shorten his life. His last days, nonetheless, were filled with sincere religious devotion to the Mass and sacraments. And Maximin revisited the ravine where the shining woman had come to see him.

Melanie lived many years beyond the restless boy who shared her life's most memorable moments. She, too, found little peace or satisfaction in the years following the apparition. She left the convent at Corenc, where visitors constantly plagued her for interviews. After other attempts to adjust in convents at Vienne and at her hometown of Corps, she was received by a Carmelite convent at Darlington, England. Melanie's fame had begun to appeal to her in her early, formative years. She found the isolation of contemplative existence too confining. Half a dozen more attempts at different convents were no more successful. Like Maximin, she moved constantly, looking for a home or a way to fit in.

The bishop of a diocese in Italy finally befriended the troubled, aging visionary of La Salette. She attended Mass each day in Altamura, where she had a rented room. On December 15, 1904, she was found dead in her room there. The seventy-three-year-old seer of the La Salette apparition had been freed. After that September day nearly sixty years past, life had been a sad anticlimax.

By 1879, the basilica of Our Lady of La Salette had been completed and the statue of Our Lady of La Salette consecrated. The La Salette Fathers were founded on the spirit the Lady had called for in 1846. In particular, they worked in the ministry of reconciliation.

Lourdes, France

1858

*L*ourdes — the name has a marvelous meaning for millions of believers today. As the most renowned healing shrine of modern times — possibly of all times — the very name carries a sense of hope and deep devotion to a Mother who cares.

Nevertheless, there was certainly a time when this town mattered very little to anyone other than the few hundred country people settled there near the Pyrénées in the southwest of France. This was merely Lourdes, a modest little market town of about four thousand by the 1850s. In this neighborhood, Bernadette, the oldest child of François and Louise Soubirous, was born in 1844.

Through a series of financial misfortunes, the Soubirous family gradually sank into a desperate state of affairs. In the winter of 1857-58, there was almost no money at all. François, a miller, had no head for business and was too generous with credit. Outlay exceeded income until Soubirous, with scarcely a sou to his name, was forced to ask if his family could take a foul-smelling room at the old prison, which his cousin owned. The place was cold and damp. Everyone in the town then knew that the miller's family, if forced to live at *Le Cachot* (The Dungeon), was totally without resources.

Just before noon on Thursday, February 11, 1858, Bernadette pulled the door closed behind her and headed down the Rue des Petits Fosses (the Street of the Little Holes). Her younger sister Toinette and her cousin Jeanne Abadie were way ahead of her. Bernadette would not rush so fast. She was asthmatic, and her health had been delicate since she had contracted cholera at age ten. She pulled her white woolen cape more tightly around her.

The wooden sabots on the feet of this pretty, petite fourteen-year-old clacked on the pavement as she made her way down the street and across the old bridge over the Gave River. Bernadette and the two other girls were out to gather firewood on this cold, clammy day. There was none to burn to cook the noonday meal that her mother hoped to concoct from a few sorry-looking vegetables and perhaps a little borrowed bread. Lately, Bernadette's little brother Jean-Marie had been caught eating the molten wax off the candles at the church. Anything to stifle the gnawing pain of an empty belly.

She reached the rocky area called Massabielle just outside the city. A large rock grotto, hollowed out by centuries of water erosion, was located just at the bottom of the small mountain. Her sister and cousin had already stripped off shoes and socks to wade across a shallow portion of the canal to collect driftwood and bones. Some of it could be sold at the local market and some could warm the supper that would put a little something into the Soubirous' stomachs.

Bernadette looked at the icy water and shivered. Would getting her feet wet make her cough worse that evening? She called out to Jeanne, a big girl, asking her to carry her over the stream on her back. The girl and Toinette both laughed back their refusals. Whatever Bernadette would do in the way of collecting wood, she would have to do on her own. She sat down to take off her socks.

At just that moment, she heard the wind rushing and looked back to see how the poplars were being blown. They were still, motionless. She looked back again toward the grotto ahead of her. There, in a niche of the rock grotto, was a light, a bright light glowing like the sun's reflection off water on a brilliant day. In the midst of the glow, Bernadette could gradually see, was a woman in white with a blue sash. The woman was smiling at her, Bernadette realized with a quick jolt. The girl reached for the rosary beads she had in her pocket in order to make the sign of the cross with them. But her arm seemed frozen! She could not move it; she was trembling.

The smiling Lady, on the other hand, made the sign of the cross with the rosary she held in her hand. Immediately, Bernadette was able to do the same. "As soon as I had made the sign of the cross, the great fear that had seized me vanished," she reported later. "I knelt down and I said my rosary in the presence of the beautiful Lady."

Not a word was spoken. After she had completed the rosary, Bernadette said, the Lady motioned her to come closer. But the girl was still too timid for that. The sunburst woman vanished into the air. Bernadette became aware of her sister and cousin across the stream. As if recovering from a dream, she stripped off the socks, then only half off, and bounded across the stream. *How foolish of me*, she thought to herself. The water seemed almost warm.

Bernadette collected some wood on the other side, looking now and then into the grotto. When Toinette and Jeanne were back, they danced around their woodpiles there in the grotto to warm their feet. Bernadette felt uncomfortable about such activities in the place that had held something wondrous.

"Did you see anything?" she asked the two finally.

"What did you see?" they countered. The cousins had noticed her kneeling there.

"Oh, nothing," replied the visionary. She changed the subject.

Yet, on the road back to Lourdes, Bernadette told her sister about the woman in white with the rosary. Toinette scoffed but promised to keep the tale a secret. Hardly were they in the door, however, when the younger sister was telling her mother of Bernadette's vision. Louise was distraught and spanked the girls. From his bed, where he was still spending the day's best hours of light, the unemployed François warned his eldest not to bring any embarrassment to the Soubirous name.

That evening at prayers by the fireplace, Bernadette was filled with a deep sense of peace. She began to weep with the overflow of a feeling she had never known. Louise asked her why she was in tears, but Bernadette could find no adequate answer.

Later, when she was in bed, her mother told her that she did not want Bernadette to return to the grotto. "It's a dream, an illusion," Louise thought to herself. It was the first of eighteen astounding apparitions of the Virgin Mother of God to Bernadette, a child of poverty.

On the following day, Friday, February 12, the girl felt a pull toward the grotto. She fought with it. Going would mean disobedience. On Saturday, Bernadette told her story to a priest in the confessional. He was impressed with her account but thought it more likely to be girlish fantasies than anything supernatural. Nonetheless, he asked his penitent if he could discuss the matter with Abbé Peyramale, the pastor of Lourdes. She agreed.

After Sunday's Mass on February 14, a group of girls concocted a scheme to take Bernadette back to the grotto. They had heard the story of the vision from Toinette and Jeanne. Made bold by their numbers, they went to Louise, who was unimpressed. She refused to release Bernadette, instead sending them to François, who was working that day. His answer was the same, but he gave in when the man he was working for sided with the children. Bernadette set out with an escort.

As the children came closer to the grotto, a nervous excitement welled up in all of them. Bernadette, with a group of younger, less inhibited children, scrambled down the tricky rock slope to the grotto from the forest road that mounted above it. She moved with an almost crazy abandon that alarmed the others; but she was thinking of the Lady whose smile filled her with such peace.

"There she is!" she said suddenly during the second decade of the rosary. Marie, one of the girls with her, handed her a vial of holy water. Louise Soubirous had been afraid that something evil was showing itself at Massabielle. The holy water was insurance. "But the more I sprinkled, the more she smiled, and I kept sprinkling until the bottle was empty," the girl later told others.

Bernadette was clearly in some sort of trance. The girls who gathered around her could not understand or penetrate it. She seemed to hear nothing, they said, and her face was so pale. Perhaps out of jealousy for the attention her cousin had gained, Jeanne Abadie started a little rockslide into the grotto that actually endangered the children. And yet the children could not get Bernadette to budge.

They ran for help, asking Nicolau, the operator of the nearby mill, to rescue their friend from danger and from the hold of something they could not see. Shocked at the weight of this slip of a child, he struggled just to carry her back to his mill at Savy. Along the way, Nicolau remembered, "I put my hand over her eyes and tried to get her to bend her head, but she would raise her head again and reopen her eyes with a smile." Her mother, hearing of the uproar, walked out to Savy with a stick in her hand, anger in her eyes. What a display!

For Bernadette, the following day, Monday, was even worse. After school, Sister Anastasie, one of the sternest sisters, was waiting for her with Sister Sophie, a woman the children tried to avoid. After listening to their indignant outbursts, Bernadette's face was slapped. "If you go back there again, you will be locked up," one of them shouted at her.

On Thursday, February 18, two women hammered at the Soubirous' door before sunrise. Madame Milhet, a well-to-do woman of the community, and her seamstress, Antoinette Peyret, had decided that they should accompany Bernadette to the grotto that day. After morning Mass, the three were on their way along the forest road. The girl sprinted down the rock-scattered mountain to the grotto once again.

Behind her, Madame Milhet and Antoinette picked their way down to find Bernadette already on her knees praying. "She is here!" she told them after a moment. The other two could make nothing out in the grotto niche where Bernadette's eyes were riveted. They reminded her to ask the Lady to write her name with the paper and pen they had brought. Bernadette held them out at arm's length, and the apparition seemed to move toward them. But nothing appeared upon the paper.

"It is not necessary," replied the heavenly woman. Her voice was soft, mysterious, musical, yet with a quality Bernadette could find no words for. Then the Lady made a request of her own.

"Would you have the graciousness to come here for fifteen days?" she asked the girl in the local patois. Bernadette agreed instantly with a heart full of warmth. The woman had asked her with such tenderness, deference, and respect. Then the woman told her: "I do not promise to make you happy in this world but in the next."

Madame Milhet had not received the answer to her request, but the state of affairs with Bernadette was clearly interesting. "And what if it was the Holy Virgin?" she challenged the child on the walk back to Lourdes. Bernadette had no answer. By the time they had crossed the Old Bridge, the woman had told the young visionary that she should live at *her* home during the fifteen days of visits to the grotto.

Back in the dingy cell on the Rue des Petits Fosses, Louise Soubirous and Aunt Bernarde believed it was they who must be with Bernadette now. Bernadette, after all, was their charge, reasoned her mother and aunt (who was namesake for her niece). Out of respect, Bernadette did stay briefly with Madame Milhet, but only for a day or two.

Early on the mornings of Friday, Saturday, and Sunday, a group set out from town toward the region of the grotto. Each day saw the visitors growing in number. Bernadette saw the Lady each day, but they were silent visitations. The woman in white said nothing to her. There was only the smile, the sense of peace.

On Sunday evening, February 21, following Vespers, the fourteen-year-old was collared by Police Commissioner Jacomet. With no warning, she was hauled across the street to the commissioner's house for interrogation.

During this, the first of many such grillings, Bernadette was cool and unflustered in the presence of well-educated, shrewd men of the world. She retold the significant details of her visions but described the woman in white only in neutral terms. If the rest of Lourdes was saying that the Lady was the Mother of God, Bernadette was certainly not. *"Aquero"* — the local word for "That one" — was the way Bernadette referred to her.

Jacomet did not get the admissions he wanted from the girl before the noisy, distressed crowds outside persuaded him to release her. Her worried father, François Soubirous, breathed a sigh of relief. But not Bernadette. Back home a little later, she laughed at the way Jacomet's hat tassel was jiggling when he shook with the most violent threats he hurled at her.

On Monday, February 22, the girl asked her parents if she could return to the grotto. Shaken by the threats of the police commissioner, Louise and François refused to permit it. Torn between the promise she had made to Aquero and the obedience she owed to her parents, Bernadette had a difficult day. After lunch, the Lady's pull overwhelmed her. She turned toward the grotto. Once she was there, no vision occurred, and she was in tears. In the evening, she entered the confessional and laid her dilemma before Father Pomian. "They do not have the right to stop you," he consoled the girl.

By 5:30 A.M. on Tuesday, February 23, the firstborn of the Soubirous children was again making her way to the grotto. Her heart was at peace. Among the spectators watching her every move were a doctor, a lawyer, and Jean-Baptiste Estrade, the excise tax officer. Estrade had been present during Jacomet's interview of the girl. There was something compelling about her story.

Tuesday's apparition did not help to give Bernadette any further clue as to Aquero's real identity. The experience was again a silent one. That of Wednesday, February 24, on the other hand, brought something new. The Lady spoke again. "Penitence," she told Bernadette, was what she wanted from everyone. "Pray to God for the conversion of sinners." After this, she told the girl to kiss the ground as a gesture of penance for others.

On Thursday, February 25, this repeated act of penance asked of Bernadette became controversial. With hundreds of people gathered at the grotto before sunrise, Bernadette's actions on that day had many, many witnesses. A few minutes after Bernadette's face revealed Aquero's presence, the girl again kissed the ground. Then she moved on her knees to the left side of the grotto and seemed to be receiving directions. For a moment, she seemed confused and turned back to the niche and her Lady.

Then Bernadette began to dig with her hands at the dirt, scraping up muddy stuff that stuck to her fingers. Then a murmur of shock and disgust passed through the crowd. Hundreds saw her lift the mud to her mouth to drink it! The Lady had said: "Go and drink at the fount and wash yourself."

"She's crazy!" some people told others. Estrade, the excise tax officer who had been so impressed with the young visionary, was dumbfounded. "I don't understand it at all," he admitted to an associate. Then Bernadette picked off bits of a plant called *dorine* and ate them. Another moan erupted from the crowd. But the Lady had ordered that, too. "You will eat of that plant which is there," she had instructed. But among those in the crowd, Bernadette's "mad" gesture set many off.

"For sinners," she responded, when townspeople and believers besieged her with questions. But in truth, she did not know why the woman in white had asked her to dirty her face with such filthy stuff. And to drink it! It had been hard just to put the muddy mix to her lips. "For sinners," she reminded herself.

On Friday, February 26, Bernadette again discovered that she was forbidden to go to the grotto. This time the ban came not from her parents but from the police commissioner. Again, she agonized about whether she should go. A remark from her Aunt Bernarde convinced Bernadette to go. She grabbed her white cape from the hook on the wall and walked to the grotto.

Overnight, the trickle of water bubbling up where Bernadette had been scraping had created a small pool of water. When she arrived at the grotto, more than six hundred people were waiting. There was no apparition on that day, however. Bernadette was demoralized. "What have I done to her?" she asked herself, weeping. No one could answer. On Saturday, February 27, Aquero was back again. Bernadette rejoiced, but there was no special message or incident.

Sunday, February 28, brought a huge crowd of almost twelve hundred to the grotto confines. The local authorities grappled with the problems of control. Too many people were wedged in between the rocky cliff, out of which the grotto jutted, and the steep drop into the Gave River. Not knowing what else to do, they grabbed the young visionary once again and interrogated her.

Despite their threats, the Soubirous girl insisted she would return to the grotto until the following Thursday, March 4. After all, she had promised Aquero to go to the grotto each day for fifteen days.

On Monday, March 1, dawn arrived, throwing golden hues on hundreds of faces waiting at the grotto. Among them was Catherine Latapie, a mother of two small children, who was expecting a third arrival at any time. Two years before, she had taken a fall that broke her arm and left two fingers of her right hand paralyzed.

Along with others, Catherine and her toddlers witnessed the apparition on this day. When Bernadette left, Catherine made her way to the spring that had developed exactly where Bernadette's "mad" scraping and mud-smearing took place. The water was running clear and at an amazing rate. Catherine plunged her right hand into the waters. Immediately, warmth flowed through her arm and hand in the icy water and she felt at peace. When she pulled her arm out of the water, the fingers that had been doubled up were straightened.

Catherine Latapie found she could open and close her hand.

It was as good as new. But the young mother's excitement seemed to bring on labor pains. She appealed to the Virgin who, she believed, had given her a healing. She had to get home! Within hours, back at Loubajac four miles away, she gave birth to a boy, a future priest.

On March 2, more than sixteen hundred people waited and listened while Bernadette again experienced the presence of the vision they were now openly calling "the Blessed Virgin." The girl finally rose from her feet and turned to tell those around her of Aquero's words. The Lady had something special in mind that day. "Go and tell the priests that people must come here in procession and that a chapel [must] be built here." They were clear, precise directions. The crowds were excited as the message passed from one cluster of spectators to he next. To carry out her errand, Bernadette set out immediately for the rectory to talk to Abbé Peyramale, dean of the district.

This priest's position was very delicate. His flock, he knew, was already convinced that it was the Mother of God who was requesting processions and a chapel. Privately, he believed this was the case himself. But the hard fact was that the Church had not pronounced that the visions of the Soubirous girl were anything but fanciful flights of imagination. He was frustrated and stormed at Bernadette. Before she left his rectory, he insisted that she ask Aquero to identify herself. The girl promised and gratefully left the pastor to himself.

On Wednesday, March 3, the Lady again came to see Bernadette but only after the girl returned a second time. The early morning crowd of three thousand or more had thinned out, disappointed after the seer failed to see the woman in the niche the first time. Conscious of her assignment from Dean Peyramale, Bernadette asked the woman what her name was. "She only smiled," Bernadette later told the priest. She received no verbal reply.

Thursday, March 4, was the last day of the fortnight of visits that Bernadette had promised to Aquero. Expectations and the crowds were even larger. A great miracle or sign would surely take place on this day — or so everyone believed.

And yet nothing of that sort really happened after Bernadette arrived with her cousin Jeanne Vedere soon after 7:00 A.M. Bernadette asked Aquero for her name and for a sign that Dean Peyramale had suggested — the blooming of a rosebush in the middle of winter. But again, the Lady was not inclined to grant the requests. She only smiled.

There was a letdown in Lourdes after this, the last anticipated apparition. Nevertheless, many still believed that the Blessed Virgin had descended upon their village in the foothills. Two "miracles" were reported through contact with the young girl, who still lived in the old jail. But they were unsubstantiated, and believers held their breath, waiting for a future confirmation of their faith.

On March 25, the feast of the Annunciation, Bernadette awoke from her sleep with a yearning to be at the grotto. Her parents wanted her to ignore it. They could do no more than make her wait until 5:00 A.M.

Aquero came, and Bernadette saw her approaching this time from the recesses of the grotto. Her heart was beating wildly, but she was determined that the woman in white would identify herself. On the fourth attempt, the vision stopped smiling and joined her hands in prayer, raising her eyes to heaven. "I am the Immaculate Conception," the woman told her.

Bernadette graciously thanked her. After the apparition was over, she repeated the phrase over and over to herself as she took the road back to the rectory. Finally, she had an answer for Dean Peyramale.

When the words were finally spoken in the pastor's study, the priest's mind reeled. Just for a moment, he fought what his ears had heard. It could not be the Blessed Mother! Bernadette clearly did not even know what the words meant. Nonetheless, the quiet, halting belief he had held inside was then and there made firm. Just four years earlier, in 1854, the Church had promulgated the doctrine of the Immaculate Conception with the words: "We define that the Blessed Virgin was preserved from every taint of original sin ... from the first moment of her conception."

Only in the evening did Bernadette herself learn the meaning of the phrase "I am the Immaculate Conception." Then she gave in finally to the joy she had felt in the presence of Aquero since the first day.

On the Wednesday after Easter, April 7, Bernadette again felt that she needed to be at the grotto. Even before dawn's first light, she was there, falling into an ecstatic state very quickly. Several hundred people witnessed once again the transformation of Bernadette's face.

In the middle of the apparition, a physician, Doctor Dozous, appeared at the girl's side. It was his object to examine the seer in the midst of the appearance. Just as he made his way through the crowds, a gasp of shock escaped from those closest to Bernadette. When he saw what was happening, Dozous, too, was stunned.

Bernadette was holding the top of a tall candle placed upon the ground in front of her. Her wrists braced the candle with her fingers laced above the wick, obviously to protect the flame from the wind. Yet the flames were licking up into and around the girl's unprotected hands and fingers! There was no look of pain upon her smiling face, no attempt to move her hands away from the flame, which was hot enough to scorch human flesh. Doctor Dozous hurried over to her to see more closely, take her pulse, and watch her while she was in ecstasy. Afterwards, he inspected her hands and fingers but found no burns. Bernadette could not understand what he was looking for as he turned her hands this way and that.

During May and June, Lourdes was chaotic. Masses of people visited the grotto hoping to see or experience wonders. Local craftsmen built a zinc basin for the spring water, which was now flowing steadily. They also built wooden holders for the candles that now burned always at the grotto. There was hysteria, too, with as many as fifty reports of additional "sightings" of the Virgin by other "visionaries" by the end of June.

Bernadette, meanwhile, tried to remain quiet. She did not visit Massabielle but was taken to a nearby health spa to relieve her asthma. Local authorities did everything to discourage large gatherings. Barricades went up around the grotto. When the people pulled them down or pushed around them, the barriers were reinforced again and again. The Church and Bishop Laurence were conspicuously silent about the entire matter.

On Monday, July 16, the tug and attraction of the grotto were at work on Bernadette again. It was the feast of Our Lady of Mount Carmel. To reduce the risk of angering the police commissioner, she waited until dark and wore a borrowed cape and hood. A group of several hundred had already assembled, stationed behind the barricades. The visionary simply knelt down among them, holding a candle in her hands.

As the girl began the rosary, a smile of surprise lit her face. The Virgin was there for her once again. Though she was much farther away from the grotto niche because of the barriers, the "Immaculate Conception," her beloved Aquero, seemed very close, Bernadette said. "It seemed to me that I was in the grotto, no more distant than the other times. I saw only the Holy Virgin."

There was no spoken message. But as she rose, Bernadette Soubirous understood that the vision just ended would be the last. There had been eighteen.

Even after all the apparitions were over, Bernadette Soubirous laughed boldly in the faces of those who called her "saint." And yet the ceaseless comings and goings of those who wished to see the "saint," hear her tale, or even touch her, grew to be a heavy burden on the Soubirous family.

On July 15, one day before the last apparition, Bernadette

had moved to the Lourdes hospice and school run by the Sisters of Nevers. Here she would receive a good education and be somewhat sheltered from the drain of constant questioners. However, she missed her family, and Louise and François Soubirous liked it even less.

Nevertheless, Bernadette lived and studied at the hospice until leaving for the convent. On April 4, 1864, she firmly decided to join the Sisters of Nevers near Paris. Bernadette felt at home with them. On July 4, 1866, she left her beloved Lourdes by train.

The afternoon before, she had paid her last visit to Massabielle, where a sizable chapel already stood. Her aunt Basile Castérot remembered the leave-taking of Bernadette. "I was not there when she went to the grotto for the last time," she said later. "I know that she suffered in leaving it, but she put on a brave front."

On Sunday, July 8, Bernadette was at the motherhouse of the Sisters of Nevers. For the first and last time at this convent, she was asked to tell of the apparitions of the Virgin Mother of God at the Lourdes grotto. Three hundred nuns gathered to hear her.

On the following day, Bernadette, then twenty-two, was no longer to be distinctive. She hoped to disappear into a life of silence, a life of prayer. Though her short stature (four feet, eight inches) sometimes gave her away to those scanning the lines of postulants, the habit did give her a measure of anonymity. She was given the name "Sister Marie-Bernarde," and work with the sick became her ministry.

Before very long, Sister Marie-Bernarde was among the sick herself. Her asthma was often threatening, and a tubercular condition also affected her. She made her religious profession early, on October 25, 1866, when her superiors feared she might die. She survived, but her health remained a delicate matter.

During December, 1878, Bernadette's health was failing for the last time. Five years earlier, she had been forced to give up her beloved work in the infirmary. She struggled with her health, and also with the knowledge that, at age twenty-nine, she was useless for almost all work in her community. On April 16, 1879, Easter Wednesday, the little sister who had seen the Mother of the Lord breathed her last. She was thirty-five years old. Her body, marvelously preserved from any corruption, lies in state in the convent chapel at Nevers.

At the request of Mother Marie Therese Vauzous, the superior at the convent at Nevers, the investigation into the sanctity of Bernadette was not opened for a number of years. "Wait until I'm dead," pleaded the aristocratic nun who'd never been able to understand why a crude, obstinate country girl had seen the Virgin.

Once the study was begun, however, canonization came quickly for Bernadette. On the feast of the Immaculate Conception, December 8, 1933, she was declared a saint, less than a century after her birth. Confirmation of the apparitions of Lourdes as worthy of belief had taken place much more quickly. On January 18, 1862, less than four years after the visions, the bishop of the Diocese of Tarbes released the letter commending devotion to Lourdes as a Marian site.

Twenty years after the visions at Lourdes, the area around Massabielle was so transformed that Bernadette would have scarcely recognized it. Today, as much as fourteen thousands five hundred gallons of water are generated daily from the spring that started with a mudhole Bernadette dug with her fingers. By the mid-1990s, an estimated five million pilgrims visited Lourdes each year, a tripling of the number of visitors a decade earlier. Lourdes became and remains the most popular healing shrine and pilgrimage site in the world. Five thousand healings have been attributed to the intercession of Our Lady of Lourdes over the years, although the Church admits only sixty-four of them to the category it calls "miraculous."

The chapel that the Virgin told Bernadette she wanted has become four "chapels" in modern times. The newest, the

Church of St. Pius X, holds as many as twenty thousand people and was built beneath the ground. It was completed in 1958, the centenary of the apparitions. The Church of Notre Dame and the Church of the Rosary had been built into the rock of Massabielle, very near to the grotto, in the previous century.

The only chapel Bernadette saw was the first, a chapel built into the rock and dedicated in 1866 before she went to the convent. Very quickly, it had become too small to fit the needs of pilgrims who are drawn to the grotto and to Lourdes.

Pontmain, France

1871

*F*rance felt as an abandoned child might have in the fall and winter of 1870-71. She had just entered war with Prussia, but revolution had followed revolution throughout the century. There seemed to be no peace in the nation for very long.

The spiritual state of health in France seemed no better than its political state. And yet, perhaps, it should have been. The Virgin Mother of God had come to earth near French soil more than once during this century. On Paris's Rue du Bac in 1830, at La Salette in 1846, and at Lourdes in 1858, she had come to speak and to be heard. Nonetheless, France in 1870 was a country that bothered little with matters of the spirit. The churches were empty, lifeless.

About two hundred miles to the west of Paris, Pontmain, a village of about five hundred, provided a fortunate exception to the prevailing religious indifference. Pontmain's people were farmers and devout believers. The unique spirituality of the community was largely due to the great example of its pastor, Abbé Guerin. He was well into his seventies as the new decade began. He had served the town as a pastor for thirty-five years.

In 1871, however, life looked bleak even here, a place where faith was as well rooted as the region's potatoes. In 1870, as war had begun, Prussia was bidding to form a German empire to the east of France under Prince Otto von Bismarck. Thirty-eight young men from Pontmain had been conscripted and were serving in the defense of their homeland.

But the newly drafted soldiers were really only farmers carrying guns. Their families and friends were desperate with fear for them and for the nation. The general climate of fear was soon justified by a national state of siege. In September, 1870, Paris was surrounded. By Christmas-time, the capital was being shelled by the Prussians every day.

France was desperately fighting for its survival as winter closed its icy grip upon the northern provinces. These were the regions that the Germans were now boastfully considering either as "already conquered" or "about to be conquered." The French wondered how long it would be before Napoleon III would be forced to sue for surrender terms.

Twelve-year-old Eugène Barbadette of Pontmain was thinking of such grim possibilities as he rose at six o'clock on the cold morning of January 17, 1871. He had heard that the Prussians were closing in on Laval, the capital of the region in which tiny Pontmain was situated. Eugène was worried about the threat, but he was more worried about his older brother Auguste. Auguste was one of those from this farming village who had been called to battle.

"Come on, get up, Joseph," Eugène called to his ten-year-old brother. They were the youngest of the three Barbadette sons. They were up early each day to pray the rosary for their brother, then were off to serve the morning Mass for Abbé Guerin. At church each morning, the Abbé prayed in a special way for villagers in the army.

On this morning, as the Prussian General Schmidt was leading his soldiers closer and closer, the priest offered prayers of hope. "Let us add penance to our prayers, and then we may take courage," the Abbé told his villagers at Mass. "God will have pity on us; his mercy will surely come to us through Mary." No more than eleven hours later his words began to be fulfilled for Pontmain and for France.

At about five that afternoon, Eugène and Joseph were working at chores in the barn with their father. They were all preparing feed for the animals. The sun was down, and the evening sky was filling with stars. Even if Bismarck's soldiers were knocking at the gates at Laval, the boys' father told them, the Barbadette cows still needed attention.

It was cold in the barn as usual, but the three could ignore the temperature as long as the cutting and chopping kept their hearts pumping at a quick rate. But before they were through, Jeannette Detais, a woman from the village, stepped into the barn and closed the door behind her. Mr. Barbadette stopped work and greeted her. Jeannette was a walking, talking bulletin board of community news.

Usually, this was a woman who came to visit families in sad circumstances. Jeannette prepared most of the dead of the village for burial. Yet she had good news on this day, she told Mr. Barbadette. She had seen Auguste, and he was in good health and sent his greetings to his family. Mr. Barbadette, with a wide smile on his face, stood his pitchfork upright for a few moments and quizzed Jeannette further.

Happy to have heard that his brother was well, Eugène walked to the barn door to see whether it would snow again that night. The ground was already covered with a thin layer of white that glistened in the declining light of day.

The boy could see that the stars were already beginning to shine brightly in the winter sky. But his eyes were drawn to an area where there seemed to be no stars, as though they had been wiped out of the heavens. It was strange.

Suddenly, in exactly that section of the starless sky, before his very eyes, a young woman of about eighteen appeared. It seemed that she was suspended just above the house opposite him. She was strikingly beautiful, Eugène realized. Dressed in a dark blue dress covered with stars, she wore a black veil on her head with a golden crown atop the veil. Eugène's mouth dropped open, and a yell of surprise crackled in the frigid night air. In a moment, Joseph rushed past the barn door left ajar and also stood gaping at the vision. "Oh, I see a beautiful Lady," he shouted to his father.

A dozen steps put Mr. Barbadette and Jeannette across the barn and next to the boys. The farmer stood behind his sons searching the star-studded sky for a wonder impressive enough to entrance his two boys. There was nothing — nothing that he or Jeannette could see.

But the boys continued to insist that a most beautiful Lady was smiling at them from the sky. She seemed to be gesturing to them, they told their bewildered father. The woman was wearing shoes of blue with gold buckles, they said.

They began to describe her appearance in detail. She was beautiful, they insisted. But Mr. Barbadette, a reliable husband, father, farmer, and a man with healthy eyes, could still see nothing of the sort. He sent for his wife to see what she could make of their claims.

The mother of Eugène and Joseph was soon at the barn, where the cows were now forgotten. She boxed her boys' ears when she heard Eugène and Joseph tell her with straight faces that a wonderful woman was overlooking them from the sky. When they would not give up the story, however, she went to find her spectacles and sent for Sister Vitaline from the nearby convent school.

Sister Vitaline immediately suspected that the Mother of God indeed might be appearing to the boys. Perhaps, she advised Mr. and Mrs. Barbadette, the Virgin would be visible only to children. It was certainly well known that the La Salette and Lourdes visions were given only to simple children, she reminded the parents. She rushed back to the convent school to bring some girls back to the Barbadettes' yard.

Françoise Richer, eleven years old, and Jeanne-Marie Lebosse, nine years old, could see the woman immediately when they arrived. There had been no chance for the girls to hear the Barbadette boys describe what they were seeing in the winter sky. "Yes, her dark blue gown has stars on it!" one of them cried out with delight. Within a moment, the two newcomers had repeated the descriptions given by Eugène and Joseph to the last detail.

By this time, fifteen to twenty minutes after the vision had begun, small clusters of people were gathering near the Barbadette barn. Jeannette Detais was the perfect herald for Pontmain's latest event of interest. The curious and those who cherished a faith in miracles left hot dinners on the table and came to see if there was really something going on.

None of the gathering adults could see anything unusual in the sky. And yet they noticed that several of the very small children also seemed to be excited by something just above the neighboring farmhouse. In her mother's arms, a little two-year-old girl clapped her hands with excitement. Then she stretched out her arms toward the area of the sky where the Virgin was said to be. The little girl was acting like a child begging to be picked up.

Filled with growing astonishment and anxious joy, Mr. and Mrs. Barbadette sent for their saintly Abbé Guerin. He should be there, they told the others. In short order, the aging village pastor stood among his parishioners, searching the sky for the woman for whom he had such unshakable devotion. Though he could see that the four children were experiencing some great vision arranged by heaven, he, too, saw nothing. A small crowd of villagers continued to gather at the Barbadettes' home. They bundled their coats tighter around their necks and stamped their feet against the cold. And they wondered what this apparent favor could mean.

As the woman continued to smile from above, the four young visionaries noticed a change in the apparition suspended just above the neighboring Guidecoq family's house. Three very bright stars began to form a triangle in which the whole vision was enclosed.

"Oh!" one of the children suddenly said with surprise. A large blue oval was forming around the figure of the woman. The whole of it seemed to simulate the shape of a huge medal in the sky. As their Lady's backdrop changed, the children, separated from one another, began to report it. A small red cross appeared next on the woman's left side, as though it were a badge.

When he heard this, the pastor, Abbé Guerin, began to lead the crowd in reciting the rosary. The vision, the children claimed, grew larger in size as the prayers began. The stars on her gown appeared to multiply so fast that the Lady seemed clothed in gold, rather than navy blue. When the rosary was completed, Abbé Guerin began to recite the Magnificat. The old man's heart was full. Devotion to the Mother of God had been a passion all of his life.

At this point, all four of the children began to talk excitedly at the same time. Within a moment or two, the adults learned that a large white banner had begun to unroll just below the feet of the woman. The woman had not yet spoken, but a message written in French had begun to appear letter by letter.

"But pray, my children," the message eventually read. Then, as the group recited the Litany of Loretto, a second message materialized, letter by letter. "God will hear you in a little while." Thinking of the threat of the Prussians so close at hand, many of the people began to weep with joy as the message was spelled out. But it was still not complete.

The children then spelled out the letters of the words "My Son ..."

Shouts of joy and exhilaration erupted from the crowd now. Most of Pontmain's people who could come were gathered in the Barbadettes' field. These two words clearly identified the woman. She was surely the Mother of God. The rest of the message followed.

"... allows himself to be touched. My Son allows himself to be touched." This was a message of consolation to Pontmain.

The heavenly Virgin was telling the people of the village that God had heard their prayers and that He would answer their needs shortly. He would answer because He was a God who allowed himself to be touched with pity, with pleading, with prayers.

As the people rejoiced over this good news, the Virgin smiled ever more gloriously, the two boys and two girls maintained. Hymn followed hymn now. Pontmain sang its heart out to the Virgin in its sky. During the singing of "My Sweet Jesus," the face of the woman was suddenly contorted with sorrow. A large red cross with a darker red figure of Jesus appeared in her hands. The Virgin was clearly praying, the children reported.

One of the stars from outside the oval then moved inside and seemed to light four candles that surrounded the Virgin Mother's form. When the people heard this, they thought of the four candles they lit each Sunday at church. The candles were lit while prayers were said for their men at war. The pastor smiled warmly. The Mother of God was giving her nod of approval to Pontmain's devotion and prayers for her sons.

Finally, the cross disappeared and the Lady's arms were again outstretched toward the people of Pontmain just below her feet. Her expression once again was of joy.

As the people continued to pray, a white veil suddenly appeared at the feet of the Virgin. Slowly, the children said, it seemed to be pulled upwards over the form of the Virgin, covering her. Just as the night prayers concluded, the covered figure garbed in blue with stars disappeared from the sky. The single apparition of Pontmain had lasted about three hours.

Pontmain learned the next morning that during the very hours of the apparition, General Schmidt received an order to pull back from Laval. He had been preparing to enter it. Some Prussian soldiers also told others that they had had a vision near the outskirts of the city. "A Madonna is guarding the country and forbidding us to advance," they told some of their Prussian superiors.

Within eleven days, the Prussians had mysteriously withdrawn all troops and abandoned the country that would have soon been forced to surrender. An armistice was signed, and the war was over. The men of Pontmain, including Auguste Barbadette, returned home.

It was hardly a victory for France: Napoleon III had been taken prisoner, and the professional army had been defeated. The Paris commune had surrendered after heavy civilian casualties. The Alsace-Lorraine region was ceded to Germany by the Treaty of Frankfurt, not to return to French possession for nearly fifty years. But Pontmain and western France had been spared.

As the years passed, the two younger Barbadette boys entered seminaries to study for the priesthood. Eugène became a diocesan priest, while Joseph entered the order of the Oblates of Mary Immaculate. Abbé Eugène died in 1927, and his younger brother in 1930.

Jeanne-Marie Lebosse, one of the girls who had witnessed the vision, entered the convent of the Sisters of the Holy Family. She died in 1933, but Father René Laurentin, the renowned authority on Marian apparitions, found that she retracted her claims to the vision late in 1920 at the age of fifty-eight. The reason for her retraction, according to Father Laurentin, is not known.

The fourth of the major visionaries, Françoise Richer, did not enter religious life. In fact, she worked as a servant and schoolroom assistant. Abbé Eugène Barbadette retained her services at the rectory of his parish at Chatillon-sur-Colmont until her death in 1915.

Only a year after the Virgin came to Pontmain, the bishop of the Laval diocese, Bishop Wicart, issued his decree concerning the occurrence of January 17, 1871. The report of the apparition of the Virgin Mother, he said, "bears the character of a happening in the supernatural and divine order." He then authorized devotion at the site and announced plans to erect a shrine in honor of "Mary on the very spot where she deigned to appear."

And the barnyard that once had become the open-air church for a village visited by the Mother of God?

It was preserved, after a fashion. The Barbadette barn itself was maintained and converted into a simple chapel, while a more substantial church was begun nearby in 1872. In later years, the church was consecrated and designated as a basilica.

Here, twenty thousand pilgrims pause each year to pray to "Our Lady of Hope," the Lady who came to a French village that had faith enough to save a nation. The basilica was called the Basilica of Our Lady of Hope.

Knock , Ireland

1879

*T*hursday, August 21, 1879, had been a warm, bright day for working in the fields. If there were fewer potatoes than the people of Knock village in County Mayo would have liked, at least there were some. The fields had not always been so generous. Besides, the day had been dry enough to harvest hay and to cut turf, or peat, the Irish fuel.

Happy harvests had been few and far between in Ireland during much of the nineteenth century. The worst years had been from 1845 through 1849, when a million and a half people were counted as victims of starvation or illnesses related to malnutrition. Another million had left for American shores, thinking the land of opportunity would provide a haven from the grave as well. Thousands who left with that hope did not live to see New York harbor. In those years, the potato crop had failed all over the country.

But if the Irish were hungry for potatoes, they were even hungrier for freedom after three centuries of political oppression under English rule and Protestant bias. Catholicism had survived crushing abuse and discrimination, but there was little joy in mere survival. In 1868 the Anglican (English Episcopalian) Church had ceased to be the State Church of Ireland, a land where Catholics were in the majority by a ratio of greater than seven to one.

The potato harvest of 1879 was still another failure — the third in a row. The Irish, whose diet depended upon the potato, had no food reserves to fall back on. Knock and County Mayo, in the west, had fared better than some places, but not so well that the Byrnes and other families there had forgotten the hopelessness of empty plates.

No one thought to ask the Byrnes what they had to put on the table that night, August 21, 1879. Typically, the menu was the same from house to house. Summer fare generally offered "stirabout" (a porridge of oatmeal or cornmeal) and milk for breakfast, then potatoes, milk, and perhaps an egg or butter for dinner. Meat was generally unknown at the tables of the poor, and bacon was a dream to all but wealthy farmers.

Sometime after supper, a furious rain began to pour down on Knock. Nevertheless, twenty-one-year-old Margaret Byrne left the family home at about 7:30 P.M. to lock up the parish church nearby. She saw something brightly lit at the south end of the church, which was finished with a large gable, but Margaret did not investigate, perhaps because the rain was driving so hard. She was never sure why she didn't approach the light to get a closer look.

Margaret didn't know it, but thirty minutes earlier, Mary McLoughlin, the forty-five-year-old housekeeper of the parish priest, had casually noticed the same unusual light. She'd been on her way to the Byrnes' cottage for a visit at 7:00 P.M. A bit more light held on in the Irish sky even in the midst of the downpour. The south gable of the church was awash with an unusual glow, Mary McLoughlin had noticed.

Though she hadn't lingered, Mary had looked a little more closely than young Margaret. She thought she saw three large figures standing against the gable, silhouetted by the light. Margaret immediately thought the figures were statues. The Knock church had lost two of its statues in the previous year. A storm had toppled the statues, smashing them. Why wouldn't Archdeacon Cavanagh, the pastor, have mentioned that the new statues had arrived? But the housekeeper had hurried on, feeling just a little irritated.

Mary McLoughlin spent a little time with the Byrnes, then was ready to return to her own home. Mary Byrne, the twenty-nine-year old sister of Margaret, offered to walk the older woman home. It was probably eight o'clock, Mary Byrne remembered, when she and Mary McLoughlin passed by the church again. She became the chief witness of Knock and described what she saw later.

"... and at the distance of three hundred yards or so from the church, I beheld all at once, standing out from the gable, and rather to the west of it, three figures which, on more attentive inspection, appeared to be that of the Blessed Virgin, of St. Joseph, and St. John.

"That of the Blessed Virgin was life-size, the others apparently either not so big or not so high as her figure; they stood a little distance out from the gable wall, and as well as I could judge, a foot and a half or two feet from the ground. The Virgin stood erect, with eyes raised to heaven, her hands elevated to the shoulders or bosom; she wore a large cloak of a white color, hanging in full folds and somewhat loosely gathered around her shoulders and fastened to the neck; she wore a crown on the head — rather a large crown — and it [the cloak] appeared to me somewhat yellower than the dress or robes worn by Our Blessed Lady."

The figure of St. Joseph, according to Mary Byrne, was bent slightly toward the Blessed Virgin as though in a posture of respect to her. His hair and beard were gray; his face was older. When she looked at the other figure, to the right of the Virgin, Mary immediately thought of St. John the Evangelist. This was a young man, dressed in Mass vestments, wearing a bishop's mitre on his head and holding a book in his left hand. As Mary explained later, his right hand was raised in blessing.

Behind the whole tableau of figures was a sort of altar. On the altar was a very young lamb. "On the body of the Lamb and around it, I saw golden stars, or small brilliant lights, glittering like jets or glass balls," Mary said. The lamb was clearly a symbol for Christ, the Paschal Lamb, and for the Eucharist.

As Mary Byrne and Mary McLoughlin stared hard at the three figures in the pouring rain, they grew more and more assured that heaven was sending a wonderful message for Knock. While the pastor's housekeeper kept watch, Mary Byrne ran back to her family's cottage to alert them.

Out of the Byrne house and into the drenching rain came Mary's widowed sixty-eight-year-old mother, Margaret Byrne; Mary's younger sister Margaret, who had passed the vision by earlier; her eighteen-year-old brother, Dominick; and her eight-year-old niece, Catherine Murray. A wide generational spread of witnesses was gathering at the Knock church.

A few of the younger Byrnes left to alert some of the neighbors about the phenomenon, which all now believed to be miraculous. In contrast to some apparitions, *all* who came to view it saw it. Soon, more than a dozen people were gathered around the south gable, watching, praying, discussing the scene quietly and reverently among themselves. Nevertheless, the group was distressed that their pastor, Archdeacon Cavanagh, was not there to see the wonder.

Others from Knock came, however. Eleven-year-old Patrick Hill ran to the church after Dominick Byrne had burst into the house where Patrick was living with his aunt. Dominick had shouted, "Come up to the chapel and see the miraculous lights, and the beautiful visions that are to be seen there!" Then Dominick had run out, still panting from shortness of breath.

Off went Patrick, with his uncle (a second Dominick Byrne, aged thirty-five), a twenty-four-year-old youth named John Durkan, and a little six-year-old boy named John Curry. They grabbed rain gear and rushed out of the cottage in Dominick's tracks. When they came around the bend to face the gable end of the church, they all saw what Patrick called the "clear white light, covering most of the gable" and the figures.

Patrick Hill and little Johnny Curry and the two men joined the others from the Byrne household and nearby cottages. Johnny, as Patrick recalled, could not see over the wall that bordered the churchyard. Some of the witnesses, Patrick said, were leaning against the wall. Patrick lifted the little boy up, then decided that they would get a better look if they went closer still. He helped Johnny over and the two children crept close enough to touch the church wall — and three persons who looked as real as any on the other side. Patrick was convinced.

"The figures were full and round, as if they had a body and

life; they said nothing, but as we approached, they seemed to go back a little toward the gable," he said. Patrick went so close that he could see the "lines and the letters" inside of the book that the figure of St. John held.

Another witness was just as bold as Patrick and little Johnny. Seventy-four-year-old Bridget Trench was moved with devotion at the sight, unmatched by any other through the many years of her life. Approaching the vision, she tried to embrace the Virgin's feet. "She found nothing in her arms or hands," said Patrick, who watched it. Again, the figures receded out of reach but not out of sight.

As the hour passed, some of the witnesses left, filled with a joy and a sense that heaven knew about their problems in Knock. All noted that, despite the rain, the figures of the Blessed Virgin, St. Joseph, and St. John remained dry. The glow of light, radiating through the figures and the altar with the lamb, continued and never dimmed.

Most of the villagers knew about the apparition of Our Lady at Lourdes in France. In fact, one of the new statues on order for the church was of Our Lady of Lourdes. This rendezvous with the Virgin seemed distinctly different. These figures never moved, except to recede closer to the gable wall. There were no words — no spoken or written messages given. All who passed by were blessed with the ability to see the vision. Half a mile away, Patrick Walsh, a farmer heading home from his fields, saw the glow of light off the face of the church.

After the apparition had persisted for more than two hours, many of the visionaries from the village went off to see a neighbor, Mrs. Campbell, and pray with her. The neighborhood knew that she was dying. When they returned, passing by the church again, the vision was gone. There was no trace of the figures or the mysterious light that had brightened the night.

On Friday, August 22, an appointed group went to see Archdeacon Cavanagh, the pastor of Knock and Aghamore. He believed their stories immediately. Promptly he sent a report to the bishop of Tuam, the diocese to which Knock belonged. But the response of the institutional Church was neither immediate nor positive.

A commission was created within several months to interview the apparition subjects. Fifteen of the village visionaries were examined by the commission, although at least twenty-two people had viewed the event at the south gable.

Research later revealed that the only original investigative documents in the diocesan archives were negative toward Knock. The rest had been lost or burned or misplaced. One report, however, suggested that the figures were the work of a local Protestant policeman. The vision, it said, was a hoax arranged by the policeman, who experimented with the use of a special sort of light. He had created the images of the figures against the church wall just to mislead the faithful, it said.

Ecclesiastical voices from other quarters did show support for Knock, however. In 1882, Archbishop John Joseph Lynch of Toronto, Canada, was a pilgrim at Knock. He believed he had received a healing through Our Lady of Knock. "I was satisfied with the account of the investigation already made," explained this bishop, who listened to the testimony of just one witness. One was all he needed to hear.

Among the people of County Mayo and adjoining areas, there was also immediate trust in the alleged witnesses and in the apparition. The first "pilgrimage" to honor the apparition of Knock came from Limerick City in March, 1880, just months after the vision.

The Knock witnesses told their stories over and over to Irish believers from neighboring counties, but the first commission never met with them a second time. The experience of these "seers" was unlike the grueling cross-examinations endured by Bernadette at Lourdes twenty-one years earlier. In fact, the investigation was, in many respects, shallow.

Life changed for the Byrne family and for those who had also seen the silent but beautiful Virgin Mother and her holy escorts. Within a few years, Dominick and Margaret Byrne, brother and sister, had died. So, too, had their young niece Catherine Murray. Bridget Trench, the elderly woman who had tried to embrace the Blessed Mother, and Patrick Walsh (the farmer who had witnessed the light from a distance) had also died. Ten of the original and official witnesses then remained to tell and retell the story of the vision over and over.

Mary Byrne married James O'Connell in 1882, three years after the Knock apparition. They continued to live in the village and raised a family of six children. Mary lived a life of simple, unaffected piety, according to her children and grandchildren. Shortly before her death, in 1936, she was interviewed by questioners for the second official commission. Though she was eighty-six then, her testimony was just as confident as it had been more than a half-century before.

What was puzzling to the Diocese of Tuam and others was the wordless meaning of Knock's apparition, which continued to puzzle scholars and everyday folk. And yet, for many, there were some answers in the images themselves.

The Blessed Virgin, for instance, was immediately recognized by all gathered in the rain in front of the church. The rosary, said to be the "Irish Catechism," was a commonly recited prayer. It was almost universally said in a land where the churches had often been closed or destroyed by law, thus denying Irish Catholics their means of worship at Mass. Mary should have felt at home in Ireland because Ireland loved her so.

St. John the Apostle's appearance in the attire of a bishop and in the pose of a preacher had its meaning for the Irish, too. Here was a visual reinforcement for the people of the sacred role of priest, which they were to uphold even in times of great oppression. He held the Mass book or the Scriptures in his hand. This was an encouragement to continue devotion to the Mass, also symbolized by the altar and the Paschal Lamb appearing behind the Apostle and Evangelist John.

St. Joseph's deferential pose reminded the Church of his quiet but invaluable role as protector. In 1872, Pope Pius IX had named him "patron of the Universal Church." But Joseph had also been the provider and protector of Jesus and Mary. His presence seemed to stress his role as protector of all families and of the Church. St. Joseph's appearance was particularly intended to comfort Irish families. They had been devastated by starvation, political and religious discrimination, poverty, and the emigration of family members to other lands.

Knock's families were elated to have received this blessing in 1879, but life was never again the same. It had been a quiet village of a dozen families. One year after the vision, the neighborhood schoolchildren could no longer take lunch or recess in the field adjoining the schoolhouse. "I saw such a crowd that we [the children] could hardly go outside from school to play," one man said of Knock's sudden transformation during his boyhood days.

In fact, the church, which accommodated six hundred, was soon too small to welcome the crowds. It was widened by adding two aisles and standing room beyond the aisles on either side. And still it was inadequate. On Sundays, there was quite a crush of pilgrims and tourists.

In 1976, a new church was dedicated at Knock. It was known as the Church of Our Lady Queen of Ireland and could accommodate thousands of pilgrims. It was needed, since the annual rate of pilgrims traveling to Knock in modern times is about one million.

In 1971, the Sacred Congregation for Religious Worship granted permission to the Knock Shrine to have the ceremony of the anointing of the sick carried out at Knock. It was a privilege extended to other major Marian shrines, even though this apparition site still lacked the approval (or any statement of assessment) from the Diocese of Tuam. Rather than to issue a direct approval of the Knock apparition as "worthy of belief," the bishops of the Irish diocese were apparently content to let the event speak for itself. There seemed to be little doubt, however, that the Church unofficially saw Knock with the same eyes as did the faithful. The visit of Pope John Paul II in 1979 strengthened that sense of ecclesial sanction. And by the 1980s and '90s, every parish in Ireland sent a pilgrimage group to Knock at least once a year.

On a dreary August night, during a sad century, the Virgin Mary had come to comfort the downtrodden Irish. It was a blessing, and the Irish had never concerned themselves with studying blessings. In Gaelic, they simply thanked heaven for it. *"Cead mile failte!"* as one believer said — "A hundred thousand thanks!"

Fátima, Portugal

1917

*I*t was the saddest supper I ever remember," wrote Lucia dos Santos of an evening during her early childhood, sometime in the autumn of 1916. Her mother, Maria Rosa, had wept with grief at the dinner table.

The dos Santos family, village peasants with seven children, had come upon some hard times in tiny Aljustrel, just half a mile south of Fátima, Portugal. Fátima was about seventy miles north of Lisbon, the capital. There was worry there and all over Portugal. The nation had entered World War I against Germany in March.

Manuel, one of Lucia's two brothers, was headed for military service. Then, too, Antonio, the father and head of the family, had been turning to a life of drink and detachment from family duties. Without Manuel to help, Maria Rosa could see little to stop a steady downward slide of the family's precarious fortunes.

If Maria Rosa had been caught up in her own concerns during that year, so too, had Lucia, the youngest of her seven children. The things that preoccupied mother and daughter, however, were literally worlds apart. Already that year, nine-year-old Lucia had witnessed the apparition of an angel three times. Maria Rosa knew nothing of it.

Early in the summer, Lucia, who tended the family's sheep, had been in a sort of cave near a place called Cabeco, on land her father owned. She was with her cousins, eight-year-old Francisco Marto and his six-year-old sister, Jacinta. These two had persuaded their parents, Manuel (called Ti — "uncle" — by Lucia) and Olimpia Marto, that they, too, could tend the family flock, especially if Lucia was with them.

The sky became dark and a light rain began to fall. The three ran to the cave after driving their sheep into the shelter of some trees. This area formed part of a mountain chain called the Serra da Estrela. It wriggles down the length of Portugal well past Fátima.

What came, however, was much more than a summer shower.

Suddenly, in front of the three shepherd children stood a shining young man of about fourteen or fifteen. He was, according to Lucia, incredibly handsome and "more brilliant than a crystal, penetrated by the rays of the sun." He calmed the children and told them he was the "Angel of Peace." Then the apparition asked the three to pray with him. Imitating his motions and his words, the cousins learned a prayer of adoration before the vision was gone, dissolved into the sun.

The children saw the Angel of Peace later in the summer and again in the autumn. From him they learned of the need for frequent prayer and sacrifice. The experiences profoundly altered the lives of the three youngsters. Neither the Martos nor Lucia's parents suspected anything. Each day they sent out happy, playful children to herd and graze the sheep and goats. In private, however, the three children had begun a simple but deep prayer life and a habit of sacrifice and reparation that no one suspected.

All of this came to mind for Lucia the evening she saw her mother weeping at the table. The Angel of Peace had said, "Above all, accept and endure with submission the suffering which the Lord will send you." Lucia knew her mother was struggling to accept and endure. Lucia could not know that the following year would bring her own suffering — even from her mother, Maria Rosa. She did not know either that her heavenly Mother would bring her joy — face to face.

Sunday, May 13, 1917, was a fine, sunny day. Ti and Olimpia Marto thought so much of it that they took the cart to attend Mass at Batalha, a town to the west. After Mass, they told their children, they would head for the city's market to buy a piglet.

After they saw their parents off, Francisco and Jacinta, now ages nine and seven, gathered up the Marto sheep. They drove them to the place where they always met Lucia (now nearly ten) with the dos Santos flock. Together, they moved the animals slowly to the Cova da Iria property that Antonio dos Santos owned. Once the animals were grazing, the three amused themselves while they kept an eye on the sheep.

They were busy creating a "house" out of a tangle of bushes and rocks. "Pretend" games were fun and always made the day go quickly. As they were lugging rocks to form a "wall" for the house, a flash of light against the clear blue sky startled them. Frightened by what they thought was lightning, the children ran down the slope toward a tree. Another flash crackled close to them. They ran again — about a hundred yards — and found themselves staring at something atop a small evergreen tree called a *carrasqueira*, or holm oak.

It took three sets of normal, healthy eyes only a second to see that a large ball of light was settling at the top of the four-foot tree. Inside the glowing ball was the figure of a woman, a beautiful woman.

She was, as Lucia later wrote, "a Lady of all white, more brilliant than the sun dispensing light, clearer and more intense than a crystal cup full of crystalline water penetrated by the rays of the most glaring sun." Perhaps this description by Lucia as an adult would have overwhelmed her own childhood understanding. Her young cousins, who would never have years of life to learn to write, put it more simply. There above the bush was a woman glowing with a bright light, they told others. The three of them were petrified.

"Don't be afraid," the woman said. "I won't hurt you." The tones were soothing, warm. Somehow, the voice melted their fear and drew them out of themselves into hope. They thought of the angel. This woman's presence was more peaceful, comforting.

"Where do you come from?" asked Lucia with great deference.

"I am from heaven," came the Lady's answer.

"And what is it you want of me?" Lucia asked after a moment.

The woman told her that she wanted the three to return on

the thirteenth of each month at the same hour for six months in succession. They would see her at these times. At the end of the six months, she promised, she would tell them who she was and what she wanted. Lucia agreed that they would. Finding greater voice and courage, Lucia continued to quiz this mysterious woman.

"And shall I go to heaven, too?" she inquired.

"Yes, you will."

"And Jacinta?"

"Also."

"And Francisco?"

"Also. But he will have to say many rosaries!"

The Lady continued to answer Lucia's questions about hidden truths. Finally, the Lady asked Lucia if she and the other two would be willing to suffer all that would happen to them as a reparation for sins and for the conversion of sinners.

Without consulting her cousins, Lucia said, "Yes." Then the woman told her that they would indeed suffer but that the grace of God would support them. At this, she spread her hands, and streams of light flowed from them toward the dusty red earth where the shepherd children stood.

Immediately, they felt an infusion of the light and the presence of God. As though on cue, they dropped to their knees and began to utter prayers of divine adoration. The prayers came from somewhere deep inside. The woman watched over them until the prayers of praise came to a conclusion.

"Say the rosary, to obtain peace for the world, and the end of the war," she told them.

Then, unlike the Angel of Peace who had dissolved into the light the year before, she rose from the bush and glided away into the eastern sky. Before their eyes, the woman became smaller and smaller until she was out of sight. The children studied the sky long after she was gone. Then it was as though they themselves had to return to earth.

"Oh, such a pretty Lady!" Jacinta finally said.

In a moment, all three were talking excitedly of what they'd seen and what it meant. Lucia and Jacinta told Francisco all that the Lady said. Although he had seen her, he could not hear her, just as he had not heard the angel the year before.

The children drove the sheep back to Aljustrel early. On the way, Lucia warned her cousins to keep silent about the Lady from heaven. But looking at Jacinta made her wonder if the secret could be kept. The seven-year-old's face was absolutely radiant. Was the joy too large for Jacinta to hold inside? On the following morning, Lucia would find out.

The youngest of the dos Santos children went to bed as usual, having given no hint of what the day had brought. In the morning, she ate and went out to play alone. In a way, she was a lonely child in this family. Her oldest sisters, Maria of the Angels and Theresa, were already married when Lucia was born. Caroline, the sister next to her in age, was fifteen — too old to play little-girl games. In the midst of her daydreaming, Lucia heard the voice of Maria of the Angels.

"Oh, Lucia! I hear you have seen Our Lady at Cova da Iria!"

Lucia looked up at her grinning sister but gave no answer. Jacinta or Francisco had told. She knew that there would be trouble. She bit her lip and wondered what others would have to say. The tale would be taken from house to house before sundown.

Within half an hour, Lucia was called into the house. Her mother and father wanted to know what had happened the day before. Very simply, she told them of the flash of light, the appearance of the Lady dressed in white, and of her claim to be from heaven. She left out nothing but was troubled by what she saw upon the faces of her parents.

In fact, Antonio, her father, dismissed the matter. "Silly women's tales!" he muttered. He got up and left without giving Lucia a second glance. Maria Rosa was furious. She had taught her children to tell the truth, she shouted at her nearly ten-year-old daughter. Now her youngest would make her old age miserable by becoming a liar. Lucia could protest no further. She left the house when her mother dismissed her and, with tears streaming down her face, headed for the sheep pen.

On the road, Lucia walked slowly, tapping her sheep on the rump with a stick to keep them moving. Then she spotted Francisco and Jacinta. Even from a distance, she could see their misery. She said nothing as she neared the wide spot in the road where they were waiting for her.

Francisco was fighting back tears. Jacinta was weeping with her face in her hands. They had evidently heard of the trouble they had caused at the dos Santos house. "Don't cry any more," said Lucia, going to her cousins with her arms outstretched for them. Her own anger vanished.

As they watched the flock that day, the day after the first apparition, the children were sad. The secret joy of the experience seemed lost. Wearing a long face, Jacinta sat on a rock. Finally, the three began to talk. Jacinta said she wanted to pray the full rosary and do sacrifices as the Lady had asked. The children had always prayed a daily rosary, but they had taken shortcuts, merely saying the words "Our Father" and "Hail Mary" instead of the complete prayers. And after a discussion, the cousins settled on a sacrifice. They would give their lunches to the sheep.

As May passed, Lucia endured a continual barrage of sarcastic and threatening attacks at home. The opposition of her mother was most painful. Maria Rosa was offended by the gossip and snickering of her neighbors. At the Marto household, Olimpia was indifferent. But Ti Marto believed in his children. He knew they were not liars.

"If you don't say it was a lie, I will lock you up in a dark room where you will never see the light of the sun again," Maria Rosa fumed at Lucia. But Lucia would not deny a word of it. She suffered an agony of spirit and looked toward the thirteenth of June.

As the date of the next apparition came closer, Lucia's

mother and sisters began to tempt her with reminders about the festival that day. June 13 was also the feast of St. Anthony of Padua, one of the greatest feasts in Portugal. Lucia remembered very well that there would be a great procession, with flowers, dancing, fireworks, and a delicious bread given to all the children. It was a day she loved, but she knew she would be at the Cova.

Well before dawn on the thirteenth, Lucia had her flock out to pasture in order to return them early. She attended Mass at Fátima to honor St. Anthony. When she returned home, she found a group of neighbors who wanted to accompany her to the Cova. She did not like the idea, but Maria Rosa liked it even less. The sight of such "gullible" adults and children was enraging. A flurry of sarcastic, biting comments from her mother and sisters poured down upon Lucia.

"I felt very very bitter that day," Lucia wrote years later. "I recalled the times that were past, and I asked myself where was the affection that my family had had for me only a little while ago."

The small crowd and the three children left for the Cova at 11:00 A.M. Lucia was crying softly, but Francisco cheered her up. Just before the appointed hour, noon, they sat on the ground near the *carrasqueira* and waited. They recited the rosary, and those who had escorted the children opened picnic baskets to eat. One girl led the Litany of Our Lady until Lucia stood up and interrupted her.

"Jacinta," she said, "there comes Our Lady! There is the light!"

Everyone stood up. Bystanders noticed that the sun seemed to dim even in the cloudless sky. Others noticed that the small *carrasqueira* bent a little at the top. The Lady had appeared again.

Again, Lucia asked the vision what she wanted of her. Again, the Lady requested that the children come the next month and that they recite five decades of the rosary each day. She also told the girl that she wanted the children to learn to read, and that further instructions would follow later. Lucia then asked the Lady if she would take the three of them to heaven.

This time, the answer was more specific. The Lady promised to take Francisco and Jacinta to heaven with her soon. But for Lucia, there was a different plan. She was to remain on earth longer to help establish worldwide devotion to the Lady's Immaculate Heart.

"I stay here alone?" Lucia asked with sadness.

The woman answered her with great tenderness. She would never really be alone, Lucia was told. "My Immaculate Heart will be your refuge." With that, the woman extended her hands. Great showers of light seemed to pour forth as before, but one shaft seemed to flow down upon Lucia. The other radiated back up to the sky from the sister and brother. All three saw a vision of the Immaculate Heart. As in May, the children were flooded with an unearthly joy and peace. Then the woman rose again and traveled into the eastern sky.

When the children were finally left alone, Lucia, Jacinta, and Francisco walked back together to Aljustrel. The girls told Francisco what the Lady had said. He was delighted once again to hear that his trip to heaven was assured. When the three split up to go home, the Marto children again earned a skeptical but neutral reception. Lucia, on the other hand, encountered a household that was, if anything, more abrasive than before as she told of the encounter. The following day, Maria Rosa dragged the girl to the pastor to see if he could make her recant the story.

Father Ferreira was gentle with the girl, but he told the mother and daughter that Lucia might be experiencing visions from a diabolical source. Lucia was frightened and depressed. Jacinta and Francisco were convinced that the Lady showed no traits of the evil one. "And we saw her go up to heaven," Jacinta reasoned.

Lucia had no one to help her sort it out. Maria Rosa's brutal antagonism never let up. During this month the fear grew that the devil was disguising himself as a beautiful lady from heaven. Would the devil take her away? she asked herself. Lucia decided not to go to the Cova for the apparitions any more.

Almost at the last moment on July 13, Lucia ran to the Martos' cottage and found Francisco and Jacinta in tears. They weren't going either, they explained. "We don't dare go without you," they told her. Lucia was the spokesman, the leader, and her cousins knew it.

Instantly, the girl's heart was changed. "I've changed my mind, and I'm going," she told them. Francisco told Lucia that they had been praying for her all night long. In thirty seconds, they were out of the house and off to their rendezvous with the Lady. Two thousand to three thousand people awaited the children at the Cova. Among them were two mothers who had come with blessed candles to banish the devil. Ti Marto had also come to protect his children from the crowds.

At noon, the woman came again. Much of the apparition unfolded like the others. Lucia again asked what the Lady wanted. Again she passed on the requests for healings. Again the Lady asked the children's return on the appointed days and requested the rosary each day for peace. She did refer to herself as "Our Lady of the Rosary." Then something totally new took place.

The Lady spread her hands as before, but this time the light poured through the children into the earth below them. The inner regions of the earth seemed to open and the three children looked into hell. "A sea of fire; and plunged in this fire the demons and the souls, as if they were red-hot coals," Lucia wrote of it years later. The crowd could see that the children were oppressed by some horror.

The Lady acknowledged that they had looked into hell but explained that many souls could be saved from damnation by devotion to her Immaculate Heart and by reparation. Prophecies continued: If offenses against God did not stop, the Lady told them, another, more terrible war would begin during the reign of Pope Pius XI. If this meant little to the three peasant children, the warning astounded others who knew that Pope Benedict XV was the reigning pontiff.

The Lady had other requests to make, global requests. "I come to ask the consecration of Russia to my Immaculate Heart and the Communion of reparation on the first Saturdays," she said. "If they listen to my requests, Russia will be converted and there will be peace. If not, she will scatter her errors through the world, provoking wars and persecution of the Church." Some of these persecutions would touch the Holy Father, the Pope, she continued.

"In the end my Immaculate Heart will triumph," she said finally. "The Holy Father will consecrate Russia to me, and it will be converted and a certain period of peace will be granted to the world. In Portugal the dogma of the Faith will always be kept."

Then there were private things to say to the children. The Lady of the Immaculate Heart told Lucia and Jacinta to share all of these messages with Francisco. Then she gave the children a final secret not to be told to anyone.

When the Lady rose into the east this time, the children were pale. They stared at one another but could think of no words to describe what they had seen or heard. Somehow, the crowd knew that this appearance was different from the others. As they mobbed the children, throwing questions at them, Ti Marto scooped up his youngest, Jacinta, and started to lead the children away. All three seemed to carry away the weight of profound promises and threats on which the world would turn. Something of their childhood was left behind.

After the July apparition, all Portugal knew of Fátima. Steady streams of visitors descended upon Aljustrel. There was no privacy now for the Martos or for the dos Santos family. "It's too bad you didn't keep quiet," a frustrated Francisco complained one day to Jacinta. When they saw visitors heading down the road toward their homes, they would hide.

In Lucia's household, however, there was renewed anger over the matter. Her father discovered that the crowds had trampled and destroyed his vegetable gardens at the Cova. A hungry winter was more likely for Lucia's family. They would not let her forget it. Only in the hills with the sheep was there any peace. But the negative attitude went far beyond Lucia's house.

In 1910, a Portuguese republic had come to power following the assassination of King Carlos. The republic was openly anticlerical and hostile to religion. The Fátima-generated upsurge of piety had to be stopped for political reasons, many Portuguese officials reasoned.

With this thought in mind, the administrator of Ourem arrived in Aljustrel on August 13, 1917. He claimed to have had a religious conversion. He would personally take the three children to the apparition, he promised. The Martos were reluctant. Antonio dos Santos did not care how his daughter got there. Finally, however, the visionaries were driven off in a wagon to the Cova by the newest "believer."

Halfway there, the administrator turned around and took them back to his house at Ourem. They missed the apparition and were grieved about it. For two days, the children were locked away and threatened with death unless they revealed "the secret" Our Lady had given them. On the second day of captivity, they were taken out of the jail cell one by one. The administrator told them that they would be boiled in oil. Jacinta was carried away first and sequestered to frighten the others. "What do we care if they kill us?" Francisco whispered to a pale Lucia. "We go straight to heaven!"

At that, the agnostic administrator of Ourem knew that he was defeated. On August 15, he took the children back to Aljustrel and left them on the steps of the rectory. On Sunday, August 19, the Virgin came to the children during the afternoon in a hollow or low valley called Valinhos.

After she was gone, the children cut branches from the

carrasqueira on which she had settled and took them home. The scent of them was particularly sweet to Maria Rosa, but she still did not believe in the Lady or in Lucia's claims.

Early on the thirteenth of September, the three young visionaries struggled through a crowd of thousands to get to the Cova. This apparition was very short. The Lady promised that at the next appearance the children would also see the Lord, Our Lady of Sorrows, Our Lady of Mount Carmel, and St. Joseph with the Child Jesus. "Continue to say the rosary to bring about the end of the war," she reminded them. Then after promising the cure of some who had asked for healings, she disappeared into the east.

The time between this and the last appearance on October 13 passed quickly for Aljustrel and for the three young visionaries. As the thirteenth dawned rainy and windy, more than seventy thousand people were camped at the Cova waiting for noon and for a break in the rain. With anxiety, the parents of the children prepared to go. They feared that if there was no miracle the children would be killed by an angry crowd.

Just before noon, Lucia and her cousins waited for the Virgin. Though she could not explain why, she told the crowd to close their umbrellas. The rain continued to come but changed into a lighter mist. Looking into the east, Lucia was suddenly transformed.

"Watch out, daughter, don't let yourself be deceived," cautioned her doubtful mother.

The three children did not hear this last expression of disbelief that Maria Rosa would make. On their knees, they gazed up at the Lady who had come again to rest on the little *carrasqueira* decorated with flowers and garlands. A fine mist sprayed their faces.

"What do you want of me?" Lucia began again for the last time.

"I want to tell you to have them build a chapel here in my honor. I am the Lady of the Rosary. Let them continue to say the rosary every day. The war is going to end, and the soldiers will soon return to their homes."

The child asked again for the cures of many of the sick. The Lady of the Rosary promised the healing of some, but added that they must amend their lives and ask pardon for their sins. "Let them offend Our Lord God no more, for He is already much offended," she added.

These were the last words the Lady would speak to Lucia and to the world at Fátima. She opened her hands again, and the light that came from them shot skyward. "Look at the sun!" Lucia shouted. The promised miracle was beginning, but the Virgin Mother of God vanished.

The crowds looked up to see clouds roll back and reveal the sun. But it was now like a disc of white light that all could look at without blinking. Meanwhile, all three children viewed a tableau in the heavens of scenes representing the mysteries of the rosary. At the joyful mysteries, they saw the Holy Family and watched St. Joseph bless the crowds three times. The Christ Child was in his arms. Lucia then saw visions of Our Lady of Sorrows, and then of Our Lady of Mount Carmel.

At the same time, the crowds watched in awe as the sun bobbed in the sky like a bright silver top. Then the "dancing sun" stopped and began to spin. As it whirled, bright rays representing every color of the spectrum shot off and washed everything on the earth. Green, red, violet worlds appeared momentarily to surround the people, who shouted and praised God.

Then the 70,000 people at the Cova watched the sun plunge in a zigzag path toward the earth. In every heart was a fear of death. People fell to their knees by the hundreds. Just as the sun seemed about to strike the earth, it stopped and was suddenly returned to its proper place and its proper brightness. The crowd noticed that all clothing, previously soaked with rain, had dried. The "Miracle of the Sun" was seen in nearby cities. There was no serious talk of mass hallucination. Portugal was convinced.

Lucia, Jacinta, and Francisco were mobbed, then hoisted onto the shoulders of some sturdier men. After hours of trying to break free of the questioners, they returned home pale and exhausted.

In the following months, the mothers of Lucia and Jacinta agreed to send the girls to school so they could learn to read. The Lady had requested that. Francisco declined the opportunity, knowing that he would leave the world before reading could be useful. He spent much of his time praying in the Church of St. Anthony at Fátima.

On April 4, 1919, Francisco died of bronchial pneumonia. He was not quite eleven years old. "What a man he would have been," said his father sadly. Long before the apparitions, he had been very proud of this youngest son, a handsome boy who loved nature and never showed fear. Lucia visited him every day during his long illness. Seeing that he was close to death, she asked him to pray for her from heaven.

Jacinta was sick as well. She was devastated by the loss of her brother but rejoiced in his better fortune. Over the summer and fall she developed pleurisy, which became increasingly serious. On February 20, 1920, in a Lisbon hospital, she died at 10:30 P.M. As she had predicted, there was no one with her when Our Lady of the Rosary came to welcome her.

Left alone to bear the burden of witness, Lucia remained for several years with her family. At age fourteen, in June, 1921, she left Aljustrel in the middle of the night for a school run by the Sisters of St. Dorothy at Porto.

The move was arranged by the bishop of the newly created diocese of Leiria in which Fátima and Aljustrel were located. After visiting the Cova and the grave of Francisco, Lucia traveled incognito and assumed a different identity at the school. Until the Church affirmed the apparitions, it was best, the bishop thought, to keep the girl in obscurity.

In 1925, Lucia decided to enter the convent of the Sisters of St. Dorothy. Still, none in her convent knew of her real identity as the surviving child of Fátima. In 1930, the bishop recognized the apparitions at Fátima, declaring that they were indeed "worthy of belief." Cures by the hundreds were being reported there, although a massive wave of anti-Catholic fervor was otherwise threatening the nation.

In 1936, Sister Maria das Dores (Mary of Sorrows) penned the first account of the apparitions in obedience to a request by the bishop. Three other accounts were produced, one in 1937 and two in 1941. In the fourth, she revealed the third part of the so-called "Secret of Fátima" for the eyes of the Holy Father alone. It was to be opened in 1960, or earlier in the event of Lucia's death.

The first two parts of the secret had been already known. The first had to do with the July 1917 vision of hell and the warning about a second world war "if men do not cease offending God." The second related to the Virgin's request for the worldwide devotion to the Immaculate Heart of Mary.

In more recent times, rumors periodically circulate in the Italian press about dire punishments predicted in the "third secret." Dozens of articles have speculated about why the secret had been suppressed by four pontiffs in succession. After each sensational article, the Vatican had restated its position. Those close to Pope John Paul II explained why he chooses not to make the content public. First of all, that is the pope's prerogative. Secondly, the message in the secret adds nothing to what is already contained in Sacred Revelation. And finally, the Vatican has explained, the Pontiff wishes to avoid the possibility of sensationalism by the media and pseudo-prophets attempting to lead the faithful astray. Some suffering is inevitable, he has said, but Our Lady of Fátima has already predicted the ultimate triumph of her Immaculate Heart.

It is clear that Pope John XXIII read the secret — the third part — in 1960. "This makes no reference to my time," he said. He had the document filed. Pope Paul VI also read the secret and visited Fátima in 1967, the fifty-year anniversary of the apparitions. There he met Lucia, who was by this time Sister Mary of the Immaculate Heart, a Carmelite sister living in Coimbra. A pillar inside the basilica marked the spot where the holm oak, or *carrasqueira*, once received the Mother of God.

On May 13, 1982, Pope John Paul II traveled to Fátima, where he, too, met Lucia, the only living witness of the apparitions. The Pope told the seer that he owed his life to Our Lady of Fátima after a would-be assassin had shot him on May 13, 1981, in St. Peter's Square. During the weeks and months of recovery, the Pope had read and reread the documents about Fátima. Later, he sent the bullet removed from his stomach to Fátima where it was set among the jewels that encrusted the crown on the statue's head.

In a quiet way, Pope John Paul had a small chapel built in the woods, near the border of Poland and Russia. A replica of the Fátima statue was placed facing Russia. The Pope believed that Russia really would be converted.

In 1984, Pope John Paul II consecrated the world and Russia to the Immaculate Heart in collegial union with the world's bishops. Pius XII had done something similar in 1942 and had later consecrated the Russian people in 1952. Pope Pius XII also instituted the feast of the Immaculate Heart of Mary and declared that the shrine at Fátima was a basilica.

Within five years of the consecration of Russia to the Immaculate Heart of Mary, the Soviet Union was peacefully breaking apart. Some people said that the disintegration of the Communist block had begun when the blue mantle of Our Lady was thrown across it.

Today, millions visit the shrine at Fátima in Portugal. Millions more have been transformed by the message brought by Our Lady to three children. Gradually, the Christian world realized that the apparitions were the most important in modern times.

Fátima had profoundly touched the world. New devotions to the Immaculate Heart and the five first Saturdays were created. And historic devotions, like the recitation of the rosary, were renewed again.

Beauraing, Belgium

1932-33

Guadalupe (1531)

Painting depicts the miracle crowning the apparitions of Guadalupe. Juan Diego unfolds his mantle to show Bishop Zumarraga winter roses picked on Tepeyac Hill, unaware of the image (sunrays, etc., actually added later).

Rue du Bac (1830)

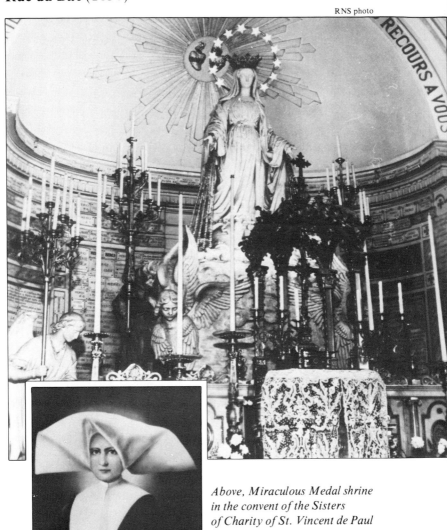

Above, Miraculous Medal shrine in the convent of the Sisters of Charity of St. Vincent de Paul in Paris notes visits of Mary to St. Catherine Labouré (inset), whose body is enshrined there. Legend on her medal: "O Mary, conceived without sin, pray for us who have recourse to thee."

La Salette (1846)

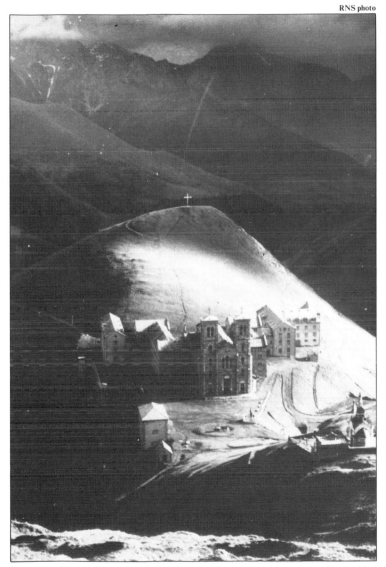

Basilica of La Salette, 5,900 feet high in French mountains near Grenoble, marks the exact spot where the Blessed Virgin is reported to have appeared one day to two young cowherds, Melanie Mathieu and Maximin Giraud.

Lourdes (1858)

Lourdes shrine (left) is cut into the rock of Massabielle, scene of Mary's appearances to St. Bernadette Soubirous. Hospitality center chapel (below), a mile from the shrine, reproduces Bernadette's sheepfold, with thatched roof and milking stools for seats.

NC photos

Pontmain (1870)

Basilica of Our Lady of Hope, west of Paris, commemorates apparition that was apparently instrumental in ending the Franco-Prussian War.

Two world wars later, as a gesture of Franco-German goodwill, Catholic pilgrims from Germany brought to Lourdes a reliquary with relics of St. Hildegarde, 12th-century Germany mystic, and St. Bernard of Clairvaux, the great French abbot who was St. Hildegarde's friend and protector.

Knock (1879)

Photograph taken in 1880 shows hundreds praying at the south gable of the church at Knock, County Mayo, Ireland, where an apparition of the Virgin with St. John was reportedly seen by nearly all the townspeople.

Fátima (1917)

Little Jacinta Marto (at right) is carried after the "miracle of the sun," Oct. 13, 1917. Below, from left, Jacinta, 7, her brother Francisco, 9, and their cousin Lucia dos Santos, 11, are shown at about the time of the apparitions.

NC photos

Beauraing (1932-33)

Shrine of the Blessed Virgin was erected when she appeared to five children in December and January. Albert Voisin (at right), spokesman for the children, returned to Belgium as a teacher and lecturer in the sixties after years of teaching in the Belgian Congo.

Banneux (1933)

The "Virgin of the Poor" (sculpture at right by Dupont) was sighted from the upper right window of the house below by Mariette Beco (lower right, holding a younger brother) and asked that a "small chapel" be built in the front-yard garden the Becos had used to grow onions during the Depression.

Belgian Tourist Bureau

Akita, Japan (1973-81)

Statue of Akita (left) that wept tears and exhibited the stigmata.

Above is the simple convent that is the home of Sister Agnes Sasagawa (in center of picture at right), the seer of Akita.

Medjugorje (1981-?)

Above, from left to right, Vicka Ivankovic, Jakov Colo, and Ivanka Ivankovic react during one of their reported apparitions during the early '80s. At right, Vicka Ivankovic in the '90s. She continued to receive apparitions into this decade. Jakov continues to see Mary daily; Ivanka, yearly on the anniversary of the first apparition.

At right, a grown-up Ivan Dragicevic during a 1991 visit to the U.S. Ivan married Laureen Murphy, an American, in 1994. Below, pilgrims from around the world gather for reconciliation with Franciscan priests outside St. James Church in Medjugorje.

CNS photo

NC photo

Kibeho, Rwanda (1981-89)

Above, Alphonsine Mumureke during a reported apparition at the convent school in Kibeho. Alphonsine was the first to receive a visitation from the Blessed Mother.

Anathalie Mukamazimpaka, above, was the second student to receive apparitions.

San Nicolás, Argentina (1983-90)

Above, the statue of Maria del Rosario de San Nicolás (Our Lady of the Rosary of San Nicolás). At right, Gladys de Motta, the seer, at prayer.

Betania, Venezuela (1984)

Above, pilgrims praying at the farm in Betania; below, part of the crowd of people witnessing Our Lady's appearance.

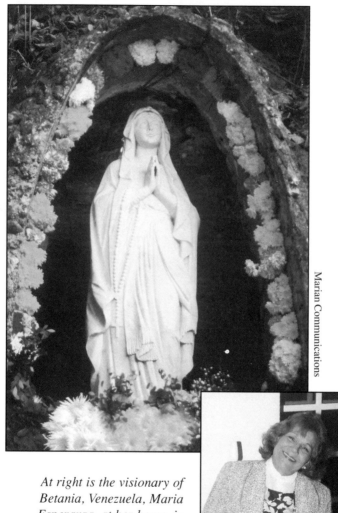

At right is the visionary of Betania, Venezuela, Maria Esperanza, at her home in Caracas. Above is the Marian shrine at Betania.

*I*f they knew of it at all, Belgians in the early 1930s thought of Beauraing as nothing more than a quaint but undistinguished town. Then, too, they might have remembered that it was close to the French border, about sixty miles southeast of Brussels, on a railroad line.

Beauraing was south of an imaginary line that bisected the nation. North of that line, Belgians spoke Flemish, a language similar to Dutch. To the south, the everyday tongue of people in this village and hundreds of others was Walloon, a French dialect.

The 2,000 or more residents of Beauraing would not have had too much more to tell about their town. They had to admit that the trains that rumbled through their village set on a wooded slope provided the only disturbance to shake an otherwise placid farming community. And yet *"Beau-raing"* (an old French name that meant "Beautiful Branch") had already been set apart as a place for a special blessing. However, in 1932, Beauraing and Belgium in general were hardly thinking of blessings.

The political spirit of the nation was heavy. The year 1932 had been the most damaging of the worldwide economic depression. In Belgium's metropolitan areas, breadlines and unemployment were as common as the cold. And Belgians grew increasingly nervous about the angry words and fist-clenching of neighboring Germany, especially of a demagogue named Adolf Hitler.

Moreover, much of Belgium had borrowed more from France than its language. As in France, Belgian Catholics viewed the Catholic Church as their birthright, but devotion was distant. Anticlericalism had poisoned France in the previous century. A lukewarm, halfhearted practice of the Faith was therefore the norm in Beauraing on that late November day in 1932.

Evening was closing in on the hundred or so houses lining Beauraing's old streets. Anyone out on this night knew that winter was surely in the air. It was cold, damp, foggy. Everyone moved with a pace that would put them inside, near the fire, a little more quickly.

Because of the cold, eleven-year-old Albert Voisin and his sister, fifteen-year-old Fernande Voisin, had reason to have wings at their feet on this Tuesday, November 29. Albert, in particular, made use of them. He flew down the street and around the corner to stop at a three-story stone house built at the intersection of three streets. The Degeimbres lived there.

During the time that the Degeimbres and the Voisins had lived as neighbors, the three Degeimbre girls and the three Voisin children had become fast friends. On this evening, as they often did, Albert and Fernande were stopping by to pick up Andrée and Gilberte, the two younger Degeimbres.

The four children had made an almost nightly habit of walking together to the academy run by the Sisters of Christian Doctrine down the street. There they waited for thirteen-year-old Gilberte Voisin to come out the academy doors. She was the only one of them enrolled at this school as a semi-boarder. When Hector Voisin could not meet her himself, he sent his youngsters and their friends to pick up his daughter. Neither the Degeimbres nor the Voisins were particularly concerned about a religious education. Little Gilberte Degeimbre also attended there, but came home earlier in the day.

Just inside the house, Germaine Degeimbre sat in her warm kitchen with two guests and her three daughters. Widowed the previous year, Germaine now served as mother and father for Jeanne, seventeen, Andrée, fourteen, and little Gilberte, nine. She knew exactly who was at the door when an impatient visitor hammered on it at this hour.

"Come on," urged a grinning Albert Voisin as he stuck his head inside the door. Andrée and Gilberte needed no more prodding. Pulling on their coats, they kissed a quick good-bye to their mother and were out the door.

In five minutes, the winded children stood at the door of the academy and convent. Albert took charge of ringing the doorbell. Inside, Sister Valeria hurried Gilberte Voisin, knowing who was making such a noisy nuisance of himself at the door. Meanwhile, Albert and the three girls passed the chilly moments by hopping about to keep their feet from freezing.

"Look!" exclaimed Albert. He had turned toward the street and the railroad viaduct that arced up above the convent enclosure. "The Virgin dressed in white is walking above the bridge!" Though the boy's voice was serious, the three girls knew him for a trickster. For the moment, none of them would turn around to see what Albert was seeing. But he remained quiet, not breaking into laughter as the joking Albert usually did.

"It's a reflection from car lights," one of the children suggested as the silence lengthened. None of the girls wanted to turn around to "bite" at Albert's bait. Nonetheless, after a few more moments, Fernande, Andrée, and little Gilberte were impressed by Albert's control.

Finally, the three turned. There was a luminous woman in white moving through the air above the bridge and the Lourdes grotto inside the convent yard. And it wasn't as though a statue were being hoisted or transported on a pulley! They could see the movements of her knees push the folds of her gown as she walked.

Suddenly, the vision was too much for them. They turned and knocked frantically on the door. Every second or two, one would timidly turn around to look at the bridge. The children tasted fear, mixed with exhilaration.

At exactly this moment, the convent door was swung open by an upset Sister Valeria. *Was so much pounding necessary?* Sister Valeria couldn't help but wonder, she later admitted. The children looked at her with a strange curiosity, then looked back at the bridge, claiming to see something like the Virgin.

Gilberte Voisin was at the door in short order. Her eyes followed the pointing fingers and anxious glances of the other four children. "Oh!" she exclaimed instantly. There didn't seem to be anything else to say. Gilberte now stood as if frozen to the doorstep.

Sister Valeria gazed up in the direction the children pointed but saw absolutely nothing. "A statue can't move on its own," she assured them, thinking the Virgin they were speaking of was that of Our Lady of Lourdes in the garden grotto. "Hurry home, you silly children," she dismissed them. The convent door closed on the five young visionaries. Sister Valeria hurried to tell Mother Théophile the disturbing tale the children had tried to tell her.

"Oh, Sister," responded the superior, "how can you tell such a story? You are as childish as those children!"

Meanwhile, the three Voisins and two Degeimbres put as much distance as they could between themselves and the walking woman in white. They ran straight toward the Degeimbre home. Along the way, little Gilberte tripped, fell, and lost her shoe. The others stopped and anxiously waited as the older Gilberte helped her put the shoe back on. A backward glance over their shoulders told the children that the vision was still there.

Within moments, all five burst through the doorway at the Degeimbres. It had just been a few minutes since the four children had left the house to pick up Gilberte Voisin. When Germaine heard the tale of the walking woman on the bridge, she became a little angry. "Be quiet, you silly children," she warned them. "Don't tell any of this foolishness to your parents," she told the Voisins.

As the three Voisins walked to their own home, they shivered. They knew they would tell their parents and everyone else about what they'd seen. They simply had to. At the Voisin home, the reaction of Hector and Marie Voisin was just about like Germaine's. There was a scolding, and then the three "taletellers" were sent to bed.

The next day, Wednesday, November 30, the two Gilbertes

could not contain the story of the night before. The older girl tried to talk to Sister Emilie about it.

"Sister," Gilberte began, "a miracle took place in Beauraing last night. We saw the Blessed Virgin over the bridge." Sister Emilie could find no reply to make and merely looked at her. Gilberte Voisin finally shrugged and went about her business.

That evening, the four schoolchildren once again headed for the academy on the same errand. This night, however, they were afraid of the vision that no one else believed in. As they passed the small Lourdes grotto in the convent yard, they hid their eyes. It was right below the place where the bridge rose above the fence. Once Gilberte Voisin came out of the academy door, the five began to run.

As the children left the convent yard, they turned back only to see that the figure in white was walking again above the railroad bridge. But this time the fear within them melted away. They felt elated, thrilled to see the wonder a second time. They ran again toward home. They would surely be believed now — or so they thought.

At the Degeimbre home, the reception from Germaine was once again icy, even indignant. She thought that the game was going much too far. Yet her girls and the Voisins held their ground. They had seen just what they described — no more, no less. Germaine later walked the block or so to the Voisin home. "Hector," she said, "you must go yourself to meet your daughter at the school. If this keeps up, we'll be the laughing-stock of the town."

On the following evening, as the clock struck six in the Degcimbre kitchen, Germaine could see that her younger two were restless. She had told them that they could not go to the academy to pick up Gilberte with the Voisins. But something else was beginning to make her think they should.

Suppose someone was playing a trick on her girls and the other three? That made her angry. She grabbed a heavy stick she used to coax their heifers into the barn. She and their oldest sister, Jeanne, would accompany them, she told Andrée and Gilberte. She would get to the bottom of the mystery and quickly.

Outside the house, five other adults wanted to see if Germaine would welcome company. By all means, she agreed. The whole group headed for the academy with the Degeimbre children plus Albert and Fernande Voisin.

Encouraged by Germaine Degeimbre, the four children hurried ahead of the "investigators" and entered the convent grounds. It was Germaine's plan to have the adults spread out around the grounds to assure the apprehension of the one fooling the youngsters. Moments later, the adults heard the children shouting.

"She is here," gasped one young voice. This time, on December 1, the Lady had not come to the railroad bridge but to the middle walk, which led from the convent gate to the front door. Frustrated that the "apparition" had not pulled the usual trick, Germaine ordered the four to go to the convent door to get "Big Gilberte."

As the thirteen-year-old closed the convent door behind her moments later, all five children suddenly shrieked with delight. The Lady appeared even closer then, and they could see that she was absolutely beautiful. For a moment, she stood about halfway between the little Lourdes grotto and the front door of the convent. It was a vision that lasted only a second or two.

In this brief glimpse, they saw a wondrous young woman suspended just a little above the ground. Her feet, it seemed, were partially hidden by a little cloud. She was dressed in a glowing white gown, and her hands were joined in a pose of prayer. She gazed at them with kindness and smiled at them. Then her beautiful blue eyes were raised to heaven. She opened her hands and arms and disappeared.

The five children ran toward the adults, yelling as they came. As they approached the gate where Germaine and the others still searched for the culprit, they stopped short once again.

This time, the Lady stood near the shrubs between the grotto and the gate. Again, the children were overwhelmed. The six adults and seventeen-year-old Jeanne Degeimbre scanned the yard with their eyes, trying to find what the children apparently saw.

Inside the convent, the Sisters of Christian Doctrine had heard the shouting taking place within their convent yard. Two of them, returning from an errand, walked up to the group and laughed when the five children reported the vision of the Virgin.

Now the five had no hesitation in describing the woman they believed was the Mother of God. The apparition had touched each one deeply, but for the rest of the townspeople the story would stir up almost endless controversy.

Inside the academy, Sister Ludovica told Mother Théophile that the boarding students knew all about the evening's events. They were too frightened to go upstairs to the dormitory. The superior became angry but went to settle the girls and send them to bed. As the five young visionaries walked home, little Gilberte sobbed in the arms of the older Gilberte. To think that neither her mother nor the nuns would believe her!

As she headed home, Germaine decided to return later to the convent grounds. She would take some of the older children; little Gilberte was just too upset. The situation had to be sorted out. Someone must be creating an optical illusion of some kind. The children, she now believed, were not trying to fool anyone.

Little Gilberte was left in the consoling care of Gilberte Voisin when Germaine started on her way with the others later that evening. Again, several adults went along to help the widow. Albert walked at the head of the group, while Fernande and Andrée were walking farther behind, listening to their mothers. As the group entered the darkened convent grounds, the three children again began shouting.

Then, at precisely the same moment, the three children fell

to their knees as if pulled there by mysterious magnets. With one voice, they began to recite the "Hail Mary," but with high-pitched voices. They sounded unnatural. Repeating the prayer over and over, the children continued, with Andrée interrupting her recitation only once. "Oh ... she is so beautiful," the girl said softly.

Germaine and the other adults were mystified. She could see that the three children were looking in the same direction at the same invisible object. She walked in the direction of their gaze, toward a rose hawthorn tree about ten feet from the convent fence.

"Stop, Mother, you will walk over her," pleaded Andrée. The girl feared that her mother would offend the Virgin by treading too close to sacred ground. A chill shot through Germaine. For the first time, she thought that the children might be really seeing something.

In a moment, the Virgin again extended her arms and disappeared. The three children moaned with disappointment. The adults meanwhile scrambled, stumbling once again around the dark garden to intercept the fraud working this trick on the children. But there was no one to be found. This, the sixth appearance of the Virgin to these Belgian children, was over. She had been seen four times in one day.

At school the next morning, December 2, Mother Théophile made it a point to remind the academy students in the schoolyard that she wanted no discussion of the apparitions. When she spotted Gilberte Voisin, her tone was even more insistent. "I forbid you to say another thing about it," she told the girl. Sister Sainte-Croix felt a bit sorry for Gilberte and joked that the girl had probably seen her out walking in the convent garden. "In your nightgown, Sister?" the teenager countered.

Motivated by fear of a popular uproar in the community, Mother Théophile came to some hard resolutions on this Friday morning. She knew well that the historic response of the

Church, when first confronted with the claims of apparitions, was always silence. If the apparitions were authentic, events would unfold to verify them. Then it would be time to break the silence.

Silence was also becoming the goal of Father Léon Lamber, Beauraing's pastor. Father Lamber, a man with a great devotion to Our Lady of Lourdes, had heard of the convent-yard happenings earlier in the week. Mrs. Degeimbre and Mrs. Voisin had come to him with Fernande and Andrée. The confused mothers were beside themselves. The priest promised to dedicate the Mass of December 8 for the intention they requested. Germaine Degeimbre and Marie Voisin needed to know if the Mother of God was indeed visiting their children. "If it is the Virgin, do not take it as a misfortune," the pastor gently advised the worried women.

On Saturday evening, December 2, the apparitions at Beauraing continued. As they had warned, the sisters had locked the gates of the academy and convent yard. They released dogs in the yard to further discourage gatherings outside the gates. But the five children and a small crowd nonetheless walked to the academy at about 8:00 P.M.

"If it is really the Blessed Virgin, that will not keep her from appearing," insisted one woman, noting the padlocked gates.

As though her words were a cue, the five children were again thrown to their knees with their eyes fixed on the hawthorn beyond. "There she is," they exclaimed. Standing in the midst of the transfixed children, the adults suggested that they speak to this vision. The girls could say nothing.

"Are you the Immaculate Virgin?" Albert finally asked.

Following a pause, he asked, "What do you want?"

In another moment, the girls responded to an unheard request with deep sincerity. "Yes, we will always be good," they said.

And just as quickly as it had begun, the vision was over. The children rose to their feet in tears. They could hardly believe that the others had not heard the Virgin speak. When Albert had asked that first question, she had nodded her head "yes." But when asked what she wanted, the woman in white had spoken to them in a tone they could never forget. "Always be good," she told them.

On Sunday, December 4, the children again went to the convent compound at about 7:00 P.M. This time they took with them a young boy suffering from polio and the blind thirty-year-old uncle of the Degeimbre girls. The Mother of God came to them quickly.

She nodded in the affirmative when asked if she was truly the "Immaculate Virgin." Then Albert asked the Virgin to heal the young boy and the blind man, but the Virgin made no response.

On the following night, Monday, December 5, Albert, now spokesman for the group, again asked the Virgin for some kinds of signs to substantiate her appearances. There was no answer, though she did request that they return "at night" for the appearances.

When the five youngsters walked to the convent yard in the evening, crowds had pushed into the area where they usually stood. Each evening the group had grown larger, attracting more and more Belgians, who traveled to the village at the end of their workdays.

Tuesday, December 6, was the feast of St. Nicholas, "Little Christmas" in Europe. On that night, the Virgin instantly became visible for the children. This time, as Albert told the crowd, the woman had a rosary. It was hanging on her right arm, partially hidden in the folds of her gown. For the first time, too, later in the evening, the children recited part of the rosary during her second visit. After that, the children always recited at least part of the rosary while waiting for the Virgin or during her appearance.

On this Tuesday, too, the children were told to come next on December 8, "the day of the Immaculate Conception." This feast, proclaimed by Pope Pius IX in 1854, had preceded the Lourdes apparitions to Bernadette in 1858. The children and the crowds began to hope that something dramatic would take place on this great Marian feast.

In just a week or so, news of the events at Beauraing had come to most of the citizens of Belgium. Apparently, many of them planned to be there in the little village in the Meuse Valley on the feast of the Immaculate Conception. When Mother Théophile looked out the windows of the academy on December 8, she was shocked. Between ten thousand and fifteen thousand would-be pilgrims had journeyed to the town.

Something wonderful did happen on this day of apparition. And yet it was not what the crowds might have wished for. For the first time, the children experienced an ecstatic state, and the Blessed Virgin was said to be more beautiful than ever. Nevertheless, there was no message, no wonder performed for all to see.

Dr. Fernand Maistriaux, Beauraing's physician, studied the physical reactions of the children during the vision on December 8. So did other doctors, much as they had flocked to observe Bernadette at Lourdes almost seventy-five years earlier.

"Dr. Lurquin of Houyer lit a match and held it to the underside of Gilberte Voisin's hand," Maistriaux later wrote. "He held it there until the fire had consumed half the match. I saw and others witnessed the flame lick the back of her hand. The child showed no reaction. In the examination that followed, no trace of burn was visible...."

Similar tests were performed on the other children during the Lady's visit. None of the children suffered burns or pain from the pinching the physicians inflicted upon them. Gilberte Voisin and Andrée Degeimbre never flinched or blinked as high-powered flashlights were turned on and directed into their eyes.

In many respects, one phase of the Beauraing apparitions was over on December 8. The Virgin continued to appear near the hawthorn tree in the convent yard, but not with the same regularity. Some nights the children and the crowds came to pray, but the Virgin did not come. Albert, something of a spokesman up to this point, became less prominent. On three occasions, he did not even see the Virgin when she appeared to the others.

On the evening of December 21, several of the children suspended their "Hail Marys" for a question. "Tell us who you are," they said to the Lady. "I am the Immaculate Virgin," came the response. Yet Gilberte Degeimbre, the nine-year-old, had not heard the response. For the first time, the testimonies of the five were not unanimous.

The lack of unanimity in what the children reported now bothered some observers at Beauraing. Were the apparitions coming from an evil source? Some now worried about this. Mother Théophile was also burdened over the growing trust hundreds were placing in the visions taking place in her convent yard. After the twenty-first, she took action, and on Christmas Day she had a medal of St. Benedict tied to the hawthorn tree where the Virgin came. St. Benedict, she had heard, was a powerful adversary of the devil. For three days following, there was no apparition.

Then, on December 27, Our Lady came again to the children. On the following evening, she came once more and the children heard her say, "My last apparition will take place soon."

As this word spread across Belgium, the crowds grew larger. On December 29, about eight thousand people crowded around the grounds near the convent and academy. Just as the Virgin was vanishing that evening, Fernande saw her display a gold heart surrounded by rays of glowing light. The other four had not seen it.

When Fernande learned that she alone had seen the heart of the Virgin, she wept. The fifteen-year-old was sure she would not be believed if she alone had seen something new. Almost every apparition experienced now was followed by interviews of each of the young visionaries, one by one. A team of doctors, lawyers, and community officials quizzed them until they were exhausted.

On December 30, three of the children — Fernande Voisin, Andrée Degeimbre, and Gilberte Voisin — saw the gold and glowing heart of the Mother of God. Fernande alone heard the Lady's counsel to "Pray, pray very much." When she heard that she had been singled out again, Fernande broke down in tears. "It is because I am the only one who heard," she moaned. "No one will ever believe me...."

As the year drew to a close, all five children knew very well that the extraordinary visions of the Queen of Heaven were also about to end. Anticipation and the crowds grew. The diseased and crippled came by the scores hoping that a "new Lourdes" was coming into being. But no cures were being reported.

On the last day of the year, all five children saw the golden heart of the Virgin as she opened her hands and withdrew from their sight. On January 2, 1933, the Immaculate Virgin told Fernande that on the next day "I shall say something to each of you." They all sensed that the words they would hear that day would be her words of parting.

Between thirty thousand and thirty-five thousand people traveled to tiny Beauraing on January 3. The main thoroughfare, the Rochefort Road, became hopelessly clogged with cars by midday. When ninety Belgian doctors had applied for special reserved sites, the police would admit no more.

When the children arrived, they were stunned by the size of the crowd. Within moments, however, four of them were thrown to their knees, praying the Hail Marys in ecstatic, high-pitched voices. Fernande alone seemed to search the hawthorn tree in vain. She knelt only after the other four had done so.

As the children continued to pray, each grew silent for a few moments and seemed to listen. The Virgin gave a private message to each of the four children in turn. Gilberte Degeimbre, Gilberte Voisin, and two other children, Andrée

Degeimbre and Albert Voisin, heard messages that touched them deeply. Tears rolled down the cheeks of the girls. Then each of the four continued to pray and soon the last apparition was nearly over. As the five children stood up, a light rain was falling. Peace, a sad peace, was descending as well. It seemed to fill every heart but one.

Fernande Voisin, the one who had wept when the Virgin had singled her out as a solitary messenger, was grief-stricken. She had not seen or heard the Virgin. She had not received any message. "I want to see her," she sobbed when onlookers encouraged her to leave for the grotto with the other children.

The girl knew very well that the Virgin had promised to speak to each. She couldn't be budged from her stance or from her heavyhearted fear that she had somehow become unworthy. As the other children left for the little grotto, she prayed the rosary.

Suddenly, as witnesses report, a tremendous flash of light enveloped the hawthorn, throwing sparks into the air. Something like a thunderclap snapped through the air. At that instant, Fernande Voisin once more dropped to her knees. The Virgin had come back just for her.

As observers watched, the girl recited a few Hail Marys and then stopped to listen to the Lady. "Yes," she responded to a question from the visitor no one else could see or hear. "Yes," she answered again with great feeling. And then it was truly over. Fifteen-year-old Fernande rose to her feet with a heaviness that seemed to say that the rest of her days would never match this moment. The most remarkable month of her young life was over.

In the interviews of the children that followed, it was learned that the youngest three — Gilberte Degeimbre, Albert Voisin, and Gilberte Voisin — all received private messages that they were not to reveal to anyone. The Virgin had bent forward to tell nine-year-old Gilberte her "secret." She had also told Gilberte Voisin that "I will convert sinners." To

Andrée, she had said, "I am the Mother of God, the Queen of Heaven."

"Do you love my Son?" the Queen had then asked the kneeling Fernande. "Do you love me?" she had added, pointing to herself. When the girl answered "yes," the Virgin responded, "Then sacrifice yourself for me." As she had for the other children, she showed her golden heart and said "good-bye."

Once the apparitions were over, the controversies started. The notoriety that had begun to swirl around Beauraing on December 8 was followed by dozens of claimed apparitions all over Belgium. Both secular and Catholic writers now began finding fault with the Beauraing reports.

Why would Our Lady appear to children whose families weren't even practicing the Faith? Why would she come at night, the time of day during which the evil one was said to roam? Why was there nothing new, nothing distinctive about Our Lady's message? Why, why, why?

To consider these questions and many others, the Holy Office in Rome asked for the investigation of all of the apparitions reported in Belgium in 1932 and 1933. On May 17, 1935, the bishop of the Diocese of Namur convened a special commission to study Beauraing in particular. From that day until its final meeting on July 21, 1936, it held seventy-two sessions and interviewed ninety-four people.

On February 15, just a few weeks after the last apparition, ten-year-old Pauline Dereppe experienced a remarkable healing that was attributed to a prayer answered at Beauraing. For three years, the child had been the victim of a bone disease that left open sores. Albert had first asked the Virgin to heal her on December 4. When the Lady smiled at his request, Albert told Pauline's parents that he believed that the girl would be healed. After that February 15 prayer at the hawthorn bush, Pauline's disease and illness were never again noted.

On June 23, 1933, Maria Van Laer, a thirty-three-year-old woman from Turnhout, was cured of a tubercular condition she had suffered from for more than half her life. She was quite literally recalled from death's door when she was healed. Before that she had clung to life as an invalid and also suffered from a deformed spinal column and a diseased leg.

Taken to Beauraing that June day by ambulance, Maria managed to visit the enclosure near the hawthorn tree, then was taken to see little Gilberte and her mother at their home. The Degeimbres urged the woman to visit the apparition site one more time before returning home. On the way back to Turnhout, Maria felt better but fell into a deep sleep. When she arrived home at about midnight, she found that she had no more pain, deformities, or disease. She was completely cured. The news of her story spread throughout the country. In 1933 alone, two million pilgrims came to Beauraing.

In the meantime, the commission pursued its work as the five favored young people pursued their callings. "Always be good," she had said. Even though the apparitions had stopped in early January, 1933, the children continued to gather near the hawthorn each evening. At about 6:30 P.M., they recited and prayed the rosary together with the pilgrims. All five of the children had become devoutly religious, and their example touched many others. Mr. and Mrs. Voisin returned the practice of a faith abandoned for many years. Germaine Degeimbre, who had doubted the Virgin's presence even at the last apparition, was finally won over.

The Second World War was brewing in Europe, however. It was to touch the lives of each of the children and also the work of the commission. Over a decade elapsed before a report could be released. But finally, on July 2, 1949, the bishop of the Diocese of Namur confirmed that the commission had thoroughly studied the events at Beauraing. The group's report, he wrote, "wins our conviction of the supernatural character of the events."

Sixteen years had come and gone. The four girls and one boy had grown up and survived the war. Albert had served his country for a time as a soldier. He was stationed in the south of France and later worked in the French Underground, which attempted to foil the work and conquests of Germany. Each of the girls had married and started a family of her own. After the war, Albert married and took his new bride to the Belgian Congo, where he became a teacher. He taught in the mission schools there, served as principal, and later returned to Beauraing in 1961 with his wife and three children.

The hawthorn and the memories of the Virgin must have drawn each of the visionaries when they were in Beauraing. They visited to pray the rosary and to stop at the chapel built there in 1947. The railroad bridge where they first saw the mysterious woman walking still arcs up above the convent enclosure where the Mother of the Lord came close to be with them.

Today, thousands of pilgrims find their way each year to the small village in Belgium that once was remembered only because trains passed through it. In the United States, devotion to Our Lady of Beauraing is encouraged by the Marian Union of Beauraing and by the Pro Maria Committee.

Banneux, Belgium

1933

*I*t was already dark and very cold on January 15, 1933, a Sunday evening. The winter of 1933 had not been easy in Belgium. Eleven-year-old Mariette Beco had spent many evenings just like this one. Inside the simple two-story brick house her father had built, there was decent protection from the bitter winter, but the place was not without drafts. The landscape was frozen and bleak just outside of the village of Banneux, near the Ardennes mountain region, twenty miles southeast of Liège and fifty-six miles east of Beauraing.

Mariette, the oldest of seven children, was born on the feast of the Annunciation in 1921. She had good, even features and wore her hair cut in the straight, short "bobbed" style that was also common among American girls in the "Roaring Twenties."

The "little mother" in Mariette was pulled in two different directions at this moment. She was watching over one of the younger Becos asleep in a cradle nearby — the child was ill. Then, too, she was worried, very worried, about Julien, her ten-year-old brother. He had been sent upon an errand, but she didn't like that he had not returned before winter nightfall had overtaken Banneux. Mariette had always believed that the night held special terrors that daylight could dispel. At any rate, she hoped Julien would be home at any moment.

The girl lifted a corner of the bedsheet hung as a curtain over the second-story window where she was an unofficial lookout. She began to scan the distance toward the horizon — along the fence and down the road to town — for Julien.

Just this moment, however, the eyes of Mariette met instead with a glowing shape, hovering near the vegetable garden. (Her father, Julien *père*, had been unemployed for some time. In their season of need, the front yard of the Becos had gradually been given over to a garden. The share of space for vegetables had grown until it occupied the whole of the yard that separated the domain of the Becos from the road.)

Mariette rubbed her eyes in disbelief. And yet, a second

glance confirmed that there was indeed a bright thing standing there where cabbages had been growing months before. With a quick, rushed heartbeat, the girl could now easily see that it was a woman — an unbelievably beautiful woman — who had stationed herself in this most unlikely setting. Dressed in a flowing white gown and white veil, with a brilliant blue sash, the woman also held a rosary in her right hand and was nodding and smiling at Mariette.

A round of eye-rubbing and head-shaking failed to clear the garden of this visitor among the cabbage leaves. But Mariette still could not believe what her eyes were finding there. She turned from the window and suddenly grabbed the oil lamp sitting on the table next to the cradle. Perhaps the lamplight was creating a strange reflection.

Mariette carried the burning lamp into the next room. She left it on a table there, ran back to the window near the cradle, and whisked the curtain aside once more.

"Still there!" Mariette exclaimed. Now her heart was pounding wildly. "Mother," she called out, "there's a beautiful Lady in the garden. She is smiling at me!" Busy with a younger child in another room, Louise Beco could scarcely be bothered with her eldest's silly fantasies. Visions can easily be concocted out of winter shadows, she knew very well.

But Mariette would not quit shouting. She insisted that her mother come and take a good look. With patience nearly gone, Louise finally rushed over to her daughter and the window. Holding the younger child in her arms, she squinted out into the darkness in the direction of Mariette's pointing finger.

For an instant, she thought to herself, there did seem to be something white hovering just about where the girl saw something. But it certainly had none of the detail her child was seeing. "Perhaps it is the Blessed Virgin!" scoffed Louise, trying to shame the girl. She turned and carried the little one away.

But the words of scorn worked in reverse. Mariette begged her mother to let her have a closer look outside. She ran to her room, where she had set aside a rosary she once found lying in the road to Tancremont. Then Mariette made for her hat and coat.

Louise would have none of the girl's plans for a closer look at this phantom. She locked the door and firmly told her daughter she could not go out. Like many of the village people in this area, Louise put more stock in superstitious fears than in religious creeds. What if there was some witchcraft at work outside? Would her little girl be carried away? Now, when a disappointed Mariette turned to the window again, the wonderful vision was gone.

Later in the evening, the reported vision of their oldest child caused the first ripples of disturbance on the surface of the Becos' home life. When little Julien had returned and was warming up, Mariette excitedly went through the events point by point. Like his mother, the boy laughed away the story. It was wild, fantastic.

Only her father, Julien *père*, let the account sink in a little deeper. He quietly told his little girl that her story was unbelievable. But privately, the head of the house turned the tale over and over again in his mind. He and his wife were hardly religious types. So why would Marlette make up such a thing? Was it to impress or please them?

Like many of his Catholic countrymen in these dreary, hard times, Julien Beco maintained only a token faith. It was comfortable, traditional, and yet certainly insignificant in his everyday life. It is true that the older children were enrolled in the religious education program at the parish church of Banneux. But Beco himself never bothered to see that they attended. He was an unemployed wiremaker, and having no work deadened him. It was more and more difficult to leave the house, read a paper, or reach for anything beyond what he could see in front of him. But now this. What did it mean?

On Monday morning, the morning after her vision, Mariette went to school for the first time in two months. During the day, she took her best friend aside. Within a few moments, Josephine Léonard had heard all about the Virgin in the garden. But she, too, laughed at the storyteller. Suddenly Mariette was in tears. To have no one who believed her was devastating.

Seeing Mariette so upset made Josephine reconsider. Perhaps Mariette *had* seen something. In the town of Banneux, a community of about 300, the Becos were well known. They were not flighty folk. Mariette, in fact, was a matter-of-fact sort of girl, somewhat rough in manners, lacking in polish.

And so, after the school day was over, the two girls, Mariette and Josephine, went to tell the story to the parish priest. This was Josephine's idea. Mariette shrank with embarrassment in the presence of Father Louis Jamin. She ran from the presbytery as she heard Josephine relating the story of the vision in the cabbage yard.

Monday, Tuesday, and Wednesday passed. Those who knew this oldest Beco child wondered what had gotten into her — or had left her. The change in her behavior was dramatic.

Mariette was now preparing her religion lessons and was able to recite them flawlessly. The girl who had scoffed at schooling was now attending each day. And she was attentive. What's more, before school began each morning, Mariette was seen at Banneux's parish church.

On Wednesday, January 18, this something new inside of Mariette moved in her as darkness poured out over the Belgian village. Just before 7:00 P.M., she walked out of the house into the yard and garden. Julien, her father, followed her.

Immediately, Mariette was kneeling on the frozen ground, praying the rosary with the beads she had found. Suddenly, she stretched out her arms in a gesture of welcome. As she later told it, she could see the same woman in white descending from the distant sky toward her as she knelt in the garden. At first, the image was small but glowing brightly, and it became larger as it seemed to float down between two distant pines.

In a moment, the vision of Sunday evening was before the girl once again. But this time, to her great joy, Mariette was close to this wonderful woman. The child could now see more clearly how beautiful this creature was who stood before her, radiating a golden light. The woman seemed suspended about a foot and a half above the earth, standing on a sort of gray cloud. "It was like smoke," Mariette later explained.

Julien Beco could see nothing of this woman, and yet he was moved by what he saw reflected in his firstborn's face. He ran to his bicycle to bring others back to see this miracle touching his child. *Father Jamin should see this*, was the thought that took hold of him.

Within ten minutes Mariette's father had found that the pastor was not at the rectory, so he hurried instead to a neighbor's house. Within moments, Michel Charleseche and his eleven-year-old son trotted behind the pedaling Beco.

The three spectators arrived at the house in time to see Mariette walk out of the yard and head down the road. She walked past the three as if she were being pulled. Julien Beco was frightened. "Where are you going? Come back," he insisted.

"She is calling me," Mariette reassured her father.

The entourage of three followed as the girl proceeded down the road. Twice Mariette fell to her knees with such force that the witnesses shuddered. With a twelve-degree frost, the ground was bitterly cold and hard as rock. She quickly rose again and walked still farther down the dark road. Then Mariette turned off the road to the right, toward a small stream. Julien and the two Charleseches were three steps behind her.

As the child later explained, the Lady had led her down the road and then stood on the other side of the stream, beckoning her toward it. Mariette had then knelt down near the tiny stream. "Plunge your hand into the water," the Lady instructed her. When the girl had done so, the woman told her, "This spring is reserved for me." At that, the woman in white bade the child

Au revoir, assuring her that she would return. When Mariette arose, this second apparition — about an hour in duration — was over.

Later in the evening, Father Jamin came to the Becos' home to go over the matter with the head of the house. He had heard the story of Mariette's second vision. As the girl was asleep, the priest discussed the matter only with Julien Beco. Beco, it was clear, was convinced that his daughter was seeing the Mother of God. He made arrangements to see the priest the next day to receive the sacraments of penance and the Eucharist. It had been so many years ...

On Thursday, January 19, and again on Friday, January 20, the eleven-year-old Mariette saw the Lady. The apparitions began at about the same hour as the first two, around 7:00 P.M. Eleven witnesses were clustered around the Beco yard on Thursday night, but the number had doubled by the following night. Again, the Virgin appeared to the girl to be moving out of the southwestern sky, coming to rest finally in front of the only human being who could see her.

"Who are you, Madame?" Mariette asked on Thursday evening.

"I am the Virgin of the Poor," the Lady replied.

Then the girl was drawn again to the icy stream. The small brook, the Virgin told her, was to be "reserved for all nations ... to relieve the sick." Mariette did not fully understand the words "nations" and "relieve" but relayed the message to her questioners at home when the apparition was over.

On the following evening, Friday, the woman who called herself "The Virgin of the Poor" told the girl that what she wanted was "a little chapel" at Banneux. Then the Virgin extended her hands over the head of the child in blessing. She made a sign of the cross above Mariette's head and was gone. That night Mariette collapsed in a faint.

After that apparition of Friday, January 20, there was time for the puzzled villagers of Banneux to reflect upon the remarkable events of the week. Though Mariette continued to pray each night in the garden, there was no further appearance of the Virgin until three weeks later.

During the interim, Mariette suffered from the scoffers. When the apparitions seemed to have stopped, the villagers no longer came to the Becos' house. Among some of the children of Banneux, Mariette quickly became the object of a new game, which involved belittling and tormenting the girl who faithfully continued to look for the Blessed Virgin in her front yard. She was hurt in more ways than one.

The Virgin of the Poor appeared to her again on Saturday, February 11. Exactly seventy-five years before, the Virgin had appeared for the first time to another young girl in neighboring France. On that day, Bernadette Soubirous had encountered the Queen of Heaven at the grotto of Massabielle near Lourdes.

During the vision of February 11, Mariette was again called to the spring. There, the Virgin again directed her to plunge her hand into the cold water. Toward the end of the vision, the Virgin told the girl that "I come to relieve suffering." But the apparition faded, and the girl lapsed into a fit of tears. It was all too wonderful, but the Virgin's leave-taking was always so terrible.

Father Jamin interviewed the child later in the rectory. She repeated the short messages of the Virgin and then, as Bernadette had in the previous century, asked about receiving her First Communion. The pastor favored delaying the event until spring, but Mariette was now insistent. "It would please her," she told the priest, who finally agreed to it.

On the evening of February 15, the following Wednesday, Mariette Beco again walked out of the house into the garden, carrying her rosary beads. For the first time, Louise, her mother, accompanied her. Within a few moments, it was clear that the girl could see the Virgin. On this occasion, the child had something to ask the woman from heaven.

"Blessed Virgin, the priest told me to ask you for a sign," Mariette blurted out. At first, the Virgin did not answer the request but smiled at the girl instead. The request was repeated. Finally, the Virgin looked at Mariette and told her, "Believe in me; I will believe in you." This was a call for faith but not a promise that a "sign" would be given.

Our Lady then gave a private message to Mariette and told her to share it with no one, not even her parents. And with an admonition to "Pray a lot," the Virgin left her.

Five days later, on February 20, a Monday evening, the Lady came again. As they waited along with Mariette, eight spectators tried to put the piercing cold out of mind. But suddenly such concerns were irrelevant for the young visionary. She was led again to the stream. "Pray a lot," the Virgin told her. Then it was over once more.

Almost two weeks later, on March 2, Mariette received the eighth apparition. A warmer evening than the previous nights of favor, it was pouring rain. Only five women were present when the girl came out of the door at 7:00 P.M. One of the women protected the kneeling child with her umbrella as the eleven-year-old began the rosary. In the midst of the third decade, she suddenly stood up, stretched out her arms, then knelt again. The downpour came to a halt.

Mariette resumed the prayer, but her verbal responses were now quickened; her voice was pitched higher. This phenomenon had been part of each of the apparitions. As this vision came to an end, the wondrous woman in white told the child that she was indeed "the Mother of the Savior, Mother of God." She blessed the girl and then gave her a good-bye that Mariette knew would be a final one. The Virgin had used the French word *Adieu,* or "Good-bye," rather than the term *Au revoir,* or "See you again," as she had seven times before.

The apparitions to Mariette Beco at Banneux were over, but as at nearby Beauraing, the Virgin's visits to this village and this eleven-year-old caused almost endless controversy.

Even Father Jamin, the community's pastor, had initially suspected that Mariette had dreamed up the visions after hearing of the Beauraing happenings. By the time Mariette had seen the Virgin for the third and fourth times, Louis Jamin *the man* had become a believer. Louis Jamin *the priest*, on the other hand, maintained the careful attitude of neutrality that the Church asked until a judgment could be made.

For her community, however, the special privilege of Mariette Beco was more difficult to accept. Somehow, in Banneux, this child seemed an unlikely candidate for the attention of the Mother of God.

Wouldn't heaven have chosen a child who had at least some of the patterns of piety? And wouldn't the apparitions — if they were genuine — occur in a setting more conducive to devotion than last year's vegetable garden? Banneux's people puzzled over it throughout 1933. And yet, despite circumstances they found very strange, many came to believe that the Queen of Heaven, as the "Virgin of the Poor," had come very close to them.

In January, 1935, Cardinal Joseph E. Van Roey, Metropolitan of Belgium, established a commission to study the recently reported apparitions. The Banneux and Beauraing apparitions, occurring just weeks apart, had been followed by a virtual epidemic of similar stories all over Belgium. In Banneux's local diocese, the Diocese of Liège, another commission of inquiry was set up to study just the claims of Mariette Beco. The constant cross-examination by both official and unofficial questioners weighed heavily on young Mariette during the years she grew into womanhood. One day she said: "If I'd known all that was to happen, I wouldn't have said a word to anyone. I'd have built a little chapel myself in the garden." Bernadette had often had the same thought.

The "little chapel," was all the Virgin had really asked for. And such a monument was built soon enough. The last apparition to Mariette was barely over when a committee was formed to build one. It was up and dedicated to the Virgin of the Poor on the feast of the Assumption, August 15, 1933. Only seven months had elapsed since the last vision of the Virgin. Respecting canonical procedures, the bishop of the diocese then authorized the chapel's consecration but made no judgment about the apparitions.

Yet many who visited Banneux made their own unofficial judgments. Mrs. Goethals of Anvers, Belgium, became an ardent supporter on May 21, 1933.

Just about a year before, this wife and mother of four children had been injured in a car accident. A bone in her jaw and another in her temple were fractured. She had gone completely deaf, could eat no solid food, and lived with constant, sharp pain. With her husband and four youngsters, Mrs. Goethals traveled to Banneux to seek the intercession of the Virgin of the Poor. When she had sipped a few drops of the spring water, which was intended to "relieve the sick," she immediately felt worse. Pain shot through her face with an almost unbearable intensity for about thirty minutes. Her husband then led her to rest beneath some trees, out of the summer heat.

After a few minutes in the shade, the woman turned to her anxious husband and told him she could open her mouth properly — and without pain. She began to eat solid foods again, regained full hearing, and returned to her doctors, who could no longer find evidence of any fracture or damage.

The spring that did such wonders for Madame Goethals, now yields two thousand gallons each day. A stone basin encloses the spring, and nearby an altar marks the place where the Virgin stopped to speak to Mariette. The reported path of the Virgin's footsteps from the garden to the spring offers the only place in the world where pilgrims can literally follow the path of the Blessed Mother.

In September, 1933, a young woman twenty years of age, Laura Pletinck, was completely freed from the effects of cerebro-spinal meningitis. For seven years she had been bedridden and paralyzed in both legs. The day after her pilgrimage to Banneux, she walked out of her bedroom, free of pain and paralysis. Many other wonders were reported by those who visited the tiny town where the Mother of God had once visited a young girl in the dead of winter.

The onset of World War II in 1938 inhibited the work of both Church commissions studying the apparitions at Banneux. Belgium was soon invaded and overrun by Germany, making communication and travel difficult. In 1942, with the war still raging, Cardinal Van Roey published a letter to tell occupied Belgium that the reported Beauraing and Banneux apparitions were worthy of further study, but within two years the Ardennes region was to witness the "Battle of the Bulge" and some of the most bitter fighting of World War II (as it had been ravaged nearly thirty years before in World War I). It was three more years before actual acknowledgment of the two sites and claims seemed near.

Finally, on August 22, 1949, the Bishop of Liège declared in a pastoral letter that Our Lady had made eight appearances to Mariette Beco at Banneux. The letter also assured all that the claims made supporting these visions were worthy of belief. The little town in the south of Belgium knew a matchless joy that day.

With the conclusion of the war, Banneux was now free to welcome many more pilgrims. In respect for the wishes of the Virgin of the Poor, the chapel built there was indeed a "small chapel." It was thought that she would not want a lavish, expensive structure that would drain away the limited resources of the poor. Twenty-four feet wide and only thirty-four feet high from the ground to the top of the belfry, the Banneux chapel is a modest monument built in the Becos' garden. Today, a marble mosaic square marks the place where the Virgin stood.

Because its design and construction were far from costly, it has been duplicated by believers all over the world. There are at least one hundred fifty "small chapels" dedicated to Banneux's Virgin of the Poor, while statues honoring her are found all over the world.

But what of the young girl whose eyes found the Virgin smiling at her from the frozen cabbage garden?

Unlike some visionaries, Mariette Beco did not feel called to religious life. Clearly, her visions of the Blessed Virgin profoundly touched her life and the lives of others in her family. In later years, she married a restaurant owner but apparently suffered from an unhappy marriage.

Some reports maintain that later she did not practice her Catholic faith regularly, but the same has been said of many whose lives were embattled and later vindicated. It is certain that she was often seen returning to pray at the garden where the Mother of God had come to seek her out. There, on winter nights, she had known a warmth and seen a light that came from the Blessed Mother in heaven, the Virgin of the Poor.

Akita, Japan

1973-81

*P*rivately, forty-two-year-old Sister Agnes Sasagawa may have been relieved — even happy — that the six other nuns who resided in the convent had left her alone on this summer Tuesday morning. It was June 12, 1973, and the petite, pretty sister quickly made her way down the hallway to the chapel for adoration.

Sister Agnes was no longer afraid of being left alone there. As well as anyone could, she had adapted herself to her noiseless world. But the adaptation was not without pain. Constantly reading the lips of others in order to know what was being said was exhausting. One could so easily feel detached, left out, stranded on an island of silence. Less than three months earlier, Sister Agnes had been plunged quite cruelly and suddenly into total deafness. Six months earlier, she had noticed that sounds seemed muffled, indistinct, and distant in both ears. But she thought little about it. Physical complaints and health problems had always been constant companions.

Born prematurely on May 28, 1931, Agnes Katsuko Sasagawa had been a physically weak but spiritually resilient child. Her parents and older siblings were protective of their little "Kako-chan," as she was called. Although she had often been ill, adversities never bowed her. There was a strength, a determination in her, even when she'd been paralyzed at age nineteen by a bungled spinal anesthesia given during an appendectomy.

For almost ten years, Katsuko was in and out of hospitals. Then, under the loving care of a Catholic nurse, she made an astonishing recovery, after almost ten years of paralysis. The nurse and a return to health inspired Katsuko to become Catholic in 1960, at the age of thirty-three. And later still, she decided to dedicate her new life to God. She became a nun.

On May 12, 1973, she had arrived at this small hilltop convent that belonged to the Institute of the Handmaids of the Eucharist. The house was in Yuzawadai, a suburb of Akita, a busy city of three hundred thousand that hugged the Sea of

Japan. Beyond the city were breathtaking views of majestic mountains.

The Institute was a new congregation founded in the early 1960s by Bishop John Ito of the local diocese of Niigata. The handmaids, or sisters, worked as catechists and also devoted themselves to prayer, especially to Eucharistic adoration. But they were poor. Their convent was sparcely furnished and winds off the Sea of Japan often shook doors and the traditional Japanese paper screens that divided many rooms. All of this — even the rattling screens — had attracted Sister Agnes when she first visited.

On this June day, however, the thought of Eucharistic adoration drew Sister Agnes to the chapel. She walked up to the altar to open the tabernacle door. A brilliant light broke forth, much whiter and brighter than the sun. Sister was overwhelmed by the light, and what it meant.

Instinctively, she dropped, face to the floor, and began to pray. She sensed that the light came from Jesus, who was truly present in the Eucharist. During her month at the convent, she had prayed the congregation's Eucharistic Prayer over and over again. It began, "Most Sacred Heart of Jesus, truly present in the Holy Eucharist...." With her heart racing, Sister Agnes Sasagawa prayed intensely on the hard floor for about an hour. A force seemed to prevent her from moving. However, when she finally was able to arise and leave the chapel, she began to doubt the experience. Had she been hallucinating?

The next day, June 13, Sister Agnes again headed to the chapel to privately pray in Eucharistic adoration. As she opened the tabernacle door, the blinding light once again shone inside. Again, the little sister collapsed to the floor and began to praise the living God. But this time, she experienced also a feeling of peace. The light was not an illusion; it was simply a sign that the tabernacle truly held the body of Jesus.

On the following day, a Thursday, Sister Agnes again saw the light, which this time was surrounded by a red flame. She felt a deep new love of Jesus in the Eucharist, and wondered whether her fellow sisters were quietly witnessing the same thing. Later, in a guarded way, she asked about it at the dinner table. But no one else could see the tabernacle fire. Fearing perhaps that their newest member was trying to set herself apart, the superior brusquely told Sister Agnes that the "vision" was apparently for her eyes only. She was to remain silent about the matter.

Over the next several weeks, Sister Agnes ached to speak about what she had seen. On the eve of the feast of the Sacred Heart, she saw the splendid tabernacle light for a fourth time. This time she also saw, as she put it, "an adoring crowd of spiritual beings" who were clearly worshipping the Host on the altar. Were these angels? Strangely, neither the word "angels" nor the thought of them came to Sister Agnes' mind right away.

Later that day, she broke her silence and shyly went to discuss it with Bishop Ito, who had come to visit and celebrate Mass for a week. The bishop listened gravely, and suggested that the "spiritual beings" might be "angels." Then, he counseled Sister Agnes to continue in humility and silence. He saw no signs of emotional or psychological imbalance. Referring to Fátima, he reminded her that supernatural apparitions did occur at times. "But in your case, it is still not made clear," he advised her. "Try to live an ordinary life as every other sister does."

On the evening of Thursday, June 28, Sister Agnes noticed a sharp pain in the palm of her left hand. A small rose-colored cross seemed to be etched across her palm. By Friday, the mysterious wound had become excruciatingly painful. The pain continued into Saturday. On Sunday, July 1, however, the pain was gone and the wound faded and disappeared. But on Thursday, July 5, Sister Agnes knew that the wound was returning, and she could no longer conceal it from her sisters.

On Thursday evening, July 5, the novice mistress, Sister

Saki Kotake, was so concerned about Sister Agnes that she went to her room to investigate. It was all Sister Agnes could do to unclench her bleeding hand and allow her superior to examine it. Tears of pain stung her eyes and poured down her cheeks. "It hurts me so (much) that I took out my work," she explained, nodding toward her crocheting needle and thread that lay on the bed. Some of the little nun's bottled-up feelings and fears then flowed with the tears.

"If I have come to this, it is perhaps that my sins are grave?" The words and a sense of shame and abandonment tumbled out of Sister Agnes. Agnes was new to the house, but Sister Saki knew a good deal about her previous life. Agnes was not a religious fanatic. The stigmata — which was what the wound seemed to be — was not an illusion. Making sure that her deaf sister could see her face to read her lips, she tried to put the sense of guilt to rest.

"I felt that this must have been sent to her by the Lord," the novice mistress later reported. She told Sister Agnes, "It seems to hurt you very much, but try to bear it by thinking of the sufferings of the Lord. Excuse us for causing you to bear the consequences of the sins of us all." Then she and another nun bandaged the hand and made Sister Agnes as comfortable as they could. But Sister Agnes could not sleep that night.

At 3:00 A.M., Sister Agnes rose to pray, since sleeping was out of the question. The pain in her left hand was excruciating. Out of nowhere, a voice spoke to her, saying:

"Be not afraid. Pray with fervor not only because of your sins, but in reparation for those of all people. The world today wounds the most Sacred Heart of Our Lord by its ingratitudes and injuries. The wounds of Mary are much deeper and more sorrowful than yours. Let us go to pray together in the chapel."

A beautiful figure suddenly stood near the right shoulder of Sister Agnes. The figure resembled Tomi, Agnes' older sister who had died many years before. "My sister," Agnes blurted out. But the figure smiled and shook her head no. "I am the one who is with you and watches over you." Sister Agnes understood this to mean the being was her guardian angel.

In the chapel, the angel vanished. Sister Agnes approached the three-foot-high wooden statue of Mary to look at her palms. The whole statue was instantly ablaze with the same brilliant light she had seen in the tabernacle! She fell in awe to the floor to pray. It seemed as though the statue was coming to life and about to speak. Face to the floor, with ears that were deaf to ordinary sounds, Sister Agnes then heard these words:

"My daughter, my novice, you have obeyed me well in abandoning all to follow me. Do you suffer much because of the handicap which deafness causes you? You will be assuredly healed. Be patient, it is the last trial. Does the wound in your hand give you pain? Pray in reparation for the sins of humanity. Each person in this community is my irreplaceable daughter.

"Pray very much for the pope, bishops, and priests. Since your baptism you have always prayed faithfully for them. Continue to pray very much ... very much. Tell your superior all that has passed today and obey him in everything that he will tell you. Your superior is wholeheartedly seeking prayers now. He has asked that you pray with fervor."

Then, the light, the voice, and the angel were all gone. Sister Agnes noticed now that another sister was praying quietly beside her. The nuns of the house were gathering for morning prayer. Later in the day, after she had asked Sister Kotake, the novice mistress, to examine the statue's hand, she found the nun in prayer with tears filling her eyes. Sister Kotake pointed to the statue's hand. There was a wound in the middle of the statue's right hand and blood flowed out of the hole made where the two lines intersected.

Soon, of course, all the other sisters of the convent knew about both the bleeding wounds — on the hand of their own Sister Agnes, and on the hand of their statue of Mary. As the summer weeks passed, their deaf sister found that her pain increased on Thursday evenings and was most intense on Fridays, the day of the Lord's passion and death. By Sunday, the pain was gone and her wound had disappeared. In a way, the stigmata of the statue was even more remarkable: A three-foot-high wooden image of the Blessed Mother made by a Buddhist from a "katsura" tree was apparently bleeding out of anguish for the world.

On Tuesday, July 24, Bishop Ito again visited the house to say Mass and to provide any spiritual counsel or help. It was about 150 miles from the diocesan see city of Niigata to Akita. As devoted as he was to his Institute sisters, he did not have time to visit often. He had hoped to locate a chaplain who could say daily Mass for the sisters in their house. But he had not yet been successful — and that was fortunate.

"How are you?" he asked Sister Agnes that afternoon when she brought a tray of tea to him. Then, in an unassuming but thorough way, she told him about the appearance of her guardian angel, the message from the glowing statue of Mary, the wound in her hand, and the bleeding wound in the hand of the statue.

Sister Agnes was happy to finally share her experience with a wise and balanced spiritual advisor. And the "Voice of Indescribable Beauty," as she called it, had told her to "Tell your superior all that passed today and obey him in everything that he will tell you." Bishop Ito asked to see the wound on her hand, then went to the chapel to inspect the statue. When he returned, he encouraged her but offered again the advice he'd given six weeks earlier.

"Be careful," he told her, "not to say to yourself: 'It is a phenomenon especially destined for me. I am a special case.' Strive for humility."

Sister Agnes was confused by his words. She presumed that the visions and "voice" had come to her because of her sins and her personal need for reparation. She also assumed that her handicap and limited usefulness to the Institute made her the practical recipient of any special suffering or messages from God.

Two days later, on Thursday, July 26, her hand began to hurt again with an intensity that almost made her scream. It was the feast of St. Ann, the mother of the Virgin Mary. One of the sisters, Sister Yoko Ishikawa, was to renew her vows at the 5:00 P.M. Mass. At Communion time, Sister Agnes received the Host on her tongue because opening her hand was impossible. Because of this special celebration, however, Sister Agnes tried to hide her agony. At the same time, the wound in the statue's hand began to bleed. In fact, the blood was flowing at a much faster rate than before.

"Such a quantity of blood! What does it mean?" Sister Agnes whispered anxiously to the bishop as they later knelt to say the rosary in the chapel with another sister. The tall, distinguished-looking bishop of Niigata, who'd been named to the diocese by Pope John XXIII in 1962, shook his head in wonder.

During the night, Sister Agnes Sasagawa endured unmerciful pain in her hand. Bishop Ito examined the wound. It looked much worse, and he advised a visit to a doctor. After a sleepless night, however, Agnes headed downstairs to the chapel to pray near the Blessed Sacrament. All during the morning and early afternoon, the pain would not leave her. At about 2:30 P.M., she went again to the empty first-floor chapel. The small vigil light near the tabernacle welcomed her. With her left hand throbbing, Sister Agnes quietly knelt on her cushion, grateful for that tiny spark near the Real Presence of Jesus. Immediately, the voice of the angel came to her and said:

"Your sufferings will end today. Carefully engrave in the depth of your heart the thought of the blood of Mary. The blood shed by Mary has a profound meaning. This precious blood was shed to ask your conversion, to ask for peace, in reparation for the ingratitude and the outrages toward the Lord. As with devotion to the Sacred Heart, apply yourself to devotion to the most Precious Blood. Pray in reparation for all men.

"Say to your superior that the blood is shed today for the last time. Your pain also ends today. Tell them what happened today. He will understand all immediately. And you, observe his directions."

Then, the angel voice was gone. Sister Agnes continued in prayer but the pain had disappeared! She opened and closed her left hand quickly, with no pain. A quick glance confirmed it. The wound was gone, just as the angel had promised. Agnes was glad to be released from the agony. "Never will I forget that pain," she later admitted with a shudder.

But she felt grief — even guilt — about the wound that still could be seen in the hand of the statue. Mary's sufferings continued, and the statue's hand began to bleed profusely once again. Alerted, the nuns of the house on Yuzawadai hill kept a prayerful vigil in the chapel that day. With a special intensity, they prayed and watched. As predicted, the bleeding from the wooden statue ended for good that day, although the wound remained.

On August 3, the First Friday of the month, while Sister Agnes was praying the rosary in the chapel, the angel appeared once more. Within a few moments, however, the nun heard a voice from the statue of the Blessed Virgin. Mary told her:

"My daughter, my novice, do you love the Lord? If you love the Lord, listen to what I have to say to you.

"It is very important. Convey it to your superior.

"Many men in this world grieve the Lord. I seek souls to console Him. In order to appease the anger of the Heavenly Father, I wish, with my Son, for souls who will make reparation for sinners and for the ungrateful by offering up their sufferings and poverty to God on their behalf.

"In order that the world might know the wrath of the Heavenly Father toward today's world, He is preparing to inflict a great chastisement on all mankind. With my Son, many times I have tried to appease the wrath of the Heavenly Father. I have prevented the coming of the chastisement by offering the sufferings of His Son on the Cross, His precious Blood, and the compassionate souls who console the Heavenly Father, a cohort of victim souls overflowing with love.

"Prayer, penance, honest poverty, and courageous acts of sacrifices can soften the anger of the Heavenly Father. I desire this also from your community: please make much of poverty, deepen repentance, and pray amid your poverty in reparation for the ingratitude and insults toward the Lord by so many men. Recite the prayer of the Handmaids of the Eucharist with awareness of its meaning; put it into practice; offer your life to God in reparation for sins. Let each one endeavor by making much of one's ability and position, to offer oneself entirely to the Lord.

"Even in a secular community, prayer is necessary. Already souls who wish to pray are on the way to being gathered in this community. Without attaching too much importance to the form, pray fervently and steadfastly to console the Lord.

"Is what you think in your heart true? Are you truly prepared to become the rejected stone? My novice, you who wish to become the pure bride of the Lord, in order that you, the bride, become the spouse worthy of the Holy Bridegroom, make your vows with the hearty readiness to be fastened to a cross with three nails. These three nails are honest poverty, chastity, and obedience. Of the three, obedience is the foundation. With total obedience, follow your superior. Your superior will understand you well and guide you."

This message, as all could see, was not meant just for Sister Agnes Sasagawa. It was an appeal for prayer, reparation, and obedience from all of the sisters of the Institute. From that day, all seven sisters were increasingly involved with the messages and requests that apparently came from Our Lady. As a community, they prayed more fervently than ever before their beloved Eucharist. And, in a sense, they waited, not knowing what they waited for.

On September 29, the feast of the archangels, Sister Agnes

and another sister were in the chapel completing the rosary when Sister Agnes glanced at the statue of Mary. It was ablaze with light. With her heart racing, Agnes tugged on the sleeve of her companion, motioning her to look at the statue. When the other nun clasped her hands tightly to her chest in excitement, Agnes knew that another pair of eyes was finally seeing that unearthly light. Heaven was opening a door a little bit wider. Soon, both sisters noticed that the hands of the statue blazed intensely. Then, the companion of Sister Agnes pointed to the statue. She turned her head so that Agnes could read her lips and said: "The wound has disappeared."

That evening, Sister Agnes again became aware of the angel's presence. The angel told her, "Mary is even sadder than when she shed blood. Dry the perspiration." When she looked up, the statue was glowing. But drops of clear liquid were beading and flowing down the statue. Not knowing what else to do, one of the sisters hurried away to find a sack of cotton balls to wipe away the sweat that was literally flowing out of their Mary.

Only later as they talked about it did the nuns discover that each sister had been privately overwhelmed by a sense of grief as she wiped away the sweat. And only later did they find that the drops of perspiration had a wonderful fragrance of flowers. That wonderful sweet aroma stayed with them for seventeen days. As October began, the women on Yuzawadai hill prayed still harder. And yet, they must have wondered where each new phenomenon was leading.

The thirteenth day of October, 1973, was Saturday, a day set aside to celebrate Mary. And though Sister Agnes Sasagawa probably hadn't thought of it, it was also the fifty-sixth anniversary of the last apparition of Our Lady at Fátima in 1917. During early morning prayer, Sister Agnes saw the tabernacle burn once more with the dazzling white light. Then, the statue of Mary gave off a wonderful fragrance, which filled the chapel. As she began the rosary later in the morning, the voice sounded in her ears:

"My dear daughter, listen well to what I have to say to you. You will inform your superior.

"As I told you, if men do not repent and better themselves, the Father will inflict a terrible punishment on all humanity. It will be a punishment greater than a deluge, such as one has never seen before. Fire will fall from the sky and will wipe out a great part of humanity, the good as well as the bad, sparing neither priests nor faithful. The survivors will find themselves so desolate that they will envy the dead. The only arms which will remain for you will be the rosary and the Sign left by my Son. Each day recite the prayers of the rosary. With the rosary, pray for the pope, the bishops and the priests.

"The work of the devil will infiltrate even into the Church in such a way that one will see cardinals opposing cardinals, bishops against other bishops. The priests who venerate me will be scorned and opposed by their confreres ... churches and altars sacked; the Church will be full of those who accept compromises and the demon will press many priests and consecrated souls to leave the service of the Lord.

"The demon will be especially implacable against souls consecrated to God. The thought of the loss of so many souls is the cause of my sadness. If sins increase in number and gravity, there will be no longer pardon for them.

"With courage, speak to your superior. He will know how to encourage each one of you to pray and to accomplish works of reparation.

"Today is the last time I will speak to you in living voice. From now on, you will obey the one sent to you and your superior. Pray very much the prayers of the rosary. I alone am able still to save you from the calamities which approach. Those who place their confidence in me will be saved."

When Sister Agnes raised her head, the statue of Mary seemed to have a sad expression. Another glance, however, soon showed her that the appearance of the statue was normal. As she gazed at it for a moment, sadness washed over her. In her deafness, she had heard the Mother of Jesus. She rose to her feet, trying to hold on to the memory of the glorious voice.

The Virgin's words of warning that predicted calamities and fire falling from the sky were frightening, unspeakable. Many in Japan remembered the terrible falling fire of atomic bombs at Hiroshima and Nagasaki in 1945. This falling fire would be worse. Sister Agnes shivered when she thought of it and of the way Our Lady predicted that the devil would stir up dissension and sin within the Church.

Later, Sister Agnes shared this third and last message of Our Lady with Bishop Ito. She asked him the meaning of Our Lady's word "cardinal." The voice had used this English word pronounced in Japanese. "But it is the English word for '*sukikyo*'" [cardinal], he answered. To Bishop Ito, it seemed to be one more sign that Sister Agnes was not inventing these messages from heaven. She didn't know the meaning of a word used in the message.

As autumn blew colder winds across the Japanese islands, the sisters of the Institute wore more sweaters. There were many chinks and holes in their poor house. On October 15, the feast of St. Teresa of Ávila, the nuns enjoyed the heavenly and mysterious aroma of flowers for the last time. The next day, another kind of smell — in fact, a putrid stench — waited for them as the first sisters opened the door to begin morning prayer. Even the stalwart Sister Agnes cupped her hand over her nose immediately. She and others immediately searched for a dead animal but found nothing.

The sisters gathered to pray anyway, and soon concluded, as the Virgin Mary had requested, with a rosary. As one of the sisters extinguished the candles, she suddenly pointed with horror at a small white thing crawling on the floor. Soon, all of the sisters were pointing at small white worms. They were all over the floor. Like the stench, the worms appeared out of nowhere. The next day, the worms were gone, though the stench polluted the chapel for three days.

Later, it seemed to the sisters that the wonderful scent of flowers was a reminder of Mary's holiness. The unexplainable stench and the disgusting worms, on the other hand, seemed to symbolize sin — their own sin. The smell had been strongest in the sacristy that also served the sisters as the confessional area.

Life in the convent at the edge of Akita continued more or less normally through the winter months, which brought some unprecedented snowfalls. In March, the nuns at Yuzawadai hill finally received a chaplain, Father Teiji Yasuda, O.S.V. Heaven's hand, not chance, led him to the sisters during a February snowstorm when no priest had been able to come to say Mass. In town, he heard the sisters criticized because they had no real work and because they lived in shameful poverty. But something powerful and virtuous at their house touched Father Yasuda deeply. Within weeks, he resigned as pastor of a large and prosperous parish to become chaplain.

In the years ahead, Father Teiji was to become an invaluable spiritual advisor of Sister Agnes. At first, however, "she appeared to me as one of the most ordinary women. What I heard seemed to be something of a dream or a world disconnected from reality." October 13, 1974, was a day that Father Yasuda must have prayed for. It was another Fátima anniversary. It was also the day on which Sister Agnes regained her hearing. In May, the angel had told Sister Agnes that her deafness would be cured soon. The healing would be temporary, the angel reminded her. A full and permanent healing would be given later.

During Benediction, Sister Agnes heard the bell ring. Then, she heard the voice of Father Yasuda saying, "Blessed be God ...." Confused and then filled with joy, she prostrated herself to weep quietly. Later, she joyfully phoned Bishop Ito and her parents. One year and seven months had passed since she had become deaf. The little community of sisters had a new reason for joy and thanksgiving in the waning months of the year.

On January 4, 1975, Father Yasuda sat in his presbytery office, preparing a talk for the last day of a retreat he was giving his Institute sisters. Meanwhile, the rest of Japan observed the traditional New Year's Festival, the biggest celebration of the year. During the first days of the new year, everyone visited friends and relatives to exchange gifts. Women dressed up in their finest kimonos, and many parades and sporting events were held all over the country.

A nun suddenly knocked at Father's door, calling his name. When he answered, the excited sister gasped, "The statue of the Virgin is weeping!" Father Yasuda hurried to the chapel to see for himself. The statue of Mary was so dried out that there were cracks in the wood in several places. Nonetheless, small beads of water were gathering in the corners of her eyes. Then, the tears flowed over the eye lid to her cheek and chin below.

The way the tears were forming and flowing was so lifelike, Father Yasuda later reported, that he and the sisters simply stood around the statue, watching and praying. They all felt as though they were watching a living person cry. Although no one thought of taking a photo until later, there were other opportunities. The weeping of the statue occurred twice more that same day. Over the next six and one-half years, the statue was to weep a total of one hundred one times. The last occasion was September 15, 1981, the feast of Our Lady of Sorrows.

Toward the end of the 1975 New Year's retreat, Sister Agnes again saw her guardian angel. The angel told her:

"Do not be so surprised to see the Blessed Virgin weeping. She weeps because she wishes the conversion of the greatest number. She desires that souls be consecrated to Jesus and to the Father by her intercession.

"He who directs you told you during the last sermon today: Your faith diminishes when you do not see. It is because your faith is weak. The Blessed Virgin rejoices in the consecration of Japan to her Immaculate Heart because she loves Japan. But she is sad to see that this devotion is not taken seriously. Even though she has chosen this land of Akita to give her messages, the local pastor doesn't dare to come for fear of what one would say. Do not be afraid. The Blessed Virgin awaits you all...."

Within a few weeks after the lachrimations — or tears — began, Professor Eiji Okuhara, M.D., a Catholic physician and member of Akita University's Department of Biochemistry, analyzed the three kinds of liquid from the statue — tears, perspiration, and blood. Two weeks later, Dr. Okuhara passed the samples along to a non-Christian forensic specialist, Dr. Kaoru Sagisaka, M.D. Okuhara did not tell his colleague where the samples came from.

Two weeks later, the second report came back. It echoed the findings of the first, stating: "The matter adhering on the gauze is human blood. The sweat and tears absorbed in the two pieces of cotton are of human origin." Furthermore, the analysis indicated that the blood was Type B, while the sweat and tears were Type AB. A second analysis completed later yielded the same results. That the blood and other body fluids were of different types was to help build the case for the authenticity of the Virgin's messages in years to come.

Word began to spread throughout Japan that human tears were coming from a statue of Mary at Akita. The convent began to receive phone calls, visitors, letters, and requests for interviews from the media. By March 6, Sister Agnes was unable to answer any of the phone calls. On the same day that the newsmen arrived from a Catholic newspaper, the statue wept again for the fourth time. On this day, too, Sister Agnes went to Father Yasuda to tell him that she could no longer hear. To verify her condition, he took her to Municipal Hospital of Akita. Doctors certified that there was no hearing left in either ear and that the chance for any improvement or cure was virtually nonexistant.

By now, secular newspapers and magazines had begun to report on "the statue which weeps." Bishop John Ito was beginning to be pulled in many directions over events in the convent at Akita. Many in the Church wanted nothing said about the situation. In 1975, the bishop opened an inquiry into the reports of supernatural happenings. On the advice of another bishop, he appointed a Mariologist, Father Garcia Evangelista from Tokyo, to lead the commission. Father Evangelista came to Akita to visit, asking the sisters many questions. Before he left, he borrowed the personal diaries of Sister Agnes.

By the middle of May, 1976, Father Evangelista had come to his own conclusions about the matter. They were negative. All of the phenomena described by Sister Agnes Sasagawa, the sisters, and other witnesses were not supernatural at all, he contended. The bleeding, sweating, and tearing seen in the chapel statue was a result of certain "ectoplasmic powers" of the seer, Sister Agnes. By these ectoplasmic powers, he later argued, she could transfer her own body fluids to the statue.

Even though he had not yet shared his negative views about events at their house with the sisters or their chaplain, Father Evangelista accepted an invitation from Father Yasuda to come and preach a weeklong retreat at the convent in May of 1976. Father Yasuda had agreed to give a talk in Suzuka. During these same days, Sister Agnes was also away, visiting her dying mother.

During the retreat, Father Evangelista took the opportunity to attack the veracity and claims of Sister Agnes. As the handmaids sat before him in their small chapel, the priest characterized Sister Agnes as a "special psychopathic case." The visions that she claimed to have, he told the nuns, were a result of her disassociation from reality and of her double personality. The statue had exhibited bleeding, sweating, and tearing only through the ectoplasmic powers of Sister Agnes. Once they learned what ectoplasmic powers were, none of the nuns thought to point out that the statue had often bled or cried when Sister Agnes was far from Akita. By the end of the week, however, the nuns were weighed down with a leaden doubt and dread. They were humiliated, shamed, defeated. Father Evangelista, after all, was a scholar. He had studied the matter — at their bishop's request.

When Sister Agnes and Father Yasuda returned, the chill and spiritual gloom were immediately apparent. Although the nuns greeted Sister Agnes with affection, she soon discovered that her credibility with them had been destroyed. As June, 1976, began, she was in agony, believing that no one really trusted her. At the suggestion of Father Yasuda, she meditated often on Jesus abandoned on the cross.

Nonetheless, small unofficial groups of "pilgrims" began to visit and pray in the sisters' chapel. The months and even the years seemed to pass by so quickly for Sister Agnes and the sisters of the Institute. The statue produced tears only six times in 1976 and none at all in 1977. In 1978, the sisters counted twelve different occasions of weeping by the statue.

During these two years, clouds of doubt hung over the convent at Akita. Bishop Ito was wounded by it all. Even more disturbing, however, was the spirit of distrust and confusion among his sisters at Akita. He went to the Apostolic Delegate to ask for advice. In 1976, the delegate advised him to ask the Archbishop of Tokyo to appoint an official Commission of Canonical Inquiry into the Akita claims. Though the views of Father Evangelista were already known to be negative, he was mysteriously named to lead the commission's study.

In Akita, Sister Agnes was grieving over the death of her mother. Soon after the commission was constituted, she was summoned to Tokyo for a daylong inquiry with Father Evangelista. With Father Yasuda and her own brother and sister to support her, the slender nun listened as Father Evangelista calmly informed her that she had misled many people and that her spiritual director — Father Yasuda — had used her to write articles for pay in the media.

Later, she wrote about this excruciatingly painful cross-examination. "I saw coming the moment when I was going to be squarely labeled mentally ill, but this word was not pronounced a single time. It was when he declared that I had ectoplasmic powers that I began seriously to be disturbed."After more than eight hours of this treatment, she left exhausted and grieved. At home, however, peace returned. Though her sisters were uncertain about what to believe, Sister Agnes could see even more clearly that even the painful doubts and charges against her were all in God's plan.

In 1978, the report of the Canonical Commision of Inquiry, written by Father Evangelista, was published. It was negative. Except for Father Evangelista, no other commission member had traveled to Akita to try to determine what had happened. But the matter was now closed, and no details of the report were sent to Akita. Bishop Ito, though clearly troubled, ordered the sisters and their chaplain to accept the verdict in silence.

Within a few months, however, he traveled to Rome to share his doubts about the commission's procedures with the Congregation for the Doctrine of the Faith. He was told that he had the authority to form a new commission. It was the local ordinary who was supposed to have primary responsibility to direct study into apparition claims, but Bishop Ito had not even been a member of the first commission.

In 1979, a second Commission of Canonical Inquiry was set up under the direction of Bishop Ito. The seven members studied the claims and released their findings on September 12, 1981. By a vote of four to three, they approved the supernatural character of the events. Even as the commission was preparing to vote, Sister Therese Kasiwagi, the mother superior, phoned to report that the statue of the Virgin was again shedding tears. The weeping had occurred only two other times during the year. The last tears of the Akita statue flowed three days later on September 15, 1981, the Feast of Our Lady of Sorrows.

Though the commission hadn't heard about it, a Korean

woman, Theresa Chun, a forty-three-year-old wife and mother of four children, had been cured of a brain tumor. Her older sister had placed a photo of Our Lady of Akita near her pillow, praying for her healing. On August 4, 1981, Theresa awoke and was soon declared miraculously free of any tumor.

After the approval of the second commission, the nuns at Akita now found a new joy, a new peace, and a new unity. The official Church had declared as "authentic" events that they had always deeply believed in. Somehow, it had never seemed possible that Sister Agnes had duped them and herself.

On May 1, 1982, the guardian angel of Sister Agnes alerted her that her deafness would be healed before the month was done. She went to Father Yasuda to share the good news. On May 30, the Feast of Pentecost and the Vigil of the Feast of the Visitation, Sister Agnes again heard the Benediction bell sound. The nuns enthusiastically sang a "*Te Deum*" with tears of joy. On May 31, the Red Cross Hospital, which had declared her incurably deaf, now retested Sister Agnes. For reasons that couldn't be explained, her deafness was now totally cured.

On Easter Sunday, April 22, 1984, Bishop Ito released a pastoral letter to his diocese, declaring the events of Akita to be supernatural. He authorized veneration of the "Holy Mother of Akita." The messages given there, he said, were the same as those given by Our Lady at Fátima. Within a few years, Akita became a place of international pilgrimage. There in the small chapel of poor sisters devoted to the Eucharist, the world had found a new place of prayer.

Medjugorje

1981-?

*T*here is a village in Bosnia-Herzegovina, as millions of people now know, named Medjugorje, or "Between the Hills." Even this name shows the good sense of the local people, because the place is tucked into a valley surrounded by several sizable hills. One is called Crinca and is flanked by a smaller hill called Podbrdo, or "Under Hill." Nearby, too, is Krizevac, or "Cross Hill."

Although the name Medjugorje had been used since the sixteenth century, Krizevac was given its name in 1933. In that year, the people of Medjugorje and other nearby villages erected a twenty-five-foot stone cross on top of the hill. The monument marked 1,900 years since the death of Christ.

All of this history was quite familiar to sixteen-year-old Vicka Ivankovic, who had just completed school exams on the morning of June 24, 1981. It was the feast of St. John the Baptist. Vicka had worked hard, and by midafternoon she was tired. She told her mother, Zlata, that she needed some extra sleep and headed for bed.

Zlata Ivankovic and her husband, Pero, had eight children, including Vicka. For fifteen years, however, Pero had been working in West Germany to support his family. The land the family lived on near Medjugorje was his, but raising sheep and the region's principal crops — tobacco and grapes — just didn't feed his family.

The late afternoon was, as usual during June, hot and dry. The young people in the area often gathered at dusk, when it was a little cooler, to walk and talk together. Video arcades and movie matinees had not yet invaded the villages.

While Vicka napped, fifteen-year-old Ivanka Ivankovic and Mirjana Dragicevic, sixteen, walked along together from their village of Bijakovici, which neighbored Medjugorje. The two were close friends, and Mirjana's companionship had helped to dull the pain Ivanka was still suffering after the death of her mother a month before. Ivanka's father, like Vicka's, was far away, working in West Germany. Both Mirjana and Ivanka lived in other cities but spent summers here, visiting with their grand-mothers.

Along the way, Ivanka glanced up toward the small hill called Podbrdo, and gasped.

"Look, it's the Virgin Mary!" she exclaimed.

"No, it couldn't be the Virgin Mary," responded Mirjana, without a second thought. Still, when she, too, looked, it did seem as though there was something up there that had a hu-man shape. It was white or gray, and was moving. Mirjana and Ivanka were instantly filled with a nervous fear. They hurried to the house of Marija and Milka Pavlovic, located not far from the bottom of Podbrdo.

Although Marija, at sixteen, was closer to their age, Ivanka and Mirjana soon left with thirteen-year-old Milka, who had to gather in the family's sheep.

As the three talked on the way to the pasture, Ivanka was unable to get her mind off what they had seen. When they neared the place where she could view the top of the hill again, she took another glance.

"I saw the Madonna, holding Jesus in her hands," she later told a priest, Father Svetozar Kraljevic, O.F.M., "and then Mirjana and Milka looked and saw her." The two older girls were more frightened than ever. They hurried off to Vicka's house to see what she would make of it all. Because Vicka's mother didn't want to wake her still-sleeping daughter, the girls left a message for her: "As soon as you get up, come to Jakov's house."

Jakov Colo, aged ten, had been born in the house, and was a first cousin to Marija and Milka Pavlovic. Marija knew that Jakov's house had an excellent view of the top of Podbrdo, and of the mysterious sight.

By this time, Vicka was awake, had heard the message from her mother, and was on her way to Jakov's house. When she finally caught up with Mirjana and Ivanka, they directed her attention to the top of the hill. Vicka was afraid and wouldn't look. Instead, she ran in the other direction until she met with sixteen-year-old Ivan Dragicevic and twenty-two-year-old Ivan Ivankovic.

Vicka felt pulled. She wanted to see the vision, but was almost consumed with fright. The two Ivans were picking apples when she blurted out her dilemma. They quickly agreed to go back with her to see whatever there was to see. When these three came within viewing distance, however, Ivan Dragicevic suddenly realized what had terrified Ivanka. After one look, he turned and ran.

In fact, the object of the young people's scrutiny and fear was a healthy distance away. Later, Vicka estimated that the Madonna stood about two hundred meters (about two hundred twenty yards) away. The young people were close enough to identify a general shape, but were too far away to see critical details.

As Vicka stood there, she could began to distinguish the figure's gown and dark hair. "It looked as if she were showing something. Then she called to us to come closer — but who was going to get any closer?" After a few more minutes, Vicka left with Milka. The others followed a a short time later. Little was said. All of them were troubled by the figure standing atop Podbrdo Hill.

Vicka and Milka returned to the Pavlovic house at 6:30 P.M. Marija would not believe her younger sister or Vicka. Later on, Vicka's sister had her own explanation: "Maybe they saw a flying saucer."

The following day, June 25, was a fine day to harvest tobacco. Many of the valley people spent the day doing just that. Sometime during the day, four of the young people — Ivanka, Mirjana, Vicka, and Ivan — met and decided that it would be good to have a closer look at whatever stood atop the hill. They decided to meet again later in the day, at about 6:00 P.M. If they saw a "Madonna" again that night, Vicka planned to notify little Jakov Colo and Marija. Both of them wanted to see any new vision.

As the four teenagers and several curious adults approached Podbrdo, Ivanka whispered, "Look, the Madonna!"

When the other three looked up at the hill, they had to agree. The Virgin's features were much easier to distinguish than they had been the night before. And on this night, there was a different feeling about the mysterious presence up there. Gone was the cold grip of fear. In fact, joy filled Ivanka as she jogged away to retrieve Jakov and Marija.

These young people — Mirjana, Ivanka, Vicka, Marija, Jakov, and Ivan — witnessed the second vision of Mary at Medjugorje. In fact, these six comprised the group that reportedly began to receive daily apparitions.

At the bottom of the hill, the six quickly felt a pull to approach the Madonna at the top. "The Madonna called us," Vicka told others. With no discussion whatsoever, the young people immediately raced up the hill. They ran over the rough rocks, ignoring the path. They traveled so fast that the adults watching couldn't understand it. Vicka was barefoot but suffered no cuts or bruises on her feet.

Suddenly, the six young people stood within a few feet of the shining and beautiful Madonna. She was so beautiful, all said later. It was impossible to describe her adequately. "She has black hair, a bit curly, blue eyes, rosy cheeks, slender, beautiful," one of the children said later. Her gown, they all agreed, was a hard color to fix with words. It was sort of gray, but then again like coffee with cream. A wonderful veil covered her head and flowed down over her body.

A sense of peace overtook them for a few moments. Then, Ivanka spoke up. She asked the Virgin if her mother was in heaven. The Virgin said that she was. Then Ivanka asked if her mother had any messages for her children. The Virgin replied in Croatian: "Obey your grandmother and be good to her because she is old and cannot work."

The Virgin then told the children that she had come to the region because she found faith there. She told them to pray seven "Our Fathers," "Hail Marys," "Glory Bes," and the "Creed." Mirjana told the visitor that no one would believe that she was appearing. The Virgin only smiled. She seemed to be suspended in the air as she looked at them and said: "Go in God's peace." Then, she was gone.

At the bottom of the hill, spectators noticed that all of the young visionaries had turned and looked in the same direction during the apparition. No one else saw anything.

On Friday, June 26, several thousand people from nearby villages prepared to travel to the hill in the early evening. Word had traveled so quickly. The six didn't know if the Virgin would return, but they sensed that she would.

At 6:15 P.M., a light appeared three times near the hill of the apparitions. At this, the six children ran up Probrdo again. They approached the Madonna even more closely. They sang canticles and prayed the rosary in her honor. Down below, at the bottom of the hill, several thousand people did the same.

Vicka had brought holy water to throw in the vision's direction. She feared that the apparition might be from the devil.

The Lady only smiled. "Oh, no, I am '*Gospa*' (The Madonna)," she told the girl.

The young people asked her if she would return, and the Virgin made a motion with her head that seemed to say "yes."

"Who are you?" they asked at the end of this third encounter.

"I am the Blessed Virgin Mary," she said simply. Their fears about a diabolical manifestation vanished. Then, the shining Lady spoke to them of peace. "Peace, peace, peace," she repeated. "Be reconciled."

The messages from the Virgin on this night were simple, familiar, vital, and yet fresh. When the six youths went back down the hill around 7:00 P.M., they were almost crushed by the crowds. A neighbor, Marinko Ivankovic, immediately became a sort of bodyguard. She ushered the children through the crowd with great authority.

On the following morning, the young people were summoned by the police to Citluk, the area's principal city. Interrogations failed to weaken the stories of any of the six. Interviews with a police psychiatrist turned up no abnormalities. Back in their homes by noon, the visionaries prepared for the trip back to Podbrdo that evening.

About fifteen thousand people came to accompany them on the fifth day of vision, June 28. By now it seemed as though the apparitions would be daily.

On the following day, the police cross-examined all six again in Citluk. Despite the hopes of the authorities, no rationale for committing any of the children to psychiatric wards could be uncovered. It was already clear to Communist authorities that the events were fostering the cause of religion.

On Tuesday, June 30, at the usual time, the Virgin appeared to five of the children near the side of a road. Two women had offered them a ride to Podbrdo, then detained them so that they would be late for the apparition. The visionaries were about two miles from the apparition site when they got out of the car and began to pray. Ivan was not there because of illness.

After praying and singing in the Lady's presence, Vicka asked the Virgin if they could wait for her apparitions in the church. The police had forbidden public gatherings at the hill. After a moment, the Virgin agreed and disappeared.

For a while, apparitions occurred at private homes. In early July, Mass was celebrated at St. James Parish Church each evening after the apparitions. The Franciscan pastor believed that prayer was needed. It wasn't yet clear that these reported apparitions were coming from God.

On July 13, 1981, just two weeks after the apparitions began, the Communist Yugoslavian government closed off access to Podbrdo Hill with a blockade. On August 6, some people thought they saw the word *"Mir"* (Peace) written in the sky. They presumed that the "skywriting" was a message from Our Lady: blockades wouldn't stop or intimidate her.

On August 15, the feast of the Assumption of Mary, great crowds traveled to Medjugorje, a village of three hundred. Government officials were enraged. Two days later, they arrested the pastor, Father Jozo Zovko, O.F.M. Though he had originally been skeptical about the apparition reports, he had come to believe in their authenticity. Father Zovko was sentenced to three and a half years in prison for "subversion." Because of protests, his time in prison was reduced to eighteen months.

As the hot, dry summer months of 1981 finally yielded to the colder, crisper days of autumn, grapes ripened in the vineyards near Medjugorje. "Zilavku" wine made from this region's grapes had been famous throughout Europe for centuries. The time for harvesting came and went as usual, but it was clear that many other things in this valley would never be the same.

For one thing, there was little peace between the bishop of Mostar, Bishop Pavao Zanic, and those who believed in the apparitions of "the Queen of Peace," as she called herself. The bishop had been upset with the Franciscan priests who staffed many of the parishes in the area. When he tried to change some of the Franciscan parishes to diocesan, there was an uproar. As the conflict continued, the bishop tried to defrock priests who remained in the parish that the diocese was now claiming.

When the six seers put the conflict before the Virgin, she reportedly sided with the priests, whom she said were innocent of wrongdoing. She also said that the bishop had acted in haste and should reconsider his actions.

When he heard about it, Bishop Zanic was furious. "The Mother of God would never speak to a bishop that way," he thundered. The bishop was never again able to consider events in Medjugorje in a favorable light.

In the early months of 1982, the daily apparitions began to take place in the parish church, St. James, because the police were trying to shut down all large gatherings outdoors. The messages Our Lady gave to the six young people were simple and always focused on reconciliation. Apparitions were as long as forty minutes. During that time, the seers remained transfixed by visions of an extraordinarily beautiful woman of average height who looked as though she was about twenty-five years old. She spoke to them in Croatian and her voice, they said, was like a bell that rang softly.

"Prayer and fasting can prevent even war," she told the young people on July 21, 1982. Some months earlier, she had recommended a Friday fast on bread and water as the most effective way to make reparations for sin. She told priests to "believe firmly and watch over the faith of the people." Russia, she said on another day, "is the people in which God will be most glorified. The West has advanced civilization, but without God, as though it were its own creator." Our Lady also recommended monthly confession, frequent attendance at Mass with reception of the Eucharist, and prayer, especially the rosary. Mary appealed to the villagers of Medjugorje for special help in her efforts to save people. The response was impressive. Almost everyone began to attend the three-hour-long evening Masses at St. James.

In 1982, the Queen of Peace had begun to separately instruct each of the young visionaries, telling them that they would eventually receive ten secrets about the end times. Physical signs would appear at Medjugorje that would convince all that Mary really appears there. Mary told the young people that when they had received the ten secrets, she would no longer appear to them on a daily basis.

Mirjana was the first to receive all ten secrets. She learned the tenth one on Christmas Eve, 1982. Knowing that she would no longer see the Queen of Peace each day made that appearance bittersweet, Mirjana later said. She was grieved that she would no longer see that glorious face each day. During the apparition, however, the Virgin consoled the girl by telling her that she would appear to her each year on her birthday, March 18. Nonetheless, on Christmas day, when Mirjana realized that she would not see Our Lady, she wept bitterly. Later on, the Virgin began again to appear to her on the second day of each month.

As the months went by, Ivanka, too, learned the tenth secret. Daily apparitions stopped for her on May 7, 1985. Instead, she began to receive apparitions only on the anniversaries of the first apparition. In the meantime, in January, 1983, Our Lady began to tell Vicka the story of her life over a two-year period.

The apparitions reported at Medjugorje continued month after month, year after year. "I stayed this long so that I could be of help to you in your trials," Mary said, explaining the astounding duration of her visits. The news about these appearances therefore spread around the world. The longevity allowed millions of people to travel there. Hundreds of physical cures were reported. But even more numerous, perhaps, were reports of conversions or spiritual healings.

"Medjugorje is the world's confessional," remarked a priest, referring to the enormous numbers who seek sacramental reconcilation there. The support of the bishop of the neighboring diocese, Archbishop Frane Franic, was much stronger.

The archbishop said that "the happenings in Medjugorje have done more for the faith and awareness of the world's life in faith than all the pastoral work through the last forty years."

And yet, the themes of Medjugorje continued to be simple. In short, Mary was asking the world to seriously embrace faith, peace, prayer, fasting, and reconciliation.

Privately, the six young people grew up, finished school, and went about their lives as normally as they could. They all retain deep commitments to prayer and spreading the message of the Virgin who came to see them.

Ivan completed his two years of required military service. Later, he entered, then withdrew, from a seminary, then married an American girl in 1994. Vicka and Marija planned to enter religious life when the apparitions concluded. Mirjana studied at the university in Sarajevo, but later married Marko Soldo. The Soldos now have two children. Ivanka married Raiko Elez and they also are raising two children. Jakov, the youngest seer, lost both of his parents and was said to be the most free-spirited of the group. All but Marija live still in the little village of Medjugorje.

In the last months of 1990, the bishops of Yugoslavia felt the pressure to make some assessment of the apparitions that had been reported for almost ten years. In a private session on November 27, they discussed the results of a study conducted over several years.

"On the basis of research conducted so far, one cannot affirm that supernatural apparitions or revelation are involved," they stated. The bishops said that they would continue to study events at Medjugorje and that they wished to provide pastoral care for the pilgrims who traveled there.

Soon, however, all of former Yugoslavia was plunged into a ruthless and bloody civil war. Although Medjugorje has never been directly damaged or attacked, most of Bosnia-Herzegovina around it has been devastated. The study of the apparitions at Medjugorje have been virtually suspended.

As a new millennium approaches, it is clear that the Church will take more time to make its final conclusions about Medjugorje, a tiny village where the Virgin reportedly came to see us once again.

Kibeho, Rwanda

1981-89

*A*lphonsine Mumureke smiled and chatted with her friends as she moved up and down the rows separating the long wooden dining room tables at Kibeho College, a school run by the Benebikira Sisters. The teenager was serving tables at the noon meal that Saturday, November 28, 1981, but it didn't seem very much like work. Like most sixteen-year-olds, this girl with a winning smile loved to be with friends.

Alphonsine was a boarding student, in her first year of secondary school. Her mother, a Catholic, had wanted this type of schooling for her daughter. For Alphonsine and many of the other boarding students, life at school was good, despite the separation from home. In the villages and the bush, the families of virtually all of the students were farmers who raised coffee and tea. Even though the parents of Alphonsine and the others worked very hard, their income was not much better than the national per capita average — $106 per year.

Rwanda, a beautiful, mountainous republic in the center of Africa, was one of the continent's poorest and most densely populated nations. As the 1980s began, a majority of Rwandans were Christians, and about fifty percent of the population was Catholic. Charismatic renewal and a growing interest in Marian devotion were creating an impact among Catholics. But in all honesty, Alphonsine Mumureke rarely concerned herself with what people did and how they lived beyond the school compound. Instead, she thought about her classwork, her friendships, and family matters.

Pouring water into the glasses and making sure that everyone had enough to eat, Alphonsine was enjoying herself while doing her job, too. Then, she heard a voice calling her "My daughter ..." Alphonsine swung around to see who had spoken. Curious about the strong but lovely voice, she headed out of the room. No one in the dining room would call her "My daughter."

Instantly, she saw an incredibly beautiful lady in the corridor.

"Who are you?" Alphonsine gasped, looking at the glowing woman dressed all in white. Though she asked the question, somehow the teenager must have already known. Alphonsine dropped to her knees the second she saw her.

"Ndi Nyina wa Jambo" ("I am the Mother of the Word"), the Virgin said, identifying herself in Kinyarwanda, the shared language of Rwanda's people.

Whether or not the transfixed girl knew what to make of the title isn't clear. She may have been memorizing every detail of the Lady's appearance. Her hands were joined at her breast, fingers pointing toward heaven. Our Lady's skin, Alphonsine said later, "was not really white like we see her in pictures. I could not determine the color of her skin, but she was of an uncomparable beauty." The Virgin wore a white veil and her white dress was seamless. And like the village people, Alphonsine noticed, she wore no shoes.

As the young lady studied her, the Virgin continued the conversation, but changed the subject considerably. "Of the religions, what do you like?" asked the Mother of the Word.

"I love God and His Mother who have given us Their Son who has saved us," answered Alphonsine without hesitation.

"It is true," said Our Lady, smiling. "I have come to assure you of this. I have heard your prayers. I would like it if your companions had more faith because some of them do not believe enough."

Mary told Alphonsine that she wanted her to join the Legion of Mary to help her realize her vocation. The Legion, a lay group dedicated to evangelization, worked in conjunction with the bishop and priests to bring the word of God to the most remote areas of Rwanda. After Alphonsine quickly agreed, the Virgin told the girl that she wanted people to trust and love her as a Mother because she wanted to lead them to her Son Jesus.

Then, Mary apparently wanted Alphonsine to witness her return to Jesus. The girl watched as Mary rose gracefully and beautifully out of human sight. When it was over, this new visionary collapsed to the corridor floor. For about fifteen minutes, she seemed to be in a stupor and couldn't be roused by the other students and teachers. Finally, the sister directress shook her back to reality.

"What happened?" the nun asked Alphonsine, speaking for the small crowd of students and staff who had left the dining room to see what was going on. Almost everyone had heard Alphonsine speaking with great animation to someone in the corridor.

When Alphonsine recovered her senses, she was bubbling with joy, anxious to tell about the wonderful "Mother of the Word." As she told her story, describing in detail the Mother's dress and radiance, she saw blank faces and expressions of scorn and disgust. None of the students, teachers, or staff members believed her. Even her closest friends shook their heads in disbelief at this "crazy" story.

During the next day, Sunday, November 29, Alphonsine saw her Lady again. It was the First Sunday of Advent, a day that initiated a season of waiting for Jesus. The apparition was brief. Again, Alphonsine fell into a state of oblivion and exhaustion at the end of it. But her return to "reality" was no more friendly than it had been after the first apparition. Her tale about the Virgin Mary was dismissed and she was ridiculed.

An essential message given to Alphonsine concerned Mary's desire to be seen as the Mother. The Virgin told the girl, "I love a child who plays with me because this is a beautiful manifestation of trust and love. Feel like children with me because I, too, love to pet you. No one should be afraid of their Mother. I am your Mother. You should not be afraid of me but you should love me."

If the nuns at Kibeho College saw Alphonsine's tricks as some new ploy to get attention, they were probably surprised that she kept it up. The girl did receive attention, but who would have wanted the teasing, snickers, and sneers? Sometimes, she was labeled "sick." Sometimes, fingers were pointed at her. A few people whispered the word "possessed" in a tone that she overheard easily.

In that same social climate, the apparitions continued throughout December. They took place mostly on Saturdays in the student dormitory. Whenever an apparition occurred, everyone in the school compound knew about it almost immediately. Some students laughed and tossed rosaries to the visionary for the Virgin to bless.

Gradually, a few students began to wonder if there was some truth to Alphonsine's story. Why would she lie or make it up? During the apparitions, they noticed, Alphonsine could not lift the rosaries of the scoffers. Mysteriously, the rosaries became so heavy that she couldn't seem to raise them for a blessing. After a while, some students began to pray that Our Lady would appear to another student as well. That would confirm the claim their friend was making.

On January 12, 1982, Our Lady acquiesced. In addition to Alphonsine, she came to see sixteen-year-old Anathalie Mukamazimpaka. Like Alphonsine, Anathalie was Catholic, as were both her parents. Anathalie was the fourth of eight children in her family. Because of her Catholic upbringing, she was already a member of the Legion of Mary and was also active with Charismatic Renewal.

When the apparitions to Anathalie began, many people from the little community at Kibeho College began to believe. The messages from this second visionary were more mystical than those given to Alphonsine. They stressed the need for prayer, deep reflection, humility, and self-sacrifice. One message Anathalie repeated many times was: "Wake up, stand up. Wash yourself and look up attentively. We must dedicate ourselves to prayer. We must develop in us the virtues of charity, availability and humility."

By mid-January, almost three weeks had passed since Alphonsine's first apparition. Although the simple brick and stucco buildings inside the compound at Kibeho College looked unchanged, the school and its students were changing inside. But once the Virgin began to visit a second girl, students and staff began to believe that heaven's Mother really was visiting their school in tiny Kibeho. Many students began to pray the rosary with sincerity and renewed faith.

On March 22, lightning struck for a third time. The lightning, of course, was the shining vision of Mary, the Mother of God, the Mother of the Word. Mary had chosen a third visionary, twenty-two-year-old Marie-Clare Mukangango. This young woman was from a Catholic family, the fifth of eight children.

When Marie-Clare rushed to tell her friends and teachers that she, too, had seen the Virgin, her classmates were shocked. Marie-Clare had been one of those who had tormented Alphonsine, calling her "crazy." She was not known to be particularly pious. In fact, Marie-Clare was very outspoken and sometimes unruly. She loved to be on center stage, commanding the attention of everyone, and having fun.

Marie-Clare joyfully admitted that she had been wrong about Alphonsine. She also begged pardon for her disbelief and lack of charity. What more could she do? Now, she was seeing how wrong she had been. And now she was seeing a gorgeous woman from heaven, who told her things she wanted the whole world to hear. "We must meditate on the passion of Jesus and on the deep sorrow of his Mother," Marie-Clare said. "We must recite the rosary and the beads of the Seven Sorrows of Our Lady to obtain the grace of repentance."

Word about the visions of the three girls spread quickly across the high plateaus of Rwanda. Among the Hutu and the Tutsi tribes, there was excitement about the reports. People began to travel from great distances to Kibeho, which was about eighteen miles from Butare, where the University of Rwanda was located. Rwandans wanted to see and hear more about what was really going on in the dormitory of the college.

Because hospitality is deeply respected in Rwanda, the Sisters at the college did not even think of turning away the hundreds of curious villagers. Instead, tall wooden platforms were soon erected so the crowds could watch as the apparitions occurred. Each girl received her apparitions individually at a time previously indicated by Mary. Each would sing, kneel, or pray the rosary aloud on the platform until the Virgin came. The apparitions were sometimes three to four hours long.

This was the way that Mary chose to be seen in a remote village in Africa's poorest nation.

She also chose four more visionaries at Kibeho.

On May 25, 1982, fourteen-year-old Stephanie Mukamurenzi saw the Virgin Mary for the first time. Stephanie was a student in the elementary school and would be the youngest of the seven visionaries of Kibeho. The message she was given by "the Mother of the Word" was so simple and direct that it could easily be dismissed as simplistic. But it was not.

Rather, it was stated in universal terms, in a way that people of all ages and nationalities could understand. And if the message of Stephanie seemed to lack a "fresh" quality, it nonetheless synthesized a major message of the Gospels: "Repent, pray, change your life." "We must be converted, we must pray and mortify ourselves," Stephanie said, relaying the message from Mary. "Satan tries to ruin us. God wants our prayers from the heart."

Just a week after Stephanie's apparitions began, the Virgin emerged from a spectacular glowing light for yet another young person. The new visionary, twenty-two-year-old Agnes Kamagaju, received her first apparition in her home on June second. Agnes came from a Catholic family and had attended the elementary school run by the sisters. Our Lady represented herself, not as the "Mother of the Word," but as the "Mother of Heaven." On August 9, the Virgin came as "the Immaculate Conception."

About three months after her Marian apparitions began,

Agnes also began to see the Lord Jesus. For about a year, the young woman received apparitions from Jesus while on the platform in the school compound. Our Lady, however, visited her privately. The words from Jesus echoed the messages given to the other visionaries about the need for conversion, prayer, renunciation of idolatry, fornication, and hypocrisy.

On August 18, Jesus spoke at length with Agnes about the youth. "They should not use their bodies as an instrument of pleasure," Agnes said, repeating Jesus. "They are using all means to love and be loved and they forget that the true love comes from God. Instead of being at the service of God, they are at the service of money. They must make of their body an instrument destined to the glory of God and not an object of pleasure at the service of men. They should pray to Mary to show them the right way to God."

This message for the youth of Rwanda could not have been more needed. AIDS, the deadly, incurable virus that frightened the entire world, was beginning to be reported in epidemic numbers throughout Africa.

In the next six weeks, however, visions began for the last two seers of Kibeho.

On July 2, fifteen-year-old Emmanuel Segatashya was picking beans in a field when he heard a man's voice coming out of nowhere. It scared him. Then, he saw a handsome man of about thirty years old who was dressed like a person of Rwanda. Initially, Emmanuel was frightened, but the man soon calmed him and filled him with an unexplainable joy.

The visitor then taught the Lord's Prayer to this unschooled boy, who had no religious faith or training. "He told me that he was Jesus," Emmanuel later recalled. "He said 'I am neither white nor black; I am simply Lord.' " Quickly, the news traveled over the low mountains and down into the valleys of the region: "Jesus is appearing to an unschooled boy at Kibeho."

For some Christians of Rwanda, this was too much. Some now doubted that any of the apparitions could be true. How could a "pagan" boy who had never gone to school give the world the message of Jesus? But Emmanuel made a very logical case for the authenticity of his claims. "I am a boy with no schooling," he told a crowd of over two thousand. "If I had not been sent by Jesus, how could I present myself to you?"

It was reported that Emmanuel hadn't even known how to make the sign of the cross. In fact, he had no idea what it meant when he saw it. The young man himself later agreed that Jesus and Mary could have made a better choice. No one in the Segatashya family had learned to read or write and they didn't even own a radio.

Nonetheless, the teenager began to share the messages he received in a remarkably articulate way. Jesus told Emmanuel that prayer and reparation were greatly needed because the world would be coming to an end. What was needed, the Lord said, was a turning away from sin and a return to the sacraments, especially the Eucharist and Penance. "Often we say that we are weak, but God has given us the sacrament of reconciliation," Emmanuel said.

According to Emmanuel, many priests and religious were in particular need of penance and reform. "The priests and religious do not take enough care of those who are ill physically and morally," Emmanuel was told during a vision on September 8, 1982. "If they have promised freely the vow of chastity, they must observe it faithfully." Priests and religious were also warned about being too attached to the world and to wealth.

The Last Judgment was looming closer and closer, Emmanuel said. At that last judgment, "we shall be our own judges." So purification and repentance was needed by everyone. "Do not lose time in doing good. There is not much time left. Jesus will come," Emmanuel repeated over and over.

The fifteenth of September was the feast of Our Lady of Sorrows. The visions began that day for twenty-four-year-old Vestine Salina, a Muslim. Though Vestine's mother had been born into a Catholic family, she had become a Muslim when she married Vestine's father. Wanting a solid education for their daughter, the parents had allowed the girl to enroll at the Catholic school at Kibeho. Vestine had finished elementary school but had joined another program for young people that was run by the nuns at the college.

Vestine said that the Virgin had asked her to serve as a shepherd, helping to lead people back to God. She often quoted these words of Our Lady: "The walk to heaven is through a narrow road. It is not easy to get through. The road to Satan is wide. You will go fast, you will run because there are no obstacles." After the apparitions, Vestine was often seen carrying a large walking stick or shepherd's staff. She took her shepherding role seriously, and did help many Rwandans return to Christian practices.

Alphonsine, Anathalie, Marie-Clare, Stephanie, Agnes, Emmanuel, and Vestine. These were the young people of Kibeho to whom heaven sent messages of love, but also of warning. These teenagers and young adults were quite different in personality and background. They expressed the messages they received in unique ways, but almost always using the colorful media of song, dance, and gestures. Music was the second language of their culture. Often the young people would also communicate with their hands or by walking rhythmically.

From the capital city of Kigali and from hundreds of miles away, people began to travel toward Kibeho to see and hear the young visionaries. Often, the visions would last several hours, as thousands of people watched. All the while, babies cried and were fed, as children played games. Adults sat or stood, or knelt and prayed to "Mariya."

Images of plants, animals, and the natural beauty of the land were often found in the messages the young people gave. That was understandable. Rwandans lived and worked close to the earth. As farmers, they understood that seeds well planted would yield bountiful harvests. Whether or not crops received adequate rainfall was often a matter of life or death for many people.

During the apparitions, Our Lady would sometimes ask the young people to sprinkle the crowds with the water she was blessing. Once, Marie-Clare obediently turned to do it. But the people looked as though they had turned into trees and flowers. "There are too many!" she complained to the Virgin. "The field is so big and I can not do it by myself. Please help me."

At other times, the visionaries would feel thirsty and drink a lot of water. Emmanuel once shouted: "I have a great thirst. I would like a river on my side to satisfy my desire." The thirst for water symbolized a thirst for God and His graces. It was a thirst that could never be satisfied until the person was united fully with God.

The visionaries also "spoke" to the people through fasting. At times, the fasting was extraordinary, particularly during the Lent of 1983. Anathalie was asked to fast for fourteen days, Emmanuel for eighteen days, and Agnes for eight days. Added together, the three visionaries fasted for forty days, just as Jesus did.

During the apparitions, the young visionaries would look toward heaven at a glorious image that others could scarcely imagine. Occasionally, the visionaries would stiffen and fall to the ground, rising again to kneel or stand in prayer. Several explained that their falls occurred because they were seeing sins. At other times, they fell as a prayer of expiation for the burden of sins they saw. At the end of the apparitions, several of the seers fell hard, then in a coma-like state for a while.

Always, the gestures, music, and imagery of the Kibeho apparitions were truly African and wonderfully colorful. But the messages were global — intended for the whole world. For one thing, Mary was apparently trying to reach out to people of all faiths with the Kibeho apparitions.

Our Lady never asked the Protestant or Muslim students to become Catholic. But she did want them to recognize that she was the Mother of God, the Mother of the Word. And Mary did want all people to ask for her intercession. On March 27, 1983,

Mary told Marie-Clare, "When I show myself to someone and talk to them, I want to turn to the whole world. If I am now turning to the parish of Kibeho it does not mean I am concerned only for Kibeho or for the Diocese of Butare, or for Rwanda, or for the whole of Africa. I am concerned with and am turning to the whole world."

Mary's message for Kibeho and for the whole world was sometimes accompanied by extraordinary signs seen in the sky. During the apparitions of Mary to Agnes, some spectators said they saw the sun spinning; others saw two suns. Several times, people saw a cross or a crown of thorns in the sky, near the sun.

Why were these extraordinary things happening?

Agnes explained: "God wants to show us that he holds the world in his hands and he can bring it to an end at his will." Preparation for that end was necessary. When Agnes asked for a blessing for the people, a light rain often fell.

Even though many unexplainable phenomena were discussed for months by Rwandans, some still thought that the seven young people were pulling off a good joke on their elders. The visionaries suffered verbal abuse and ostracism from people who had once been loving and supportive. "Blessed are the crazy of the Lord," the Virgin told Stephanie, who complained that many people thought they were deranged. "They are crazy but they are saying the word of God. I come upon the earth but men do not understand it. They are making a joke of it."

If some people joked that the visionaries were crazy, others noticed that their messages simply repeated Gospel values or traditional Catholic practice.

Over and over again, Mary recommended praying the rosary every day. If the prayer was not prayed daily, praying it on Fridays in memory of the Passion of Jesus was very important. To Marie-Clare, the Virgin also recommended a rosary devotion called the "Beads of the Seven Sorrows of Our Lady."

The Blessed Mother taught Marie-Clare to pray the Beads of the Seven Sorrows. First, there was a prayer (taught to Marie-Clare by the Virgin) offering the devotion for the greatest glory of the Holy Mother of God. Second, a short prayer asking for the grace of perfect contrition was to be said three times. Third, a reading of each of the seven sorrows: (a) Simeon telling Mary that a sword will pierce her heart; (b) the travel into Egypt; (c) losing Jesus in the temple; (d) Mary meeting Jesus on the way to the cross; (e) Mary at the foot of the cross; (f) Mary receiving the body of Jesus at the cross; (g) Mary at the tomb of Jesus.

After each sorrow was recited, an "Our Father" and seven "Hail Marys" were said, followed by the prayer: "Mary, full of Mercy, remind our hearts of the suffering of Jesus during his passion." Finally, the person meditated on the Gospel passages about the sorrows, and concluded with three "Hail Marys" and three "Our Fathers." Marie-Clare promised Our Lady that she would travel house to house in Rwanda, suggesting this devotion to each family. Mary declined, explaining, "You can make it known all over the world even though you will remain here. My grace is omnipotent."

For some of the seers, the time of visions was coming to an end. Several had experienced two or three months of visions; for a few others, six months or a year. The first visionary, Alphonsine, continued to have apparitions until November 28, 1989.

Before these incredible glimpses of glory were gone, the young people experienced some extended visions. Three of the young people — Alphonsine, Anathalie, and Vestine — were told by Our Lady that they would be plunged into a coma-like state while they were shown heaven, hell, and purgatory.

Alphonsine told Sister Superior not to worry about her from the twentieth till the twenty-first of March, 1982. "I will be like a dead person, but have no fear and do not bury me," she said. On the twentieth, Alphonsine's predictions came true. Her body was like a stone and no one could move her hands, which were clasped together.

Vestine, during her vision, saw a place with fire but learned that hell wasn't just a place of fire, but the privation of seeing God. Purgatory was described as a place of reconciliation. Heaven was aglow with light, joy, and happiness.

At different times, all seven of the Kibeho seers also apparently experienced a horrifying vision that lasted for many hours. They saw a river of blood that formed because people were killing each other indiscriminately. Corpses, some without heads, were strewn everywhere and were so numerous they couldn't be buried. As the visionaries saw these scenes, they cried and screamed and the Rwandans witnessing the event understood that the event was terrifying and prophetic.

As the visions of six of the young people came to a close, Bishop Jean Baptiste Gahamanyi of the Diocese of Butare prepared a pastoral letter about the events at Kibeho. The letter was released on July 30, 1983. Bishop Gahamanyi had watched the visionaries with great interest and respect.

In his letter, the bishop talked about traditional Church teaching on apparitions. He reported the findings of the commission of doctors he had appointed on March 20, 1982. The doctors had been charged with studying the visionaries and the events at Kibeho. Bishop Gahamanyi also referred to the wisdom of Scripture and the need for prudence as they pertained to reported apparitions.

"Because of the complexity of the facts and the number of the visionaries, it is hard to scrutinize each case," he wrote. "There should be no surprise if the Church expresses its judgment only after a relatively long period of time. Many years are often needed to clearly see the truth. We invite you therefore to be patient." As the bishop and all of Rwanda would see, however, there would be no time or opportunity for patience and careful assessment.

In the meantime, Our Lady came to visit Kibeho one last

time. Alphonsine Mumureke, who had seen the Virgin first, received this last apparition on November 28, 1989, the eighth anniversary of the first appearance.

About ten thousand people had gathered that day near the compound of the sisters' college. They had come by car, by bus, by foot. All morning, the crowd sang, danced, and prayed the rosary and other prayers of praise. At 12:30 P.M., as it began to rain, the first, brief apparition of the day began. Through a microphone and amplifier, the people heard Alphonsine express delight at seeing Mary once again.

Later, at 4:00 P.M., with a light rain falling, the Mother of the Word came a second time. Alphonsine expressed her commitment to live her Christian obligations faithfully. She also asked Our Lady to prevent people from idolizing her as a "saint," because she had been just an instrument. Mary reminded the twenty-four-year-old visionary that all Christians had a vocation to prayer, penance, obedience to the Church, love of the Church, and fidelity to the Gospel and to the hierarchy. Then, as Alphonsine communicated them to the silent crowds, the Virgin gave messages of love to the sick, those consecrated to God, the youth, and to those in authority.

As the Queen of Heaven began to leave Alphonsine and the people, the young woman's face became grief-stricken. She probably didn't notice that she had mysteriously remained dry in the pouring rain. "I love you, I love you, I love you very much!" the Virgin told them all. "Never forget the love I have for you in coming among you. These messages will do good not only now but also in the future."

Alphonsine then sang the Magnificat and the people joined her. Her voice quivered with sadness. Some people said that the plight of Alphonsine was like that of the African child who finally had to come down off the back of the mother to learn to walk alone.

In fact, the Mother of the Word had come, hoping that Rwandans would walk with Jesus and with her. But in 1991, those who remembered those reported visions of the river of blood believed that they were prophetic. In the faces of the young visionaries, heaven had previewed the bloody civil war of Rwanda, which began in 1991.

In that war, as the world discovered, Hutu and Tutsi people mercilessly massacred one another. Before the war, Rwanda was a nation of 8.2 million. Within a few years, one million, including Marie-Clare Mukangango and her husband, had been slain by their own countrymen. Another 2.4 million had to flee their homes for refugee camps. One hundred fifty thousand have succumbed to disease. More than one hundred clergy, including the bishop of Kigali, were also killed, while dozens of churches were destroyed.

Thousands of Rwandans must have recalled the words they heard from the seven youths of Kibeho. The young people had communicated a message from the Mother of the Word. Like the Queen of Peace in Medjugorje, she had pleaded for reconciliation, penance, and prayer! Our Lady also begged to be seen as a loving Mother of all peoples. She had come to bring a message of love and consolation to a nation that was soon put upon a cross.

San Nicolás,
Argentina

1983-90

*L*ike most women whose children were grown, forty-six-year-old Gladys Herminia Quiroga de Motta occasionally felt a wave of maternal sadness as she walked through the rooms of the house where her little ones had once played. God had given the Mottas two daughters, and they were now eighteen and twenty-two. It didn't seem possible. Added to that was another "unbelievable" reality — Gladys and her husband had become grandparents.

On this Sunday, September 25, 1983, it's possible that the springlike fresh air coming in her windows was responsible for this bit of nostalgia. Gladys didn't really know. She did sense that Argentina's spring was not far away. October and November would soon be alive with flowers in San Nicolás, a city of one hundred fifty thousand that was two hours from Buenos Aires. There would be as many flowers blossoming in the Mottas' working-class neighborhood of small row-houses as there would be around the mansions of the rich. God is generous with flowers in Argentina.

The feeling that Gladys had about the imminence of spring was simply the natural fruit of experience. For several weeks, however, she had experienced another feeling that had absolutely no root in ordinary life. Gladys hardly knew how to describe it. She was a balanced and intelligent woman, but with only four years of elementary school education, she lacked the skills to express herself with confidence.

About a month before, Gladys had seen her rosary light up in a mysterious way. She had glanced at it for no apparent reason. The rosary was hanging on the wall as usual. Suddenly, it glowed like the molten steel she had often seen at the iron and steel factory where her husband worked as a crane driver. Immediately, Gladys went to fetch her neighbors. When they confirmed that they, too, saw the rosary glowing, a new feeling of holy fear and anticipation had been born in her. What she saw was *not* produced by an overactive imagination, stimulated by boredom!

Beginning on the day that the rosary glowed, Gladys prayed the rosary prayers more carefully and frequently. She invited her friends to accompany her. They came readily. After all, the whole neighborhood was talking about the "heavenly" light that had drawn everyone's eyes to the rosary on the wall. How could believers from a parish dedicated to "Our Lady of the Rosary" refuse to pray the rosary when heaven used that sort of spotlight?

As the days went by, however, Gladys began to pray more frequently by herself. Perhaps she discovered a greater peace this way. She was a reserved person, and the need to reach out socially to each friend who came to her house was a little draining. It also took more time to arrange a group prayer. Not that Gladys didn't like praying with others; it simply seemed that she found herself more focused and peaceful when she prayed the "Hail Marys" and the "Our Fathers" by herself.

As she methodically turned over the matter in her mind one day, she began to feel an urge to pray the rosary immediately. She went to the wall and took the beads off the nails. The house was quiet. She went to her room, knelt, and began the prayers as always.

With no warning, the Blessed Virgin was in front of her. Gladys could see instantly that it was she. The Madonna's face was radiant, beautiful! Her whole figure was glowing with light. The Virgin wore a blue gown and a veil. Gladys saw that the heavenly Mother held the Child Jesus in her arms, as well as a large rosary.

The Virgin did not speak to Gladys during these privileged moments. She did, however, smile and gesture to the awestruck Venezuelan mother who knelt before her. Gladys thought that the Lady was offering her the rosary that she held in her hand. Transfixed, Gladys simply looked at the smiling Mother of God and squeezed her own beads harder. Gladys felt no fear. There was only a tingling sensation, a joy deep, deep inside of her.

Just as suddenly as she arrived, the Virgin was gone. After a while, Gladys calmed her spirit and finished praying her rosary. Then she stood up, wondering for a moment if this miracle had truly come to her house. She let the rosary slip down around her arm to her elbow, leaving her hands free. She rubbed her dark brown eyes hard. She was awake!

For a little while, Gladys walked around her small home, touching the familiar solid objects of her environment. In her mind, she was already deciding to tell no one about this miracle. And yet, she wanted to report or record the event in some way. After a few moments, she went to a cupboard and found paper and a pen. She sat down and laboriously recorded the day's date. And then she wrote simply: "*Vi a la virgen por primera vez*" (I saw the Virgin for the first time).

Never in her life had Gladys written a letter to anyone. As a little girl, she, had worn glasses. Reading had been very difficult for her, and writing was hard too. Now, Gladys looked down at the words — the truth — that she had put upon the paper. She put the paper in a special place and planned to keep it always.

Gladys had written that she had seen the Virgin "for the first time." This didn't mean that she expected a second occasion. In fact, as she talked about these experiences later, she was very firm about that. She had not expected the Lady to come the first time, and she didn't look for the wonderful blessing to be repeated.

However, on Wednesday, September 28, Gladys felt a joyful excitement in her spirit. There was no obvious reason for it. She was in her room, just as she had been when the Holy Mother came the first time. She closed her eyes and waited.

In that instant, the Blessed Virgin appeared out of a bright light, which the visionary perceived with her eyes closed. As before, the Virgin tenderly held the Child Jesus. Again, she seemed to offer her own rosary to Gladys before she vanished. Longing again to hold on to this event in some tangible way,

Gladys later took down the paper and pen she had used before. She wrote: *"La vi nuevamente"* (I saw her again).

One week later, on October 5, Our Lady appeared a third time while Gladys was praying the rosary in her room. By now, Gladys spent her days wondering why the Queen of Heaven was appearing to a short, middle-aged woman who could barely read or write. In the meantime, she carefully tended to her housework. No one else knew about the apparitions taking place in the Motta house.

With the same meticulous attention with which she kept house, Gladys formulated a question for the glorious woman who came to her. Gladys planned to ask her why she was coming. What did a heavenly creature want from her? What could the Blessed Mother expect of her?

On October 7, the feast of the Holy Rosary, Gladys had a chance to ask the question that was constantly on her mind. Later on, with her paper and pen, she carefully reported on the question and what came of it. "I saw her and I asked her what she wanted of me. Then her image faded away and a chapel appeared. I understood that she wanted to be among us." Wordlessly, the Virgin had told Gladys that she wanted a church built.

A church! Shouldering responsibility for a church for Our Lady was a bit unsettling. Gladys was a practical woman who knew her limitations. She decided to share the news in the confessional, a setting that assured confidentiality. The priest was Father Carlos A. Perez, a parish priest at the church of St. Nicholas de Bari. Father Perez heard what Gladys had to say on October 12. He listened most carefully, and encouraged prayer and the sacraments. But nothing more was said or done.

Perhaps Gladys didn't realize it, but October 13 was the anniversary of the last apparition of Our Lady of Fátima. The Virgin chose that day to appear for the sixth apparition. During this visit, Mary spoke to Gladys, saying: "You have been faithful. Do not be afraid. Come to see me. You will walk (with your hand) in my hand, and you will travel over a long road."

The message was strictly personal and Gladys must have cherished it deeply. It encouraged her to hear the Virgin commend her for being faithful. She didn't really know what "long road" she would be traveling, but knowing that she would be walking with the Mother of God calmed her anxieties and fears. Along with the warm words of encouragement given by the Virgin, Gladys also received homework. Our Lady asked her to read Ezekiel 2:4-10, a passage about the way God's prophet had to persist in the face of rebellious people.

Locating a Scripture passage and reading it carefully was undoubtedly new for Gladys. With so little education, she may have been uncomfortable with a book of any kind. If so, that feeling soon disappeared. In many ways, the Virgin was showing her who she could be and what she could really do. The visionary was growing in faith and self-esteem.

On the seventeenth of October, Gladys traveled to Rosario, a city up-river from San Nicolás. In the eighteenth century, the priests from the Rosario parish had served the people at San Nicolás, as well as the people of their own community. In a sense, Rosario, a city dedicated to "Our Lady of the Rosary," was a godmother for the Church in San Nicolás. And in Rosario stood the cathedral that Gladys wanted to see again.

Over three weeks had passed since Gladys had first seen the Virgin in her room. If her family and friends still didn't know why or how Gladys was changing, Gladys knew. She was suddenly reading the Bible and praying with great devotion. And in a way that no one else could see, she was becoming much more focused about what she needed to do for the visiting Virgin. To more fully understand Mary and her expectations, Gladys began to journey to Rosario to pray at the cathedral. In the last half of October, the apparitions had been brief, but more frequent.

On October 25, Gladys celebrated the one-month anniversary of the first apparition with a visit to Rosario. Our Lady appeared and extended a white rosary to her, saying: "Receive this rosary from my hands and keep it forever and ever. You are obedient; I am happy because of it. Rejoice, for God is with you." On this day, Mary came to encourage and support Gladys. A little later, however, the messages were more often admonitions and warnings for all people.

"You are my children, needy but loved," the Blessed Mother told Gladys on October 30. "It is time to pray, to ask for repentance, and it will be given." By mid-November, apparitions of Mary or of Christ were taking place each day.

On November 15, Christ appeared, telling Gladys, "I am the sower. Gather the harvest; it will be great." On November 17, Jesus was there again, reminding her, "Glorious days await you. You will rejoice in me, my beloved children." As Jesus left her, His Mother appeared. Gladys took holy water and sprinkled it in the direction of the vision. Mary only smiled, reassuringly. "May you be blessed today, on this day and forever," she said. When the Virgin came, she often gave Gladys Scriptural references, suggesting passages that she should read. As she had from the first appearance, Gladys recorded the event on paper, making sure she would remember every word the Virgin shared with her.

When Mary visited on November 17, she had kindly directed Gladys to speak to the bishop about her requests for a church. "Announce my request," she said firmly. Nervous about the responsibility she bore, Gladys began to consider how she would explain it to the bishop.

In the meantime, Gladys had spoken more often with Father Perez. He was very understanding, supportive, and helpful. He had learned that there was a statue of Mary in the belfry of the cathedral in Rosario. The statue depicted her as "Our Lady of the Rosary." More than a century old, it had originally found its home in the church of San Nicolás, the home parish of Gladys. Blessed by Pope Leo XIII, the life-sized image of

Our Lady had come from Rome to San Nicholas, which had been built in 1884. Immediately, a Confraternity of the rosary was begun. San Nicholas parish had initiated an annual procession and a preparatory novena.

At some point over the years, however, the wooden statue of Our Lady of the Rosary had been damaged, perhaps during a procession. Mary's hand was broken, and the statue was taken down from its pedestal to be repaired. For some reason, the statue was never restored. Instead, it was put away in the belfry of the cathedral in Rosario. When Father Perez heard about the statue, he told Gladys and invited her to view it on November 27.

"Oh!" exclaimed Gladys when she saw the dusty statue in the cathedral belfry. The statue looked exactly like "the Lady that I see," she whispered to Father Perez. Our Lady's statue was smaller than the radiant image that Gladys saw. But otherwise, the details appeared the same. She was dressed in a blue gown draped over a bright pink tunic. A white veil covered her head and she held the Child Jesus, a dark-haired, dark-eyed toddler of a year or two. A large rosary hung from one hand of the Madonna and across the Child's hands.

Immediately, Gladys had another chance to compare the abandoned statue with the glorious vision that heaven was sending. Our Lady appeared in front of the statue. She faced Gladys, who saw her this time with her eyes wide open. "They had kept me in oblivion, but I reappeared," complained the Virgin. "Put me up again since you see me just as I am."

Glancing behind the statue, the visionary then noticed a stained-glass window that represented the Trinity and the angels. Our Lady of the Rosary had more to add. "I want to settle on the bank of the Paraná," she said. "Be strong. There, you have seen my light. May your strength not weaken. Glory be to the Father Most High."

By late November, the apparitions of Our Lady of the Rosary were no longer a private concern of Gladys de Motta.

Throughout the city of San Nicolás and the Campito — a waste-land near the banks of the Paraná — the news traveled fast. *The Mother of God was appearing*, people told one another.

Just how that news affected the private family life of the Mottas isn't known. Clearly, Gladys didn't relish many things concerning her status as one of "those who saw her." She was a private person. Before September 25, 1983, her home had been a domestic sanctuary, a simple retreat for family and close friends. Now, people were pointing out her home and members of her family. People were pointing to her. In this way and others, Gladys was beginning to need every bit of the encouragement and support the Virgin was lavishing upon her. She was beginning to suffer.

What Our Lady wanted from Gladys de Motta and from the diocese was becoming increasingly clear. She wanted a renewed devotion to Our Lady of the rosary at the church dedicated to her a century earlier. She wanted her statue restored and displayed with respect. Also, it was evident that the Virgin wanted a sanctuary or basilica built at San Nicolás on the bank of the Paraná.

On the evening of November 24, Gladys and a small group of people had walked to the site Mary had chosen for the sanctuary. As they stood there, a powerful shaft of light pierced the dark and struck the soil. In addition to Gladys, the bolt of light was seen by a nine-year-old girl. A few weeks earlier, when Gladys had asked the Virgin if she wanted a sanctuary or a simple chapel, the Virgin answered with a reference to Exodus 25:8.

It reads: "They shall make a sanctuary for me, that I may dwell in their midst." Mary wanted a sanctuary, a large church. She wanted a place where many people could gather to ask for her intercession. Interestingly, the Scripture reference Mary gave to Gladys described the way the Hebrews were to build the sacred Ark of the Covenant that was thought to be the dwelling place of Yahweh.

In 1983, in San Nicolás, Mary wanted it clearly understood that *she* was the New Testament's Ark of the Covenant. She was the sacred dwelling place of the Lord. Jesus, the Son of God, had been conceived in her body, and Mary gave birth to Jesus.

On December 21, four days before the Church celebrated that holy birth, Mary pointedly told her daughter Gladys, "May what I give you be known. I do not give it to be kept in a drawer." Toward the end of the year, the apparition message for the day carried more of a warning for the world.

"All humanity is contaminated," Mary told Gladys on December 27. "It does not know what it wants, and it is the evil one's chance, but he will not be the winner. Christ Jesus will win the great battle, my daughter. You must not let yourselves be surprised; you must be alert. For this reason, daughter, I ask for so much prayer, so much obedience to God. I say this for the whole world. Preach this! Amen."

Gladys de Motta welcomed the new year, 1984, with the deepest feeling of joy. On January 1, 1983, she couldn't have imagined that the Mother of God would appear before her eyes during the coming year. Gladys wouldn't have dreamed that Mary would soon fondly call her "my daughter."

On January 4, a second shaft of light pinpointed the spot that Mary had selected for her sanctuary. Was the Blessed Mother anxious to see the building started? Yes, and yet she knew that the cornerstone would not be laid for two more years. In much of what the Blessed Mother had already said, there was an urgency, a pleading, which would become more apparent as the days of apparition came and went.

By her own decision, Gladys had begun to fast. In November, 1983, just a few weeks after the apparitions had begun, she fasted from all solid foods. Though her husband had been very concerned, the seer had taken nothing except grapefruit juice and coffee, or tea with milk, for about thirty days. During that time, Gladys later told a friend, she lost only three pounds from her normal weight of one hundred thirty five pounds. Remarkably, during her fast, Gladys had cooked each day for her husband. Cooking and smelling the food had not made her hungry. "No, during the fast," she explained, "I lose the sense of smell and there is no appetite."

The discipline of fasting and of a deepening of her prayer life apparently prepared the visionary for the sacrifices of 1984. And so, too, did the daily visits of the Virgin. Though the Virgin came at different times of the day, Gladys could sense the event a moment or two before the light and the Virgin's appearance. "I experience something like a tingling sensation in my arms," she said. "Then, I know that she is coming. I close my eyes and she appears."

The way that Gladys saw her — with closed eyes — was different than the way other visionaries reportedly perceived the Virgin. But the message and the messenger were no less real for Gladys. If she was with others as Our Lady came to her, she said nothing. But those around her knew what it meant when Gladys shut her eyes. Sometimes, too, they noticed a sudden scent of roses, or a feeling of warmth, as though sunshine was suddenly shining through the clouds.

Each new day of 1984 brought a fresh message, a new inspiration to Gladys. This woman, who had never written a single letter, now took out her pen and notebook to write each day. Sometimes, the messages from the Virgin were very brief. On February 15, the Virgin Mary said, "May your mouths not deny what your hearts cry out — the name of the Lord Our God, and make perpetual praise. Amen." The words of Our Lady on March 20 were encouraging. "You have started to pray, people of God," she said. "You are beginning to arise again, as I have risen in presence before you. You behave in a way that is pleasing to the Lord."

The Virgin was right. There was a renewal of prayer and faith in San Nicolás. And people were beginning to call upon Our Lady of the Rosary in their times of need. Father Carlos

Perez had reintroduced the perpetual rosary in the cathedral. It began on September 25, the first anniversary of the first apparition of Our Lady to San Nicolás.

In the next month, Maria del Valle Godoy de Miguel, a mother who was pregnant with her seventh child, was one of those who asked Our Lady of the rosary to intercede for her. Gonzalo, her seven-year-old son, had been diagnosed with a brain tumor. The tumor, large and growing, had quickly paralyzed the boy's right side and left him unable to speak. Doctors told Gonzalo's parents that they would have to operate to save the child's life. And yet operating, they admitted, would probably cause the boy permanent brain damage.

On October 25, the desperate mother stood in the hospital corridor, weeping and praying. The unborn child within her would never know its older brother, Gonzalo. Even as God was about to give her a new baby, He was taking back her little son. Suddenly, Mariqui, as she was nicknamed, decided to put her son's life into the hands of Our Lady of the Rosary. She became peaceful; the flood of tears stopped. God, through His Mother, would give her the strength and faith to accept whatever came.

Gonzalo's condition continued to worsen. On October 30, the parents asked for the Anointing of the Sick for him. They also asked if their young son could receive his First Holy Communion. Gonzalo had not completed his instruction for the Eucharist, but his parents wanted him to receive Jesus before he died. When the priest arrived to anoint Gonzalo, he also asked for the healing intercession of Our Lady of the Rosary. Then, as the brokenhearted Miguel family watched, Gonzalo was anointed and received the Eucharist.

Within forty-five minutes, the paralysis locking the boy in a tightening death grip had decreased. The child regained his color and seemed more responsive. Two days later, a brain scan showed that the tumor had shrunk by seventy percent! Pressure inside his brain had also decreased. Each day after that brought the little boy closer to normal activity and health. Within three weeks, a third brain scan confirmed that the impossible had taken place. Where there had been an egg-sized tumor, there was nothing but a scar.

News of this healing soon reached the ears of the new bishop of San Nicolás, Monsignor Domingo Salvador Castagna. He had heard so many things about Señora Motta and the Virgin's appearances since his arrival in the diocese on August 28. The handsome fifty-three-year-old churchman had been looking for a sign that could further confirm the good fruits of the apparitions. Naturally, he discussed the matter at length with Father Perez.

Although some critical medical records about Gonzalo's case were unfortunately lost at the hospital, one could not ignore the evidence that presented itself. A seven-year-old boy was at death's door. After he received his First Communion and after the parents had prayed for the intercession of Our Lady of the Rosary, the child had immediately recovered. Bishop Castagna wanted to begin an official investigation of the claims, but he waited a bit longer.

Like the bishop, many people throughout the province of Buenos Aires soon heard about the astonishing cure of Gonzalo. About six months later, on June 2, 1985, *La Nacion*, a daily newspaper of Buenos Aires, printed a lengthy story about the healing of the boy, changing his name to Martin to protect his family from unwanted public attention. And on September 25, 1985, the second anniversary of the first appearance, another paper, *El Norte*, published a long article about the San Nicolás apparitions and Gonzalo's recovery.

Even before the end of 1984, however, something occurred that would generate more interest than the healing of Gonzalo. On October 23, Father Perez wrote to his bishop about Gladys. The visionary was moving into deeper prayer and silence, he said. "Gladys does not refuse the physical and moral sufferings in that she understands them to be necessary for God's plan and for Redemption," he observed. The observations made by the spiritual director to the bishop were prophetic.

On Friday, November 16, 1984, in the midst of Argentina's blossoming spring, Gladys experienced the awesome pain and suffering of the passion of Jesus. The stigmata appeared upon her wrists. Graciously and generously, she endured the excruciating torment, which reproduced some of the wounds of crucifixion.

Bishop Castagna sent Dr. Eduardo Juan Telechea, a cardiologist, and Dr. Carlos M. Pellicciotta to Gladys' home to care for her and to examine her wounds. Unlike the wounds of some stigmatists, those of Gladys didn't appear in her palms, but rather through her wrists. Recent archeological study has confirmed that Roman soldiers nailed their victims to the cross through the wrists. Nails placed through the palms wouldn't have held the body, medical authorities say. The flesh of the hands would have torn away from the nails.

On December 2, 1984, Our Lady made a new request of Gladys. She asked that a new medal be struck that reminded people she was coming into the world and that she wanted them to think of her always. Mary told Gladys:

"You must strike a medal with my image and my words: 'Mary of the Rosary of San Nicolás,' and on the reverse side the Holy Trinity with seven stars." The stars, Mary explained, represented the seven graces that Jesus would grant to those who wore the medal. The medal was struck just as Our Lady had asked, but it was not distributed until 1986. Very soon, however, the "San Nicolás" medal was widely distributed throughout Argentina and South America.

During 1984, Gladys had suffered the stigmata on the Thursdays and Fridays of Advent. In 1985, the wounds also appeared during the Thursdays and Fridays of Lent. Gladys and those closest to her noticed that the wounds began with a small red bruise on the inside of her wrists. Then, the shocking, bloody wounds developed. As they formed, her thumbs bent inwards toward her palms. This, too, medical experts claimed, would be a normal physical response to crucifixion wounds in the wrist.

By 1985, living with wounds of many kinds and living a life of constant prayer, it was clear this was the calling of Gladys de Motta. She was a shy woman whose simple but profound holiness was an example for all of Argentina.

During the first few months of 1985, in the chancery office in Rosario, Bishop Castagna was studying the large folders of reports he'd received about San Nicolás. He met with the physicians he had sent to Gladys de Motta. He reviewed their reports and other testimonies and materials. He prayed and considered the fruits. In April, 1985, he nominated an Episcopal Commission of Inquiry for the claims made at San Nicolás.

Throughout 1985, the messages of Jesus and of the Blessed Virgin Mary supported Gladys. Even when the pain of the stigmata wounds was intense, the visionary found a way to record the words that were being entrusted to her for the world. Pages and pages of paper were now being filled with the observations, warnings, and loving messages of encouragement. A central theme among the hundreds of messages from heaven was this: God wants to renew His covenant with His people through Mary, His Ark of the Covenant.

On July 1, Gladys' forty-eighth birthday, Jesus and then Mary appeared to her. After Mary disappeared, Gladys saw a chalice of wine that gradually overflowed. The wine then seemed to be blood. "It is the most precious blood of Jesus being offered," the Virgin explained.

On August 3, Mary, addressing her "children," asked them to go to Church and take part in the Mass, because during it they would feed on the Bread of Life; that is, Christ Jesus. "Nourished by Him, no plague coming from outside will reach you, since Jesus will destroy it," promised the Virgin. In other visions, Gladys saw the light blue and white flag of her country next to a much larger, solid-blue flag. Our Lady said the meaning was that, "I protect your country, I protect Argentina." Still other appeals from the Virgin asked for novena prayer for priests, for prayers of praise to God, for prayers to convert atheists and those who are indifferent toward God.

Without letup, the Virgin constantly appealed for prayer, especially the rosary, from the world.

"My children," she said in one of the eighteen hundred messages Gladys was to receive, "I ask you for prayers for a soul who is not praying and decreases in love of God. Let no one pretend to be agreeable to God if he is far from God. I ask for prayers and the conversion of hearts. Gladys, pray for my errant children. Pray so that each heart will permit the love of my Son to enter, so that rebellion may cease."

On the afternoon of October 24, Gladys was in her room, praying for someone who was very sick. The glowing light that preceded the Blessed Virgin enveloped the kneeling visionary. Gladys joyfully closed her eyes while the Queen of Heaven said: "I do not take my eyes from my dear children. Blessed are those who trust in the Mother of Jesus, because their trust will be rewarded. Amen, Amen."

The Commission of Inquiry named by Bishop Castagna released its first report on the following day, October 25, 1985. The commission made no statement about the supernatural character of the apparitions. However, the priests of the commission and the scholarly professionals (theologians, psychologists, graphologists, psychiatrists) whom they had consulted announced the following:

- There were no theological difficulties (or errors) in any of the writings of the visionary. In fact, one report said the messages were truly in harmony with the Holy Scripture.
- Because some medical data for a cure said to be connected with the claimed apparitions was missing, no conclusion could be made about it. On the other hand, serious testimonies in defense of the supernatural nature of the healing had been received and noted.

• There was no evidence of psychopathological disorder or hallucination in the visionary, Mrs. Motta. Her personality seemed well balanced and in perfect harmony with reality.

At first, the commission's report may have appeared to sound a negative note regarding the appearances of Our Lady of the Rosary. Nowhere was there a statement that the apparitions or the phenomena occurring there were authentic or from God. But on February 25,1986, Bishop Castagna celebrated Mass on the Campito near the site selected for the sanctuary. After the Mass, the bishop led the first procession to commemorate the apparitions (which had begun on the twentyfiveth day of the month).

In August, the bishop was again at the Campito to lead the procession. He announced that the land for the sanctuary had been given by the municipality of San Nicolás. He also told the crowds that the cornerstone for the church would soon be laid there. On September 25, the stone was laid, although the actual building was delayed by lack of funds in the poor community of San Nicolás.

In 1987, when Pope John Paul II visited Argentina, Bishop Castagna reported to him about the prayers and healings rising from San Nicolás. Later, as the Pope left Rosario, he had his helicopter pilot descend over the site of the sanctuary in order to "visit" this new place that Mary was apparently blessing.

As the 1980s came to an end, the good fruits of San Nicolás were increasing and more apparent. Monthly pilgrimages brought thousands to the Campito. Mostly, the people were from San Nicolás but also from the rest of Argentina and neighboring countries.

On February 11, the feast of Our Lady of Lourdes, Gladys received the last public message from Our Lady of the Rosary at San Nicolás. As before, it was an appeal to "pray, make reparation, have faith!" Mary's last words promised: "All those who have faith in God and in Mary will be saved. Glory to God. Preach it."

Bishop Domingo Castagna, the bishop of San Nicolás, believed that the message Mary brought to his diocese was being preached to many people. It was true that the commission he'd founded to study events at San Nicolás had not declared the apparitions as supernatural. He believed that such study would take many years and much patience.

In the meantime, on July 25, 1990, the shepherd of this diocese expressed his own thinking about the matter in a homily at the Campito. "Undoubtedly," he said, "this event of grace will continue to grow; it has proved its authenticity by its spiritual fruits."

Betania, Venezuela

1984

From a small plane circling above, the scene at a small Venezuelan farm would have looked like a church picnic. It was Sunday, March 25, 1984. About one hundred fifty people were singing, talking, and relaxing in some cleared farm fields. Caracas was a two-hour drive away, and it may have seemed like a long distance to travel for a picnic. From the air, this place was especially pretty.

A little river ran through this farm at Betania (Bethany) near the village of Cua in the state of Miranda. The river meandered a bit, then passed in front of an old but charming farmhouse. Near a wooded area was an abandoned sugar mill, and there were also fruit trees in abundance: bananas, mangoes, water chestnuts, tangerines, avocados, and guavas.

A few adults may have been nibbling on some of the fruit or on the remains of lunch, which everyone had carried in to eat following the noon Mass. That was celebrated with much joy and singing near a man-made rock grotto, where a large statue of Our Lady of Lourdes had been placed. Fresh flowers of every sort and color filled and bordered the grotto to please the Lady on this feast of the Annunciation. There was much beauty around the grotto.

In contrast to the adults, almost all of the children were active during this drowsy time of day. They were beguiled by a spring-fed waterfall that fell playfully down a small mountain to the right of the grotto. Some of the youngsters threw leaves and sticks to see the crazy routes they would be carried by the water. Others simply yelled, playing a game of chase near the waterfall.

Around 3:00 P.M., one child ran excitedly back to the picnic tables and shady spots where the adults were relaxing. Breathlessly, the child told the grown-ups that the Blessed Mother was appearing above the waterfall, near the grotto. Word spread. Soon, everyone rushed to the rock grotto to see what they could see. There, more than one hundred people saw her.

Our Lady's glowing white figure stood out against the dark

green trees near the waterfall. Many people began to pray the rosary, cry out, and weep with joy as they pointed to the figure of the Virgin. The apparition of Mary didn't speak or move. In that sense, she initially seemed like a statue. "It's Our Lady of Lourdes," a few whispered to each other. While some people saw her facial features, which were breathtakingly beautiful, others couldn't seem to see her that clearly. A blue sash was tied around her waist, many reported. A few also said that they saw her holding a baby, the Infant Jesus.

Nonetheless, the visual presence of a woman's figure was so clear and unmistakable that a few people began to look around to see if something "natural" was producing the image. Could the figure be a reflection of the statue in the grotto? Was it an image thrown against the leafy backdrop by a hidden projector? Was there technological trickery involved?

After about fifteen minutes, it seemed as if the image of Our Lady evaporated, or was absorbed back into the trees. Suddenly, she was gone — just as suddenly as she had come. Within a short time, however, she appeared again, even as people discussed their first experiences. "There she is!" a shout arose from the crowd, heralding her return. On that day, the shouts and the appearances came six more times.

During the last (seventh) appearance, just before sundown, the Virgin Mary stayed for about thirty minutes, the longest visit. This time, everyone agreed that she looked like a real person, although a person whose beauty had no earthly comparisons. The image was sharper, more defined. None of the visionaries was now inclined to describe the figure as a statue or a filmy figure. It was a woman, a heavenly woman! As before, the Virgin spoke no words to those who prayed and sang in front of her.

There were many young people and many poor people from the city at Betania on this March day. Also among the witnesses, however, were students, doctors, lawyers, a judge, priests, an army general, and even some atheists (who had no idea that Finca Betania already had a reputation as a place favored by Mary). In all, one hundred eight people saw her on March 25, 1984. And those same one hundred eight later said that they were transformed by what they saw.

One of those who saw her that day was fifty-five-year-old Maria Esperanza Medrano de Bianchini, of Caracas. However, Esperanza, as her family and friends called her, wasn't surprised at all by Mary's visit. In fact, the pretty, brown-haired wife, mother, and grandmother knew very well that the Virgin would come so that many people would see her.

Exactly eight years earlier, Esperanza had seen Mary on this farm. That made Esperanza the first visionary of Betania. On March 25, 1976, the Virgin identified herself by stating: "I am the Reconciler of People and Nations." Esperanza was given a special role to help promote conversion, prayer, sacrifice, and to see that a church was built here.

So, on this feast day of Mary in 1984, Esperanza smiled with a knowing smile as the newest visionaries of Betania took their leave of her. They visited the wondrous waterfall one more time and prepared to leave for home. Unless they slept on the ground, there was no place to spend the night. The sun was going down now, throwing a golden glow over the pastures and the small mountains that stood guard around the grotto.

The people radiated such joy as they walked away, still filled with the memory of the Virgin's face and the unearthly peace she brought. There would be something new and rich in their lives and their faith. Some of the poor, it was true, would be returning to the "*ranchos,*" or shacks, where they lived in Caracas, usually at the edge of starvation. Maria Esperanza was grieved by that, and she and her husband, Geo, did what they could to help. But Esperanza profoundly believed that the Virgin would not abandon her children. By bringing people back to her Son Jesus, the Virgin would one day help to reconcile all things — even the plight of the poor in Venezuela.

In fact, heaven had already reconciled many things in Esperanza's own amazing life.

She was born on November 22, 1928, at Barrancas. Her mother, who had often prayed through her difficult pregnancy for a daughter, was very happy. She and her husband, Aniceto Medrano, already had four sons. Unfortunately, Aniceto had little time with his beautiful little brown-eyed girl. He died when Maria Esperanza was only two.

As a toddler and very young child, Esperanza's spiritual sensibilities were already remarkable. She often dressed her dolls as nuns and priests and prayed with a focus that surprised everyone. When she was five years old, however, something extraordinary happened at the port in Bolivar City. Her mother was going on a trip, leaving behind a sad little Esperanza. Perhaps the girl worried that she would lose her mother as she had lost her father three years before. Heavyhearted, the little girl stood there helplessly, watching her mother depart.

Suddenly, however, something urged her to look toward the Orinoco River nearby. As the child gazed at the river, she saw a smiling woman rise from it with a beautiful red rose in her hand. As the astonished youngster watched, the woman threw the rose to her in order to console her. It was a vision of the Little Flower, St. Thérèse of Lisieux, Esperanza learned later. Roses were to surround Maria Esperanza in mystical ways in the years to come.

At the age of twelve, Esperanza was again touched by the supernatural. She developed such a severe case of pneumonia that the doctors didn't think she would survive more than a day or two. The young girl prayed, asking Mary if she should prepare to die. The Virgin Mary appeared to Esperanza and assured her that she would survive in order to serve God. The Virgin told her what medication she needed. The medications were purchased and Esperanza recovered.

Maria Esperanza Medrano received several other private apparitions of Mary and of Jesus during her youth. As a young adult, she was a petite, lovely young woman with a stunning smile and sparkling dark eyes. Those who met her were immediately enchanted by her charm and obviously loving nature. There was also a unique quality in her that was mysterious and attractive to men and women alike.

In her own mind, Esperanza naturally assumed that her vocation was to the religious life. In 1954, at twenty-six, she entered a convent. But another vision of St. Thérèse assured her that her vocation would be as a wife and mother. To help see her life in this new light, Esperanza traveled to Rome. For a time, she lived at the Ravasco Institute near the Vatican. She prayed. She toured the churches and wonders of Rome.

Maria Esperanza also traveled to see Padre Pio, who became her spiritual director for a while. Immediately, he saw the spiritual charisms in Esperanza and had prophesied her coming. "There is a young woman coming from South America," Padre Pio had told one of his spiritual daughters before he met Esperanza. "When I leave, she will be your consolation."

Heaven seemed to be guiding Esperanza very carefully. In another vision, she saw a smiling young man waving a flag that was red, green, and white. It was Geo Bianchini, her future husband, an Italian. They met on November 1, 1955, in front of the Church of the Sacred Heart of Jesus. A year later, on December 8, the feast of the Immaculate Conception and Geo's birthday, they were married at the Chapel of the Immaculate Conception of St. Peter's Basilica.

Back in Venezuela, the newlyweds made their home in Caracas and Geo went into the construction business. Their first child, Maria Immaculada, was born, quite appropriately, on December 8, the feast of the Immaculate Conception and their first anniversary. In the years that followed, five more daughters and one son were born to the Bianchinis. Maria gave each of the girls the first name "Maria." Her son was named Jesus.

During the years that her attention was focused on home and children, Esperanza never failed to spend time each day in prayer. As a result, perhaps, her family was especially loving and peaceful. As her children grew up, the mother of this large family never forgot another apparition she had received as a young woman. The Virgin told Esperanza that she would one day own some land that had an old house, a waterfall, and a grotto.

"From 1957 until 1974, we searched for this land in all of Venezuela," Geo said. "In 1974, in February, we heard about a farm and decided, 'Let's see it.' We called the guy in March and went to see it. When we arrived, Maria said, 'We have to buy this farm.' " She had finally found the land where Our Lady promised to visit her. In June, 1974, together with two other couples from Caracas, they bought the property, which would one day attract pilgrims from all over the world.

The Bianchinis and their friends soon made it a practice to travel to "Finca Betania" on weekends. It was such a peaceful place. The city folk enjoyed caring for the animals, clearing brush from the fields, and praying together near the grotto. And Esperanza and Geo understood very well that the Virgin would soon claim this place for her own purposes.

In 1975 and 1976, Esperanza and Geo spent most of their time in Italy, caring for Geo's ailing mother. But in February, 1976, Esperanza felt that the Virgin was calling her home to Venezuela and to Finca Betania. So Esperanza and Geo and their children returned. She knew that she would see the Virgin at the place the Virgin had selected on March 25, the feast of the Annunciation.

Maria Esperanza fasted, prayed, and prepared for the coming of the Virgin. During those weeks of preparation, Esperanza gradually understood that the waters of the springs near the Betania grotto would heal, like the waters of Lourdes.

Out of respect for Church authority, Esperanza and Geo had contacted the diocesan bishop before the March 25 apparition. Maria Esperanza took a bold step. She told Bishop Bernal that the Virgin was going to appear to her on the twentyfifth at Betania. The bishop neither doubted her nor labeled her as a religious fanatic. Instead, he reminded her that she bore a special responsibility if the Virgin came to her. The bishop also assigned two priests to celebrate Mass and the Sacrament of Reconciliation for the people who would gather there. As yet, there was certainly no Church approval or authentication of events unfolding at Betania. But, it seemed as though the Diocese of Los Teques was anxious to encourage the growth of good fruit in the fertile fields of Finca Betania.

At 8:30 in the morning of March 25, the Virgin showed herself. Esperanza and Geo, along with family members and friends, had gathered near the grotto at Finca Betania. Esperanza never forgot this first visit of the Virgin, in 1976.

"I was in front of the grotto when all of a sudden I was staring there, looking at that grotto, and I saw a white cloud (which was) enormous, beautiful. Then a friend said, 'Maria Esperanza, the farm is on fire, the farm is burning, like a candle,' and I said, 'Yes, I see the fire,' but it was from there that the Virgin and the cloud came.

"And when she revealed herself, she went up to the top of the tree, and I saw she was beautiful, with her brown hair, dark brown, her eyes that were light brown and she had very fine, very pretty eyebrows, tiny mouth, a nose very straight and her complexion was so beautiful, it was skin that seemed like silk. It was bronzed. It was beautiful. Very young. Her hair was down to here, to her shoulders."

Years later, Maria Esperanza said that "there was something so special about this apparition that even though many apparitions were to follow, this one had placed a seal and I would be in her arms always no matter what would happen in my life." Perhaps this apparition was so special because it was the first time the Virgin came to Finca Betania. By now, Esperanza undoubtedly understood that her own life and gifts were connected with Our Lady's mission as reconciler.

Esperanza said that the young Virgin Mother of God then stretched out her hands. From those hands came light. But, on the other hand, it seemed as though "everything was (already) full of light." Esperanza said that the Virgin seemed to be fifteen or sixteen years old and that she was all in white. "Her face was a little elongated with her cheeks that could be seen as naturally-colored and rosy. She was beautiful!"

Esperanza was so overwhelmed by the light and the beauty of the Virgin that she began to shake. In a sense, it was almost too much for the nervous system of any human being to experience. "She was a ray of light that penetrated my soul, shaking all the fibers of my heart," the visionary said. "Interiorally, I felt so humble, so weak, so incapable; I was nothing compared to this beauty that was dazzling me."

Then, in her heart and mind, Esperanza received a new message from the Virgin.

"My little daughter," the Virgin Mary told her, "tell my children of all races, of all nations, of all religions, that I love them. It doesn't matter — for me, all of my children are the same. There do not exist rich ones or poor ones, ugly ones or beautiful ones, black or white. I come to gather all of them to help them to go up to the high mountain of Mount Zion to my fertile land of Betania in these times so that they can be saved.

"I love all of them — the youth, the innocent children, the beloved baby just born. To the youth I am directing myself so that they will really serve me and make me happy, so that they go to the foot of the cross and continue going through all the word to save the world." Toward the end of the apparition, Mary spoke to Esperanza again. She said, "Little daughter, you are beholding me with my hands outstretched with graces and wrapped in the splendor of light to call all my children to conversion."

About eighty people were with Esperanza and the Bianchini family when the Virgin came. No one outside of the Bianchini family knew for sure that the Virgin would be appearing. "I was afraid to say that I was going to see Our Lady, for I wasn't sure if they were going to see her as well, but they realized I was seeing her the moment she appeared." And yet, Esperanza understood that the apparitions and messages she was receiving were no longer meant just for her own spiritual growth and virtue. Much more was at stake now, Our Lady told her.

Following the March 25 apparition, Esperanza, Geo, and their children returned to Italy. "Nona," Geo's mother, needed them. But during the summer, Esperanza felt the pull toward Betania again. On August 22, the feast of the Queenship of Mary, Our Lady appeared to her again. Two weeks before, Maria Esperanza had been moved to have a large cross erected near the entrance to the apparition site. And the timing of this addition was quite literally providential.

During the apparition of August 22, Mary wore a blue sash as she had at Lourdes. She smiled so warmly and so beautifully at Esperanza that the seer melted in tears. In fact, she couldn't stop crying. Then, with great tenderness, the Virgin spoke in a low voice to her. Mary told her namesake that when people lovingly took up their crosses each day, there would be no more pain, weeping, or death. Instead, men and women "will live rising each day with my most beloved Son in a constant and living ALLELUIA! ALLELUIA! ALLELUIA!"

About seven months later, on March 25, 1977, Mary returned to visit Betania and Esperanza. About fifteen people were gathered around Maria Esperanza, including her daughter Maria Gracia. A tremendous light again preceded the Virgin. It was so bright that someone shouted to Maria that the farm was burning, an understandable assumption. What else could produce so much light, so much fire? Maria Gracia and others simply dropped to their knees and buried their heads in the soft field grass. In the same instant that the others buried their faces, Maria Esperanza raised hers. She was looking right into the unearthly light. She was seeing the Virgin Mother of God.

After that, apparitions occurred more frequently for Betania and for Maria Esperanza. Our Lady was gradually unfolding her plan and her desires to Esperanza. Betania was to be a "Lourdes" for Latin America. It was to be a place for healing, but even more so for reconciliation. Most especially, the Virgin wanted this kind of healing for the world.

On November 27, the feast of the Miraculous Medal, Mary appeared to Esperanza again. Esperanza learned that many people would see Our Lady during the next March 25 apparition.

On December 8, a day of great celebration in the Bianchini family, something special was planned for Finca Betania. Maria and Geo had purchased large statues of Our Lady of Lourdes and St. Bernadette for the grotto. With family and friends, they were singing and proceeding down through the fields to the grotto and waterfall with the statues.

Suddenly, a large blue butterfly and two smaller butterflies hovered above the procession, then followed the group to the grotto. During the procession, Noris Behrens, a longtime friend of Esperanza's, excitedly grabbed her elbow and pulled her aside.

"Esperanza," Noris said, "do you recall that Our Lady said to you on August 11, 1954, that she was going to come on December 8 in the form of a blue butterfly with two heavenly angels, when we would be on our way to the grotto to put her in place in the 'Promised Land?' " Behrens had been with Esperanza and other young people devoted to Mary on that August day, many years before. The group of young women had been praying the rosary with Maria Esperanza at her house in San José. When the two old friends looked at each other now, they smiled and shook their heads in wonder. A promise that they had almost forgotten was not forgotten by the Queen of Heaven.

As 1977 drew to a close, the Bianchinis returned to Caracas to celebrate Christmas and the birth of Jesus with great joy.

But as 1978 dawned, Esperanza received a new assignment for Betania. The Virgin spoke to her interiorly, in her heart. Around Finca Betania, there were many people living in great poverty and abuse in aluminum shanties. These people had received very little pastoral care and most had not received the sacraments. Apparently, the Mother of Reconciliation of All People wanted to reconcile these people with the Church. They needed catechetical preparation and they needed to know that the Church cared about them. The Virgin wanted many of the people to receive the sacraments of baptism, confirmation, the Eucharist, and matrimony on February 11, her feast as Our Lady of Lourdes.

Not only was the catechetical task of preparing the people a challenge. Esperanza also realized that she would have to contact Bishop Bernal to ask his cooperation and approval. Would the bishop think that she was overstepping her boundaries by doing the work of the Church? Who was she to act as a "pastor" for the poor people near Finca Betania? Though Maria Esperanza prayed diligently about the project, she could not find the resolve to phone the bishop.

Instead, Geo became involved in working with the people. A tall, capable, and articulate leader, Geo had been very involved in Catholic Action as a young man in Italy. He loved the Church and had been devoted to serving Jesus and Mary long before he even met Maria Esperanza. Geo formed a small team to teach and reach out to the people. Everyday, for two weeks, the team traveled to the shacks and banana farms to prepare the people. However, Maria Esperanza only prayed and *thought* about phoning the bishop.

On February 7, Bishop Bernal called Maria Esperanza. He gently chided her for not having contacted him. On her own, the Virgin had moved him to embrace the project. "Our Lady of Lourdes wants me to go to Betania with you, and to help you do what she requested you to do," he told her, downplaying his episcopal authority. "Why didn't you speak to me about this matter? How did I find out? As you can see, Our Lady has her way."

And so, on her Lourdes feast day, February 11, the Virgin had her way again at Betania. Many people received sacraments and the official embrace of their Church for the first time. Bishop Bernal came with several priests. Maria Esperanza and Geo were overjoyed. The unbaptized children were baptized with water from the waterfall near the grotto. The people received the Body and Blood of Christ during a Mass celebrated in this open-air church that the Virgin was building for all.

During the Mass, Maria Esperanza could not help noticing a young boy who served the bishop as an altar boy. For many years, Esperanza had had gifts of prophecy and spiritual insight. Like Padre Pio, St. John Vianney, and others with mystical gifts, she could "read" hearts. Many times, she knew things about individuals that no one had ever told her. Now as she watched the altar boy assisting, she was struck by his piety and holiness. Years later, the boy became a parish priest who served people in the town of Paracoto.

Apparently, the embrace of the Church for the poorest neighbors of Betania was something the Virgin wanted accomplished by March 25, the day on which the Church usually celebrated the feast of the Annunication. Larger groups gathered and headed down the packed clay roads to Finca Betania. This year, March 25 was also Holy Saturday.

As they had in previous apparitions, many people in the group noticed a radiant mist coming toward them from the woods. Finally, the mist settled at the top of a large tree. Then, for Esperanza's eyes, Our Lady materialized out of the mist with her hands upon her chest.

"Then her hands opened up and I saw what appeared to be rays coming from her hands," said Esperanza, in describing this appearance of the Virgin. "They came directly toward us bathing us with light in such a fashion that Nasira Mistaje uttered a cry saying, 'Everything is burning up!' Actually, the whole area appeared to be on fire. It was beautiful. The sun began to gyrate and everyone was shouting with emotion."

The power of the celestial phenomenon and the apparition of Mary were literally overwhelming for Esperanza. "I couldn't say anything and spontaneously I fell to the ground," she remembered. After the fall, however, she was raised up into the air. The soft, tender voice of the Virgin asked her to accept the task of bringing the message of peace and reconciliation to all nations. Esperanza was told that she would suffer for this task, but that she would have great joy and happiness in being faithful.

When she came to herself, Maria Esperanza was again on the ground. Her daughter Maria Gracia was weeping inconsolably. The girl had seen her mother raised into the air and didn't know what to do to get her down. Esperanza went to calm her and her young goddaughter Jacqueline, who was also very frightened by the occurrence. "The event startled all present," recalled the seer, who immediately asked those present to describe what they had seen on paper for the bishop.

By this time, Bishop Pio Bello Ricardo, a thin, bespectacled man, had become the bishop of the Diocese of Los Teques. Bishop Bernal had been a great supporter of Esperanza and her mission. No doubt, he had discussed her with the new shepherd of Los Teques. But Bishop Ricardo wasn't as sure about the mystic from Caracas and her reports of visions on a banana farm. He held a doctorate in philosophy but had studied psychology extensively. In fact, his doctoral thesis dealt with experimental psychology. Bishop Ricardo did not believe that it was time to study Betania yet. If what people said was true, what was happening there was a matter of private revelation — something between heaven and Maria Esperanza de Bianchini.

Esperanza, on the other hand, truly sensed that what she was seeing and hearing was meant for a troubled world. In the apparitions that continued to occur, Mary talked about Betania. She told her that Betania was "a place of peace and harmony to those who will come to search for this Mother, shepherdess of souls."

The Virgin was also particularly concerned about the needs of the religious and the priests of the world. "I have come to ease the burden of my sons, the priests," she confided in Esperanza. The Virgin said that she needed those consecrated to religious life to "enter fully into prayer and contemplation that are so needed at this hour of decision for humanity."

Why was the Virgin so concerned about tending to the spiritual needs of religious and priests, and establishing a new "place of peace and harmony"? Over and over, Mary spoke of her concern for the salvation and reconciliation of individuals. Again and again, she described how this reconciliation among people and between individuals and God must be established.

"You must have a hunger for God and a hunger for his gifts, and for this Mother that continues to give herself each day, in every part of the world so that people may be saved. In this land, this 'promised land,' hunger for its children must be renewed so that they may be able, together with their brothers and sisters who will come from afar, to find refuge here."

And, more and more often, the Mother of God issued a warning ... for the world.

"Children, as Mary, Mother Reconciler of People, I come to reconcile them, to seek them out, to give them faith, which has disappeared in the noise and din of an atomic awakening which is at the point of bursting out. Passions, power, material wealth have turned them cold, lukewarm, and egotistical. Behold the complaint of a great evil that is covering the earth with shadows. The inferno raised among men must be extinguished through the medium of kindness, love, and truth of the heart of this Mother. There must be pardon, reflecting that only love can save everyone. There is a great need for social justice, a redeeming spirituality, healthy and understood. Only in this way will destruction among brothers and sisters be avoided."

During the rest of the 1970s and into the early '80s, the messages given to Maria Esperanza by the Virgin and even by Jesus had a strong and persistent tone of imminence. The Mother of God seemed to be saying that there was no longer any time for delay. The eleventh hour was arriving. Reconciliation was long overdue.

"Mankind," Mary told Esperanza, "is currently abusing the graces received and is moving toward perdition, and if there is no change and improvement of life, he will succumb under fire, war, and death." But God wanted to avert or mitigate the cataclysm, the Virgin assured Esperanza. This was why she was being sent into the world. She also said that it was why "again, in this century, my Divine Son rises up so that you may follow in His wake as a shepherd of souls."

The weight of the world's evil and violence often weighed upon Esperanza. On May 12, 1981, Esperanza sensed that there would be an attempt on the life of Pope John Paul II. "I spent the whole night praying," she recalled later. "I was desperate, I was so desperate, and I was saying, 'Lord, how can this be? How can there be an attempt made against his life, Lord?' " Esperanza knew of no way to warn the pontiff. On May 13, the feast of Our Lady of Fátima, he was shot in St. Peter's Square. For three months, Esperanza said, she experienced pains in her stomach and womb. She sensed that she was suffering in solidarity with the Pope.

Other mystical phenomena also caused her to suffer. On fourteen occasions, with witnesses watching, a red rose emerged from Esperanza's chest above her breasts. Showing first as a tiny red bud, the beautiful and fragrant rose grew, flower and stem, in a matter of minutes. The event caused the seer great pain and some embarrassment, but she endured both graciously.

Mary had promised Esperanza that many people would see wonders on March 25, 1984. And many did. Immediately, it was no longer a matter of private revelation for Señora Esperanza Bianchini. On the other side of the world on the same day, March 25, 1984, Pope John Paul II consecrated the world and Russia to the Immaculate Heart of Mary. The Act of Consecration was done in conjunction with all the Catholic and Orthodox bishops of the world. According to Sister Lucia, the only surviving visionary of Fátima, this Act of Consecration finally fulfilled the request for consecration that Our Lady had made in 1917.

For Bishop Pio Ricardo, the events of March 25, 1984, set something new in motion. For some years, he had trained a watchful eye on the events taking place at Finca Betania. The farm and the surrounding area were just beyond the urban sprawl of Caracas. Word about the wonders of Betania traveled to the chancery very quickly. And Maria Esperanza herself was scrupulous about keeping her bishop informed. Soon after the March 25 appearance, the bishop launched an official canonical inquiry into the reported apparition. The philosopher in the bishop's chair had had a few years to consider his approach. He decided to conduct the inquiry by himself.

"I didn't name any commission," explained the bishop later. "I prefer to study this matter personally and not with experts, because experience has taught me that a commission is the best way to postpone a study."

Immediately, the bishop asked for written testimonies from everyone who saw the apparitions of March 25, 1984. Later, he questioned the witnesses thoroughly. Among those who were particularly persuasive were several atheists and agnostics. "One man," the bishop said, "was drinking water from the waterfall, and all of a sudden he saw the apparition without any (preconception). He was not religious. He wasn't psychologically prepared."

Privately, the bishop was already persuaded that the apparitions were authentic. But he was careful to conduct the investigation in an objective and thorough manner. In addition to credible witnesses, the bishop also found that the apparitions had produced good fruits in the visionaries of March 25, 1984. For three years, he gathered information about Betania. Reports of healings and conversions stacked up. Bishop Ricardo sent his findings and copies of statements from witnesses to Rome. Twice, he discussed Betania with Cardinal Josef Ratzinger. He also informed the Pope about events taking place in his diocese.

In Betania, he explained later, the message is quite simple. Peace and reconciliation. In a sense, these two crucial needs of the world are beyond words. And at Betania, he said, "few people have had oral communication with the Blessed Mother, perhaps five percent. Say about twenty people from about one thousand to two thousand in total.... What has happened is a strengthening of faith here, conversion, growth of Christian life, frequency of receiving the sacraments, prayer, especially Mass and the Holy Rosary."

Even before the official Church had made any statement about Betania, however, thousands of people traveled there. Each weekend, on Marian feasts and other liturgical feast days, the roads toward the tiny village of Cua were swollen with traffic. On the twenty-fifth day of the month, the crowds reached twenty thousand to thirty thousand people.

Some of those who came were ill.

Dr. Vinicio Arrieta, director of the School of Medicine at the University of Zulia, had been diagnosed with prostate cancer, which had metastasized to his spine. After two chemotherapy treatments, he traveled to Betania on May 12, 1986, to make a vigil to the Virgin of Fátima. After praying all night, feeling ill, he fell asleep on the ground while his wife and cousin tried to protect him from a heavy rain that had begun to fall.

The next morning, the Arrietas and thousands of others saw the sun lose its light, becoming green in the center. Then, as at Fátima, the sun seemed to come down toward the screaming crowds. Amid the excitement, Dr. Arrieta felt an infusion of heat throughout his body. He screamed, "I'm being cured! I'm being cured!" Medical tests performed five days later confirmed his sense. There was no sign of the cancer in his body.

By 1987, five hundred cures had been reported at Betania. At the end of the year, on November 21, 1987, Bishop Ricardo issued his pastoral letter approving the apparitions of Betania. "I declare that in my judgment the said apparitions are authentic and of a supernatural character," he said. The appearances of Our Lady, Reconciler of Peoples at Betania, became the fourth apparition of Mary to be approved as authentic by the Church in the twentieth century.

Even after the diocesan approval, reports of new miracles and wonders brought more and more reading material to the bishop's desk.

On December 8, 1991, a Communion Host began to bleed during Mass at Betania. When the priest who said the Mass told the crowd of 40,000 about the bleeding Host, he prayed that they would not become a crazed mob seeking to see the miracle. Immediately, the masses dropped to their knees in adoration. Bishop Ricardo had the Host taken to Caracas, where medical tests proved that it was human blood.

Like Fátima and Lourdes, Betania was a charming country place far from urban life and the mad materialism of the city. At fourteen, a girl named "Hope" ("Esperanza" in Spanish) had dreamed of it. But in the 1980s and 1990s, the Mother of God was personally recreating it as a place of prayer, peace, reconciliation and healing for the children of Venezuela and the world.

Recommended reading

Amatora, Sister Mary, O.S.F.: *The Queen's Heart of Gold, The Complete Story of Our Lady of Beauraing*. New York: Pageant Press, Inc., 1957.

Barthas, Chanoine C., and Da Fonseca, Pere G., S.J.: *Our Lady of Light, World-Wide Message of Fátima*. Milwaukee: Bruce Publishing Co., 1947.

Beevers, John: *Virgin of the Poor, The Apparitions of Our Lady of Banneux*. St. Meinrad, IN: Abbey Press, 1972.

Brown, Michael H.: *The Final Hour*. Milford, OH: Faith Publishing Co., 1992

Carroll, Warren H.: *Our Lady of Guadalupe and the Conquest of Darkness*. Front Royal, VA: Christendom Publications, 1983.

Connor, Edward: *Recent Apparitions of Our Lady*. Fresno, CA: Academy Guild Press, 1960.

Craig, Mary: *Spark from Heaven: The Mystery of the Madonna of Medjugorje*. Notre Dame, IN: Ave Maria Press, 1986.

Cristiani, Leon: *Saint Bernadette*. Staten Island, NY: Alba House, 1964.

Daniel-Rops, Henri: *The Book of Mary*. New York, NY: Hawthorn Books, Inc., 1960.

Englebert, Omer: *Catherine Labouré and the Modern Apparitions of Our Lady*. New York: NY: P.J. Kenedy & Sons, 1959.

Faith Publishing Company: *Messages of Our Lady at San Nicolás*. Milford, OH: Faith Publishing Co., 1991.

Fox, Robert J.: *Rediscovering Fátima*. Huntington, IN: Our Sunday Visitor, Inc., 1982.

Fukashima, Francis Mutsuo: *Akita: Mother of god as CoRedemptrix: Modern Miracles of Holy Eucharist*. Santa Barbara, CA: Queenship Publishing Co., 1994

Geradin, Amand: *The Apparitions at Banneux*, Translated from the French. Banneux-Notre Dame: Caritas, France, 1936.

Haffert, John: *The Meaning of Akita*. Asbury, NJ: 101 Foundation, Inc., 1989.

International Marian Research Institute: *Mary in Faith and Life in the New Age of the Church*. Dayton, OH: International Marian Research Institute, 1983.

Kennedy, John S: *Light on the Mountain, The Story of La Salette*. Garden City, NY: Doubleday Image Books, 1956.

Kralievic, Svetozar: *The Apparitions of Our Lady at Medjugorje, 1981-1983*. Chicago, IL: Franciscan Herald Press, 1984.

Laurentin, René: *Bernadette of Lourdes, A Life Based on Authenticated Documents*, Minneapolis, MN: Winston Press, 1979.

Laurentin, René: *An Appeal From Mary In Argentina: The Apparitions of San Nicolás*. Milford, OH: Faith Publishing Co., 1990.

Laurentin, René, and Rupcic, Ljudevit: *Is the Virgin Mary Appearing at Medjugorje?* Washington, D.C.: The Word Among Us Press, 1984.

Leies, Herbert: *Mother for a New World, Our Lady of Guadalupe*. Westminster, MD: The Newman Press, 1964.

Lord, Bob and Penny: *The Many Faces of Mary: A Love Story*. Journeys of Faith, 1987 (self-published).

Louis-Lefebvre, Madame: *The Silence of St. Catherine Labouré*. Fresno, CA: Academy Library Guild, 1953.

McHugh, John: *The Mother of Jesus in the New Testament*. Garden City, NY: Doubleday, 1975.

Marnham, Patrick: *Lourdes: A Modern Pilgrimage.* Garden City, NY: Doubleday Image Books, 1982.

O'Reilly, James P.: *The Story of La Salette*, Chicago, IL: J.S. Paluch, 1953.

Pelletier, Joseph A.: *The Immaculate Heart of Mary.* Worcester, MA: Assumption Publications, 1976.

Pelletier, Joseph A.: *The Sun Danced at Fátima.* Worcester, MA: Assumption Publications, 1951.

Rahm, Harold J., S.J.: *Am I Not Here? Our Lady of Guadalupe.* Washington, NJ: Ave Maria, 1962.

Rynne, Catherine, *Knock, 1879-1979.* Dublin: Veritas Publications, 1979.

Saint-Pierre, Michel de: *Bernadette and Lourdes.* Garden City, NY: Doubleday Image Books, 1955.

Sharkey, Don, and Debergh, Joseph, O.M.I.: *Our Lady of Beauraing.* St. Meinrad, IN: Abbey Press, 1973.

Sims, Sister Margaret Catherine, C.S.J.: *Apparitions in Betania, Venezuela.* Framingham, MA: Medjugorje Messengers, 1992.

Tindal-Robertson, Timothy: *Fátima, Russia and Pope John Paul II.* Still River, MA: The Ravengate Press, 1992.

Venancio, Most Rev. Joao, D.D.: *A Heart for All: The Immaculate Heart of Mary in the Apparitions at Fátima.* Washington, NJ: Ave Maria Institute, 1972.

Walsh, William Thomas; *Our Lady of Fátima.* Garden City, NY: Doubleday Image Books, 1947.

Yasuda, Fr. Teiji, O.S.V.: *Akita: The Tears and Messages of Mary.* (English version by John M. Haffert.) Asbury, NJ: 101 Foundation, Inc., 1989.